The History of Urban
and Regional Planning

The History of Urban and Regional Planning ≠b

an annotated bibliography

Anthony Sutcliffe

Facts On File

119 West 57th Street, New York, N.Y. 10019

First published 1981

© Anthony Sutcliffe, 1981

Published in the United States 1981 by
Facts on File, Inc., 119 West 57th Street,
New York, N.Y. 10019

ISBN 0–87196–303–5

Library of Congress Cataloging in Publication Data

Sutcliffe, Anthony, 1942–
    The history of urban and regional planning.
    Includes indexes.
        1. City planning – History – Bibliography.
2. Regional planning – History – Bibliography.
I. Title.
Z5942.S93   [HT166]   016.3616'09   80–13521
ISBN 0–87196–303–5

Published outside the USA, its possessions and Canada by
Mansell Publishing, 3 Bloomsbury Place, London WC1A 2QA

ISBN 0 7201 0901 9

This book was commissioned, edited and designed by
Alexandrine Press, Oxford

Manufactured in Great Britain

In memory of Frederick Sutcliffe, 1909–1979

Contents

Preface   x

Introduction: urban and regional planning
as a subject of historical study   1

Urban and regional planning: a definition and survey   1
The historiography of urban and regional planning:
    its authors and their motivation   7
The historiography of urban and regional planning:
    the achievement so far   8
A future for planning history   10

The bibliography   11

Terms of reference   11
Arrangement   11

1. Planning history: definitions, methods
and objectives   13

2. Encyclopaedias, guides and bibliographies   15

3. Planning as a world movement   19

4. Planning in individual countries   37

Australia; Austria; Brazil; Canada; Chile; China;
Colombia; Cuba; Czechoslovakia; Denmark;
France; Germany; German Democratic Republic;
Hungary; India; Israel; Italy; Japan; Mexico; The
Netherlands; Norway; Poland; South Africa; Spain;

Sweden; Union of Soviet Socialist Republics; United
Kingdom; United States; Yugoslavia

5. Planning in individual towns and cities   93

Adelaide; Atlanta; Autun; Baden; Barcelona; Basle;
Belfast; Berlin; Bielefeld; Bilbao; Birmingham;
Boston (Mass.); Brasilia; Budapest; Buenos Aires;
Calgary; Cambridge; Canberra; Caracas; Catania;
Chandigarh; Chicago; Cleveland; Cologne;
Copenhagen; Coventry; Dakar; Dallas; Dar Es
Salaam; Detroit; Dortmund; Easton; Edmonton;
Essen; Florence; Forlí; Frankfurt; Genoa; Glasgow;
The Hague; Halifax (Nova Scotia); Hamburg;
Hanover; Harrisburg; Hartford; Havana;
Indianapolis; Inverary; Istanbul; Kansas City; Kiel;
Leghorn; Leicester; Leiden; Leningrad; Lisbon;
Liverpool; London; Manchester; Milan; Montreal;
Moscow; Naples; New York; Newcastle-upon-Tyne;
Nuremburg; Odessa; Oslo; Ottawa; Padua; Palermo;
Paris; Perm; Perth; Perugia; Pittsburg; Portmeirion;
Pretoria; Rome; Rotterdam; St. Louis; Saskatoon;
Sheffield; Sienna; Siracusa; Stockholm; Strasbourg;
Swindon; Tokyo; Toronto; Turin; Ujung Pandang;
Urbino; Vancouver; Västerås; Valencia (Venezuela);
Venice; Verona; Victoria; Vienna; Warsaw;
Washington; Whitehorse; Winnipeg

6. Individual planners   139

Adams; Bartholomew; Bassett; Bellamy;
Blumenfeld; Buckingham; Burnham; Cerdà;
Eggeling; Fassbender; Fischer; Garnier; Geddes;
Griffin; Hegemann; Hénard; Hilberseimer; Horsfall;
Howard; Howe; Josimović; Kahn; Korn; Le
Corbusier; Lichtwark; Lutyens; McAneny; Marsh;
Mawson; May; Miliutin; Nolen; Olmsted; Paxton;
Prost; Richardson; Sant'Elia; Schumacher; Sert;
Sitte; Soria y Mata; Tange; Taut; Taylor; Tugwell;
Unwin; Verhaeren; Wagner; Wright, F. L.; Wright, H.

7. Nineteenth-century antecedents of urban
and regional planning   165

    Urban reconstruction   165
    Extension planning   171
    Park planning   174
    The utopian tradition   175
    Model communities and company housing   179
    Garden cities   189

8. Aspects of urban and regional planning   195

    Postwar reconstruction   195
    Urban renewal, slum clearance, and redevelopment   198
    Open space   203
    Conservation (urban)   204
    Conservation (rural)   206
    Transport planning   207
    Zoning and land-use planning   210
    Residential areas   214
    Urban containment and decentralization   219
    New towns   223
    Regional planning   234

9. Additional entries   241

Index of names   265

Index of authors   272

Preface

This bibliography has already passed through two incarnations. The original version was presented to the Planning History Group at its inaugural meeting in 1974 at the Centre for Urban and Regional Studies, Birmingham University. Greatly extended, it was published in 1977 as Research Memorandum no. 57 of the Centre under the title *The History of Modern Town Planning: A Bibliographic Guide*. This provisional listing of 656 titles formed the basis for the present volume of twice its size. I wish to thank the following people for providing material or making helpful suggestions: Diana Dixon, Gerhard Fehl, Victor Gilbert, Thomas Hall, David Hulchanski, Andrew Lees, Michael Simpson, Randall Smith, Gilbert Stelter, Walter Stranz, Robert Thorne, A. S. Travis, and Bernard Zumthor. My thanks are also due to Beryl Moore and Christine Marland for their careful typing of a dour manuscript. I am, of course, entirely responsible for all errors, questionable judgments, and unjustified omissions.

ANTHONY SUTCLIFFE
Sheffield, August 1980

Introduction: urban and regional planning as a subject of historical study

Urban and regional planning: a definition and survey

Urban and regional planning may be defined as a concerted effort by public authority to guide the development of land in the interests of economic efficiency and the common welfare. Its utility is now so widely recognized that few parts of the advanced world try to exist without it. It is also regarded as an essential tool in Third World development. Capitalist and socialist societies alike practise it.

Of course, public involvement in land development is nothing new. The earliest examples of planned towns date back several thousand years. In the Roman Empire a form of regional planning was carried on, with new or expanded towns and seaports linked by a system of new roads. Even in the Middle Ages many towns were founded by kings or lords, with their streets and sites often sketched out in advance of all building. The Renaissance produced a host of designs for ideal towns, some of which were actually built. In the seventeeth and eighteenth centuries the growth of royal and princely power was reflected in the planning of elegant new extensions to European towns large and small. Many new towns were laid out in recently-colonized areas outside Europe. Admittedly, in most cases this planning involved little more than the creation of a street network and the establishment of aesthetic guidelines for some of the buildings. However, by the eighteenth century many of the larger European municipalities had built up experience in the provision of main drainage networks and in the enforcement of building regulations designed to reduce the risk of conflagrations. They were also accustomed to regulating smoke and other nuisances.

These modes of public intervention in the urban environment may reasonably be regarded as the foundations of modern planning. However, even in the eighteenth century this activity was still far from the coherent, comprehensive, predictive and scientific activity which we recognize as planning today. With the great majority of the population still living in the countryside, most towns were very small and closely bound up with rural society. Their populations grew, at best, only slowly, and were subject to sharp reductions in times of epidemic or famine. There was hardly any technological change to affect them, and their industries laboured under the constant threat of competition from the countryside, where the attraction of cheap labour was reinforced by one of the few important technical developments of the pre-industrial era, the growth of water power. Even the largest cities were compact and simple in structure, and they got by with very little public investment in main services. There was no potential here for a dynamic evolution of public intervention towards comprehensive planning.

Industrialization was to change all this. Beginning in Britain in the mid-eighteenth century, it spread to Western Europe and North America in the course of the nineteenth. By 1914 much of Eastern Europe had been affected, and trade and colonization were implanting it in parts of South America, Africa and Asia. Industrialization involved the progressive application to manufacture of new methods, machinery and power sources, allowing it to become increasingly productive. This progress was accompanied by a massive shift of labour from agriculture to industry. In time, this labour began to enjoy higher earnings which enhanced demand for consumer goods and services. In eighteenth-century Britain much of the most advanced industry was to be found in the countryside, using water power. However, by the early decades of the nineteenth century the development of canals, the steam engine, and railways was permitting industry to concentrate in the towns, which offered considerable external economies to manufacturing. When industrialization spread outside Britain it took a mainly urban form from the start. Throughout the process, moreover, the towns provided most of the new services stimulated by the growth of manufacturing.

In the industrializing areas these developments produced a big change in the balance of population between town and country. Britain led the way, with a third of her people living in towns by 1801, a half by 1851, and fully four-fifths by the First World War. The other industrializing nations followed a similar trend, and in the course of the twentieth century Germany, the United States, France and a number of other advanced nations have reached the proportion of eighty to eighty-five per cent which apparently marks the maximum degree of urbanization for sovereign states. Meanwhile, industrialization coincided with a rapid increase in the population of the areas directly affected. Britain's population, for instance, increased more than five times between the Napoleonic and Second World Wars. As a result, towns grew more numerous and, even more important, they grew much bigger. The population of London increased from less than a million in 1801 to six millions in 1914. During the same period Berlin passed from 170,000 to four millions. Many of the industrial towns of Britain's North and Midlands registered a tenfold increase in population during the nineteenth century.

During the early stages of industrialization the most striking phenomenon was the rise of once quite small towns and villages, usually on or near major coalfields, to considerable urban prominence. However, as the nineteenth century wore on, the development of the railways allowed industry to free itself from dependence on local supplies of raw materials and to move to the very large centres which offered the greatest external economies. From the middle of the nineteenth century, almost everywhere, the largest cities began to grow faster than the medium-sized and small towns. This tendency was reinforced by the expansion of the tertiary sector, which also favoured very large cities. By 1914 there existed a distinct upper class of giant cities, headed by New York and the great European capitals, with between two and six million inhabitants, and backed up by a phalanx of smaller capitals and provincial centres with populations lying between half a million and two millions. Chicago, Frankfurt, Lyons, Birmingham and Milan stand out among the latter but they are representative of a whole class of towns which, although of the second rank, were larger than any pre-industrial town—except ancient Rome, medieval Istanbul, and modern Peking—had ever been.

The change was not merely one of size, however, but also of structure. Under industrialization even the smallest towns developed a distinct segregation of functions, and in the larger cities huge variations emerged in the character and requirements of the increasingly separate commercial, industrial and residential districts. The efficient operation of the city in these conditions was sustained by a big development of the physical infrastructure, and particularly by the creation of systems of wheeled transport. Meanwhile, the crude health and building regulations of pre-industrial times fell out of line with the problems generated by large-scale mechanized industry, giant office blocks, and mass working-class housing.

With the benefit of hindsight, we can detect a clear progression from the emergence of these characteristics and problems to the perfection of urban planning. However, industrialization was linked to ideological as well as physical changes. The most important of these was the establishment of a non-interventionist orthodoxy, commonly known as *laisser-faire*, according to which the common wealth was best served by allowing the market mechanism to operate without restriction. This ideology was first developed in the home of industrialization, Britain, in the late eighteenth and early nineteenth centuries. As industrialization spread, *laisser-faire* thinking spread with it, helping to displace such feudal and mercantilist attitudes as survived from the pre-industrial period. While helping in many respects to encourage the industrialization process, *laisser-faire* ideology helped to delay the growth of public intervention in the urban environment. In many British towns, for instance, piped water supplies were established by private enterprise and most systems remained in private hands until well into the second half of the nineteenth century. Urban tramway systems were initially a private initiative almost everywhere. Meanwhile, suggestions that building regulations should be extended to require the building of more spacious or comfortable dwellings were vigorously resisted.

As the nineteenth century wore on, nevertheless, the public

role in the urban environment tended to expand. On the one hand, private enterprise increasingly failed to provide the enhanced range and standard of services which economic development and rising consumer expectations made necessary. On the other, a growing appreciation of the demands of public health and general amenity sustained growing public interference in the development of private land. It was not, however, until the 1890s that the realization dawned that a programme of direct public investment in urban services, and guidelines for the development of private land, could be combined in a single, forward-looking strategy of growth and improvement. The key steps were taken in Germany, where the combination of the long-established practice of town-extension planning with an embryonic form of zoning suddenly created a perfectly practicable vision of a fully planned urban environment. Thereafter, the idea spread quickly, and by the early 1900s a lively international debate on urban planning had grown up. In fact, by 1914 the idea of urban planning, if not its execution, already existed in its mature form.

Let us pause briefly to examine the state of urban planning on the eve of the First World War. Germany remained the most advanced area. There, the growth of nearly all the larger towns, and of a good number of small ones, was directed by a general development plan. In the districts to be developed, the plan normally indicated a network of thoroughfares, distinguishing between major traffic routes (which usually included reserved tracks for electric trams), residential streets, and industrial areas. Within the blocks thus delineated, the nature of the land use, and densities and arrangement of buildings, were laid down. Land was reserved for public open space and communal buildings. Below ground, drainage and distribution systems were incorporated in the scheme of development. In many towns, much peripheral land was owned already by the municipality, but some progress was also being made towards the recoupment of betterment on private land via a tax on property sales. Within the established built-up areas, fewer changes were envisaged, but the plan indicated the main traffic-routes so that street and tramway improvements there could contribute to the smooth operation of the enlarged city. Moreover, both the established and new areas were included in a zoning plan which designated each district for a distinct function, subject to appropriate building regulations.

Even regional planning was on the scene by 1914. Because not only large cities, but quite small towns engaged in planning in Germany, the need arose even before the end of the nineteenth century to coordinate the plans of central cities and neighbouring municipalities. This coordination was normally undertaken or encouraged by the state authorities. In the Frankfurt region, and even more around Berlin, interest in regional planning built up in the early 1900s. In 1910 an important competition was held to produce a transport and open-space system for the Berlin region, and in 1912 the Prussian government set up an embryonic regional planning authority for Berlin and its surroundings. Although much remained to be done in practice, it was already possible to envisage the incorporation of the entire country into an interlocking schema of local and regional planning schemes.

Since the First World War the development of planning has basically taken the form of the spread of practices foreshadowed before 1914 to most parts of the advanced world, accompanied by a considerable development of powers and techniques. Regional planning has become increasingly important as cities have spread and decentralized, and national planning has emerged. At the same time the planning problems posed by the reconstruction or renewal of inner districts of cities have been tackled, generating new expertise. The creation of completely new towns by public initiative has become very common, especially in developing areas. The growth of public housing, virtually unknown before 1914, has allowed planners to participate more directly in the process of residential development, and the nationalization of certain industries has helped in the drawing up of general strategies of industrial location. Finally, in every field the practice of planning has become more scientific.

However, outside the socialist world, where urban and regional planning forms just one strand in the total planning of society, some of the fundamental problems perceived before 1914 remain to be solved. Land generally remains in private ownership and in most capitalist countries it is still impossible to recoup betterment effectively. Planning thus often helps private interests to make vast profits. Planning is no longer seen as an easy route to general social reform, glimpsed by some before 1914 and again in the 1940s. Instead, income and wealth are redistributed, and the public welfare is assured, by direct government provision of social security, health services, and education. As a result, some of the excitement of the early days of planning has been lost. It is not entirely insignificant that the routinization of planning has been accompanied by a surge of interest in its history.

The historiography of urban and regional planning: its authors and their motivation

We study the past for two good reasons. One is purely self-indulgent—the past has an intrinsic interest not far removed from nostalgia; we study it because it is there. The second is utilitarian—the past allows us to transcend our own personal experience and to secure a wider and firmer basis for our judgments. Of course, we could draw on the past without the intermediacy of historians, but we would then be very vulnerable to influence by legend and myth. Admittedly, historians too tend to reinterpret the past in the light of the preoccupations of their own times, but their general fidelity to a scientific method assures a basis of objectivity.

All areas of human activity tend to attract historical attention. In the case of urban and regional planning the only surprise is that so much has been written about so recent a phenomenon. There are two main reasons for this prolific output. The first is that planning, as a highly-developed professional activity, requires an academic training which is normally provided in institutions of higher education. The second is that planning, precisely because it has emerged so recently, is still subject to an intensive process of monitoring, much of which results in the production of reports or studies which are historical in character, in the sense that they describe or analyse events taking place over a given period. In fact, pure history courses do not take up much of the time of students in planning schools, but much of the reading assigned in even their theoretical and practical courses relates to planning *experience*. Of course, these reports are also read by the planning theorists and practitioners, politicians, and the informed public, at whom they are ostensibly aimed.

A very wide range of authors thus contributes to planning history. At one extreme, academically-trained historians become involved in the study of planning through their interest in towns, social policy, economic development, transport and a number of other aspects of human activity. At the other, authors with no training other than in planning itself find that their desire to elucidate planning's present and future draws them into its history. On the whole, the former are more interested in the distant past of planning, and the latter in more recent happenings, but there are notable exceptions to this generalization. We can best review the overall distribution of interest by examining the present state of planning historiography.

The historiography of urban and regional planning: the achievement so far

The accompanying bibliography lists some 1400 planning-history titles. The selection is inevitably arbitrary and some of the inclusions and exclusions might be subject to discussion, particularly in respect of nineteenth-century antecedents of planning. However, by any standards this is an impressive body of material. Overall, the work of planners, geographers and other urban scientists or artists predominates over that of academic historians. Many of these non-historians have even been tempted to write general surveys of planning history, or to look specifically at the origins of planning. In this regard, some appear to be motivated by a desire to reinforce the identity of the planning profession by establishing its historical pedigree. Others, frustrated by the limitations of contemporary planning, seek the origins of these frustrations in lines of development, or ideological orthodoxies, established in the foundation years. For still more, planning's past exercises a purely nostalgic attraction. It goes without saying, of course, that this class of author has also been responsible for most of the monitoring reports on recent planning experience.

This lack of historical training is related to a widespread inability to relate planning to broader historical developments.

Many general studies of the history of planning are somewhat dreary catalogues of legislation in which administrative accretion appears to provide the only dynamic of growth. Portraits of heroic individual planners, unrelated to their times or to those with whom they worked, are legion. Studies of planning in individual towns often fail to relate specific planning policies to the general processes of urban evolution. However, it would be unfair to press these criticisms too far, for, on the other hand, this class of author has produced some of the great international studies of planning history, whereas the professional historian has generally preferred to operate within national boundaries. Moreover, if the academically-trained historian is unhappy with the general standard of planning historiography, he has only to move into the field to demonstrate how it should be done.

Given the preoccupations of the main body of planning-history authors, it is not surprising to find that the bulk of planning historiography falls into either the pre-1914 or the post-1945 categories. The nineteenth-century origins of planning have been a constant source of fascination, while planning's great expansion since the Second World War has provided a massive corpus of material for monitoring and polemical studies. In comparison, the interwar years are a grey area. Owing partly to international economic and political difficulties, neither planning practice nor theory greatly developed during this period, if we exclude the mainly theoretical contribution of the Modern Movement in architecture. In the last few years this gap has begun to be filled, partly owing to a recognition that certain attitudes which survive in contemporary planning were formed in these years, but much remains to be done.

The distribution of studies of detailed aspects of planning is partly a function of this general pattern. The investigation of pre-1914 antecedents of mature planning is inevitably a piecemeal operation. Since 1945, on the other hand, the great growth of planning practice has produced a number of specialisms within planning, many of which have attracted historical attention. The coverage of each of these areas will be discussed below, in the detailed introductions to sections within the bibliography.

A future for planning history

There is no doubt that the volume of planning-history studies will continue to increase. The spread of planning into the Third World is bound to generate a new wave of research. The general deceleration of economic growth in the industrialized world may well produce a contraction of planning activity, courses and publishing, but the resulting shift towards the rehabilitation of the existing habitat and the conservation of resources will very soon be reflected in the literature. Study-groups such as the Planning History Group (founded 1974) and its national affiliates will help stimulate and coordinate research, and raise standards. Academic historians will move into the field in greater numbers as, with the passage of time, the twentieth century attracts more historical attention. Historical controversy, still virtually absent from planning historiography, will develop and become a potent stimulus to new thinking and research.

It is to be hoped, however, that sight will not be lost of the essential role of planning history as a source of experience for those involved in planning. Much of the present vitality of planning history lies in its link with planning practice and theory. There is room in the writing of planning history for both the academic historian and the practising planner, together with the whole intervening range of social scientists. In fact, if this bibliography indicates anything, it is that there is no valid distinction to be made between the historian and the social scientist. Both draw, as do we all, on historical experience, and both have a contribution to make to the conservation and interpretation of this invaluable legacy.

The bibliography

Terms of reference

This bibliography sets out to list all major contributions to the study of the history of urban and regional planning, as defined above (p. 1). A study is deemed a contribution to history if (a) its main purpose is to describe, analyse, or comment on changes occurring over a period of time, or (b) it describes, analyses or comments on a state of affairs no longer obtaining at the time of writing. Discretion has been used to exclude studies of a superficial, ephemeral, or purely polemical character, and those in which historical references are incidental or markedly derivative. The coverage of some areas has been weakened by difficulties in obtaining access to journals published outside Western Europe and North America, and the compiler's illiteracy in Arabic, Chinese and Japanese. Nevertheless, the bibliography provides a fair reflection of the state of planning historiography, the main development of which has so far occurred in Western Europe and North America.

Primary materials, such as published collections of letters, documents and plans, have been excluded unless their editorial elements constitute contributions to history. Autobiographies have, however, been included. Unpublished university theses have been included and are classified with the printed titles, as are cyclostyled working papers produced by institutions. Conference contributions are excluded.

Arrangement

Titles have been placed in eight major subject-categories and, where appropriate, under sub-headings within those categories. Where a title justifies a place in more than one subject-category, cross-references are provided. Materials relating to named individuals, places and institutions are best located through the index of names (p. 265). There is also an index of authors (p. 272).

Where a book has been translated into English, the English title is preferred but the original publication details are added wherever possible. The date of publication is that of the first edition, and no attempt has been made to provide full details of all subsequent editions. However, attention is normally drawn to later editions when important changes have been made.

Bibliographies relating to the general development of urban and regional planning are included in Section 2, but more specialized bibliographies appear in the appropriate subject-categories. Serial bibliographies are not included.

In order to make this bibliography as complete and up-to-date as possible, a ninth section, 'Additional entries', has been added at the final proof stage. Cross-references in the main body of the bibliography indicate the presence of relevant material in 'Additional entries', and authors' and other names from the new section have been incorporated in the indexes.

1.
Planning history: definitions, methods and objectives

It is perhaps a sign of the immaturity of the field that so little has appeared on the nature of planning historiography. On the other hand, it is no bad thing that planning historians should get on with their main task rather than wring their hands about what they ought or ought not to be doing. Several of the titles in this section are primarily attempts to justify the teaching of history to student planners—a perennial debate, this, which dates back to the early 1900s. The growing Marxist critique of traditional 'whig' planning historiography is too recent to be reflected here, but Pierotti (1976) and the discussions recorded in the same volume are worth consulting for the shape of things to come. Indeed, the Italian presence in the vanguard of planning-history debates will be reflected throughout this bibliography.

See also 9.24, 9.125, 9.134.

1.1 CHERRY, Gordon E. (1969) The spirit and purpose of town planning: a historical approach. *Journal of the Town Planning Institute*, **60** (1), pp. 12–15.

Calls for more interest in the history of planning to provide much-needed perspective for current endeavours.

1.2 GOLDFIELD, David R. (1978) The role of planning history in the planning curriculum. *Bulletin of the Association of Collegiate Schools of Planning*, **16** (1), pp. 1–4.

Justifies the inclusion of history in planning courses in the United States.

1.3 PICCINATO, Luigi (1949) Invito alla storia dell'urbanistica. *Metron*, **33–4**, pp. 7–12.

Asserts the value of the study of the history of urban development and town planning as an aid to effective action in the future.

1.4 PIEROTTI, Piero (1976) Gli studi di storia urbanistica nell'ambito delle discipline storico-architettoniche e storico-artistiche in Italia durante il secondo dopoguerra, in Martinelli, Roberta and Nuti, Lucia (eds.), *La storiografia urbanistica*. Lucca: CISCU, pp. 104–23.

Discusses some of the major Italian contributions to town-planning history since 1943.

1.5 PRESSMAN, Norman (1974) The built environment: a planning approach to the study of urban settlement. *Contact*, **6** (3), pp. 6–13.

On the relevance of the concerns and methods of planners to the study of urban history. Also published in *Urban History Review*, No. 2, 1973, pp. 8–12.

1.6 TUNNARD, Christopher (1961) The city and its interpreters. *Journal of the American Institute of Planners*, **27**, pp. 346–50.

A review of Lewis Mumford's *The City in History*, including some general reflections on the proper objectives of planning history.

1.7 TUNNARD, Christopher (1963) The customary and the characteristic: a note on the pursuit of city planning history, in Handlin, Oscar and Burchard, John (eds.), *The Historian and the City*. Cambridge, Mass.: MIT Press/Harvard University Press, pp. 216–24.

Calls for the study of planning history as a distinct discipline (and not as a branch of the history of design or architecture), integrating economic, social and ideological factors.

2.
Encyclopaedias, guides and bibliographies

This section includes only items of international or general relevance. More specific items appear in the appropriate sections later in the bibliography.

2.1 AKADEMIE FÜR RAUMFORSCHUNG UND LANDESPLANUNG (1970) *Handwörterbuch der Raumforschung and Raumordnung* (3 vols.). Hamburg: Gebrüder Janecke.

Contains many entries relevant to the history of planning, particularly in Germany, where it is the most authoritative urban encyclopaedia.

2.2 ASHWORTH, Graham (1973) *Encyclopaedia of Planning*. London: Barrie and Jenkins.

Includes entries of historical relevance.

2.3 AUZELLE, Robert (1947–) *Encyclopédie de l'urbanisme*. Paris: Vincent Fréal.

A series of fascicules analysing and illustrating specific town planning projects, in a variety of countries, with much coverage of the nineteenth and twentieth centuries.

2.4 BESTOR, George Clinton and JONES, Holway R. (1972) *City Planning Bibliography: A Basic Bibliography of Sources and Trends* (3rd ed.). New York: American Society of Civil Engineers.

A very extensive selection, including some material of historical relevance.

2.5 *Bibliografia di Architettura e Urbanistica* (1971). Milan: La Cittá.
An extensive collection of titles, many of them relevant to planning history.

2.6 *Bibliografia di Architettura e Urbanistica 2* (1973). Milan: La Cittá.
A supplement to the above, including mainly recent titles. More such supplements are promised.

2.7 BRANCH, Melville Campbell (1970) *Comprehensive Urban Planning: A Selective Annotated Bibliography with Related Materials*. Beverly Hills: Sage Publications.
Includes some entries of historical relevance.

2.8 HULCHANSKI, John David (1977) *History of Modern Town Planning, 1800–1940: A Bibliography* (Council of Planning Librarians, Exchange Bibliography no. 1239). Monticello, Ill.: Council of Planning Librarians.
Narrower than its title might suggest, as it concentrates almost exclusively on North America. Here, however, its coverage is very thorough, and it includes much primary, as well as secondary, material.

2.9 PORTOGHESI, Paolo (ed.) (1968–69) *Dizionario enciclopedico di architettura e urbanistica* (6 vols.). Rome: Istituto Editoriale Romano.
An ambitious compilation of much value for the history of planning.

2.10 SHILLABER, Caroline (1959) *References on City and Regional Planning*. Cambridge, Mass.: MIT Press.
Contains some entries of historical relevance.

2.11 SPIELVOGEL, Samuel (1951) *A Selected Bibliography on City and Regional Planning*. Washington: Scarecrow Press.
Contains some entries of historical relevance.

2.12 SUTCLIFFE, Anthony (1977) *The History of Modern Town Planning: A Bibliographic Guide* (C.U.R.S. Research Memorandum no. 57). Birmingham: Centre for Urban and Regional Studies, Birmingham University.
An earlier version of the current bibliography, containing 656

items and an introduction commenting briefly on the past and possible future of planning history.

2.13 TESDORPF, Jürgen C. (1975) *Systematische Bibliographie zum Städtebau: Stadtgeographie, Stadtplanung, Stadtpolitik*. Cologne: Carl Heymanns.
Contains some entries of historical relevance.

2.14 WANDERSLEB, Hermann *et al.* (1959) *Handwörterbuch des Städtebaues, Wohnungs- und Siedlungswesens* (3 vols.). Stuttgart: Kohlhammer.
A planning dictionary of some relevance to the recent history of planning in the German Federal Republic.

2.15 WHITE, Brenda (1970) *Source Book of Planning Information*. London: Clive Bingley.
Includes a brief survey of the historical development of planning and a longer exposition of progress in Britain since the 1947 Act (pp. 11–40). There is also a useful survey of planning historiography (pp. 288–98).

2.16 WHITE, Brenda (1974) *The Literature of Urban and Regional Planning*. London: Routledge and Kegan Paul.
A thorough survey, mainly of British planning, with much reference to historical material.

2.17 WHITTICK, Arnold (ed.) (1974) *Encyclopedia of Urban Planning*. New York/London: McGraw-Hill.
An impressive compilation including much material of historical relevance.

3.
Planning as a world movement

Modern urbanization is a world-wide process, and the growth of planning theory, if not practice, has been to a large extent an international phenomenon. There is therefore every reason for the planning historian to look beyond the boundaries of his own country, and large numbers of them have been doing so since the early twentieth century. The genre, it must be admitted, appeals mainly to those interested in the artistic aspects of planning, but Hall (1974) and others have shown that social scientists and pure historians are by no means disqualified. Of course, the broader the scope, the more derivative most of this work has to be, and some of these titles contain no more than a standard tour of planning landmarks and a recital of received judgments. However, some of the most famous planning-history studies ever written appear in this section, and much of the current debate on the nature of planning is being carried on in this area. It is here, too, that 'capitalist' and 'socialist' planning confront each other most arrestingly. Finally, we may note that Anglo-Saxon writers are less prominent in this section than in most of the others, while the French who, as we shall see, have little to say about their own planning, stand out as guides to world-wide developments. So too do the Eastern Europeans and, once again, the Italians.

See also 9.44, 9.46, 9.59–60, 9.77, 9.79, 9.126.

3.1 ABERCROMBIE, Patrick (1953) *Town and Country Planning*. London: Thornton Butterworth.

Part 1 provides an interesting, though highly selective, discussion of the historical development of modern planning by a practising planner who always showed a strong historical sense and international awareness. A new edition was published by the Oxford University Press in 1959.

3.2 *Actualité de la Charte d'Athènes* (n.d., [1978]). Strasbourg: Institut d'Urbanisme et d'Aménagement Régional, Université des Sciences Humaines de Strasbourg.

Proceedings of a colloquium held at La Tourette in October, 1976. Includes contributions on the origins and elaboration of the Athens Charter, and on its implications and influence.

3.3 ADAMS, Thomas (1932) *Recent Advances in Town Planning*. London: J. and A. Churchill.

A survey of planning progress by the noted planning pioneer, with much discussion of post-1918 developments. Main emphasis is on Britain but the author's wide experience is fully reflected in sections on the United States, the Empire, and other countries.

3.4 ADAMS, Thomas (1935) *Outline of Town and City Planning: A Review of Past Efforts and Modern Aims*. London: J. and A. Churchill.

Almost the whole volume is composed of a historical review of the struggles and achievements of the planning movement by one of its founding figures. The main emphasis is on the United States (chapters 6, 8 and 9) but chapter 10 outlines developments elsewhere. The quality of the historical analysis is not outstanding, but Adams's personal involvement makes his account valuable.

3.5 ALBERS, Gerd (1974) Ideologie und Utopie im Städtebau, in Pehnt, Wolfgang (ed.), *Die Stadt in der Bundesrepublik Deutschland*. Stuttgart: Philipp Reclam jun., pp. 453–76.

A discussion of major tendencies and issues in the development of town planning since the nineteenth century.

3.6 AUZELLE, Robert (1964) *323 citations sur l'urbanisme*. Paris: Vincent Fréal.

An anthology of quotations from planning authorities, of which Part 1 is relevant to the historical development of planning since the early twentieth century.

3.7 AYMONINO, Carlo (1971) *Origini e sviluppo della città moderna*. Padua: Marsilio Editori.

An essay on the physical development of the modern city with some reference to planning.

3.8 BACON, Edmund N. (1967) *Design of Cities*. London: Thames and Hudson.

A study of various modes of urban design, with much reference to the work of the modern planning movement. A revised edition was issued in 1974.

3.9 BARDET, Gaston (1945) *L'urbanisme*. Paris: Presses Universitaires de France.

A brief introduction to urban planning of which chapters 1 and 2 provide a useful historical survey with major emphasis on France. There have been a number of revised editions.

3.10 BARDET, Gaston (1948) *Le nouvel urbanisme*. Paris: Vincent Fréal.

A didactic planning text with much historical perspective.

3.11 BENEVOLO, Leonardo (1967) *The Origins of Modern Town Planning*. London: Routledge and Kegan Paul.

A translation of *Le origini dell'urbanistica moderna* (Bari: Laterza, 1963). This is principally a study of model-community planning over the years 1815–48, after which efforts to improve the urban environment are depicted as losing their way through lack of an overall, idealistic vision. By rejecting the view that planning is the product of a slow accumulation of administrative instruments, this study represents the very antithesis of most British and American interpretations. It remains, however, an influential work in the Italian school of planning historians.

3.12 BENEVOLO, Leonardo (1971) *History of Modern Architecture* (2 vols.). London: Routledge and Kegan Paul.

A translation of *Storia dell'architettura moderna* (Bari: Laterza, 1960 and later editions). A comprehensive study of the evolution of modern architecture since the nineteenth century, with much reference to urban design and town planning.

3.13 BENEVOLO, Leonardo, GIURA LONGO, T. and MELOGRANI, C. (1967) *La città moderna: tre lezioni*. Florence: CLUSF.

A very general inquiry into the development of certain key

elements of the modern approach to planning. New editions
have been issued.

3.14 BERNDT, Heide (1968) *Das Gesellschaftsbild bei Stadtplänern*. Stuttgart/
Berne: Karl Krämer.
Analyses the world view of leading figures in the development
of planning.

3.15 BLUMENFELD, Hans (1949) Theory of city form, past and present.
Journal of the Society of Architectural Historians, **8** (3,4), pp. 7–16.
Discusses changing ideas on desirable forms for cities from the
Renaissance to the twentieth century.

3.16 BUNIN, Andrei V. (1953) *Istoria gradostroitelnogo iskusstva*. Moscow:
Gos.izd-vo lit-r'y po stroitel'stva i arkhitektury.
A general history of urban design and planning.

3.17 BUNIN, Andrei V., POLIAKOV, N. Kh. and SHKVARIKOV, V. A. (eds.)
(1945) *Gradostroitel'stvo*. Moscow: Izdatel'stvo Akademii
Arkhitektury S.S.S.R.
A world-wide survey of the history of urban design and
settlement, with some reference to modern planning.

3.18 CARDARELLI, Urbano (1973) *Urbanistica fra storia e teoria*. Naples:
Fondazione Ivo Vanzi.
A study of the evolution of urban and planning theory,
identifying and analysing the work of major contributors to this
development since the nineteenth century.

3.19 CARVER, Humphrey (1962) *Cities in the Suburbs*. Toronto: Toronto
University Press.
Includes a historical survey of the development of 'towns-in-
the-countryside' concepts.

3.20 CHOAY, Françoise (1965) *L'urbanisme: utopies et réalités*. Paris:
Editions du Seuil.
A selection from the writings of major contributors to
planning theory in the nineteenth and twentieth centuries,
covering the ground sketched out in *The Modern City: Planning in
the Nineteenth Century* (see 3.22). Ranges from the Utopian Socialists

to writers as recent as Jane Jacobs and Kevin Lynch. Includes thinkers, such as Victor Hugo and Spengler, who were not involved directly in urban affairs. An introductory essay proposes a typology of planning similar to that set out in *The Modern City*.

3.21 CHOAY, Françoise (1970) L'histoire et la méthode en urbanisme. *Annales E.S.C.*, 25 (4), pp. 1143–54.

A discussion of general developments in the history of planning, with less emphasis on methodology than the title suggests.

3.22 CHOAY, Françoise (1970) *The Modern City: Planning in the Nineteenth Century*. London: Studio Vista.

Discusses nineteenth-century antecedents of town planning and developments in the early twentieth century, attempting to incorporate semiological concepts. In contrast to Benevolo, she is prepared to accept that nineteenth-century urban modernization and control policies ('proto-urbanisme') led to modern town planning, but she makes a stimulating distinction between 'progressist' and 'culturalist' (i.e. backward-looking) modes.

3.23 CHRISTEN, Alexander (1946) *Zur Entwicklungsgeschichte des Städtebaus*. Erlenbach/Zurich: Verlag für Architektur.

A history of urban settlement, planned and unplanned, with much consideration of the development of modern town planning between the nineteenth century and the Second World War. Main emphasis is on physical design.

3.24 'CIAM' (1976) *Parametro*, 7 (52).

A special number of the journal devoted to the CIAM (Congrès internationaux d'architecture moderne) in the 1930s, with much relevance to the CIAM's discussions of urban planning.

3.25 CLOUGH, Rosa Trillo (1961) *Futurism: The Story of a Modern Art Movement*. New York: Philosophical Library.

Of some relevance to the development of futuristic styles of urban design.

3.26 COLLINS, George R. (1959) Linear planning throughout the world. *Journal of the Society of Architectural Historians*, 18, pp. 74–93.

On the spread and development of the principles first proposed by Soria y Mata.

3.27 CONRADS, Ulrich (1964) *Programme und Manifeste zur Architektur des 20. Jahrhunderts*. Berlin: Ullstein.

An edited collection of documents representing major tendencies in the development of the Modern Movement in architecture. Some relevance to urban design and planning.

3.28 COWAN, Peter (1972–73) Utopians, scientists and forecasters: approaches to understanding the city. *Transactions of the Bartlett Society*, 9, pp. 78–100.

A rather slight discussion of the characteristics of some of the major schools in urban studies, including some comments on nineteenth- and twentieth-century founders of planning.

3.29 CURL, James Stevens (1970) *European Cities and Society: A Study of the Influence of Political Climate on Town Design*. London: Leonard Hill.

Less specifically related to politics than its title suggests, this amounts to a general history of urban design, with some discussion of the nineteenth and twentieth centuries.

3.30 CZERNY, Władyslaw (1972) *Architektura zespołów osiedleńczych: studia i szkice*. Warsaw: Arkady.

A general history of planning and architecture.

3.31 DESPO, Jan (1973) *Die ideologische Struktur der Städte*. Berlin: Gebrüder Mann.

A discussion of the ideological foundations of urban planning policies, with some historical perspective.

3.32 EGLI, Ernst (1959–67) *Geschichte des Städtebaues* (3 vols.). Zurich: Rentsch.

Modern urban planning is surveyed in Volume 3.

3.33 FISHER, Jack C. (1962) Planning the city of socialist man. *Journal of the American Institute of Planners*, 28 (4), pp. 251–65.

A discussion of urban planning in Eastern Europe, analysing

the impact of socialist planning on a number of cities, and stressing discrepancies between ideal and reality.

3.34 FISHER, Jack C. (1967) Urban planning in the Soviet Union and Eastern Europe, in Eldredge, H. Wentworth (ed.), *Taming Megalopolis, vol. II: How to Manage an Urbanized World.* New York: Praeger, pp. 1068–99.
A critical appraisal, with some historical perspective.

3.35 GALLION, Arthur B. and EISNER, Simon (1950) *The Urban Pattern: City Planning and Design.* Princeton: Van Nostrand.
A global history of town planning from the origins to the present, concentrating on physical layout. Modern planning is discussed in Part 2, 'The industrial city'. The main emphasis is on the United States but there is a certain amount of European material. A second edition appeared in 1963.

3.36 GIEDION, Sigfried (1941) *Space, Time and Architecture: The Growth of a New Tradition.* Cambridge, Mass.: Harvard University Press.
The earliest survey of the Modern Movement, and still the most famous, written from a standpoint of utter commitment. Includes an ecstatic appraisal of the Movement's now much-questioned approach to urban design. Several new editions of the book were published into the late 1960s.

3.37 GIOVANNONI, Gustavo, *et al.* (1943) *L'urbanistica dall'antichità ad oggi.* Florence: Sansoni.
The first major study of relevance to the history of modern planning to appear in Italy.

3.38 GRUSHKA, Emanuel (1963) *Rasvitie Gradostroitel'stva.* Bratislava: Academy of Sciences.
A general survey of the development of town planning, with special emphasis on Eastern Europe and the Soviet Union.

3.39 GUENOUN, Michèle (1971) La cité, in Brion-Guerry, L. (ed.), *L'année 1913: les formes esthétiques de l'oeuvre d'art à la veille de la première guerre mondiale.* Paris: Klincksieck, pp. 181–202.
Tries, with only a degree of success, to summarize the main

currents in European planning on the eve of the First World War.

3.40 HACKETT, Brian (1950) *Man, Society and Environment: The Historical Basis of Planning*. London: Percival Marshall.

Chapters 11 and 12 deal with the development of planning in the 'machine age', looking mainly at the contributions of individual theorists and practitioners. The author tries to set planning in the context of the features of urban development and its problems, but does not achieve great depth.

3.41 HALL, Peter (1974) *Urban and Regional Planning*. Harmondsworth: Penguin.

Despite its title, most of this book is purely historical, covering the evolution of planning in Britain and abroad with all the author's customary vigour and clarity.

3.42 HEGEMANN, Werner (1911, 1913) *Der Städtebau nach den Ergebnissen der Allgemeinen Städtebau-Ausstellung in Berlin* (2 vols.). Berlin: Ernst Wasmuth.

A handbook to the General Town Planning Exhibition, Berlin, 1910. Throws much light on the world-wide development of town planning in recent years. Part 1 provides a general history and critique of the development of planning in Berlin, similar to Hegemann's later *Das steinerne Berlin*. Part 2 contains shorter studies, not all of them markedly historical, of Paris, Vienna, Budapest, Munich, Cologne, London, Stockholm, Chicago and Boston.

3.43 HEILIGENTHAL, Roman (1929) *Städtebaurecht und Städtebau. Band 1: Die Grundlagen des Städtebaus und die Probleme des Städtebaurechtes: Städtebaurecht und Städtebau im deutschen und ausserdeutschen Sprachgebiet*. Berlin: Deutsche Bauzeitung.

Principally a study of planning powers and practice current in Europe at the time of writing, but with frequent historical references to the development of planning in Germany and other European countries since the nineteenth century.

3.44 HELMS, Hans G. (1970) Die Stadt—Medium der Ausbeutung: historische Perspektiven des Städtebaus, in Helms, Hans G. and

Janssen, Jörn (eds.), *Kapitalistischer Städtebau*. Neuwied/Berlin: Hermann Luchterhand, pp. 5–35.
A lengthy critique of the 'capitalist city' and the 'capitalist town planning' which it has engendered.

3.45 HERBERT, G. (1963) The organic analogy in town planning. *Journal of the American Institute of Planners*, **29**, pp. 198–209.
A critique of the biological approach to the understanding of cities, with some reference to its earlier advocates.

3.46 HIORNS, Frederick Robert (1956) *Town-building in History*. London: Harrap.
A general history of urban design, with main emphasis on Britain and the United States.

3.47 HOUGHTON-EVANS, William (1975) *Planning Cities: Legacy and Portent*. London: Lawrence and Wishart.
A general history of town planning, with emphasis on physical design.

3.48 HRUŠKA, Emanuel (1970) *Stavba miest: jej história, prítomnost' a budúcnost'*. Bratislava: SAV.
A general history of urban design and planning.

3.49 HRŮZA, Jiří (1964) Ke vzniku soudobých urbanistických teorií. *Architektura Č.S.S.R.*, **2**, pp. 81–90.
On the origins and development of town-planning theories.

3.50 HRŮZA, Jiří (1965) *Teorie Města*. Prague: Československá Akademie Věd.
See 3.51.

3.51 HRŮZA, Jiří (1972) *Teorie goroda*. Moscow: Stroiisdat.
A general history of urban planning chiefly in terms of physical design, with some emphasis on Czechoslovakia and Eastern Europe. Originally published in Czech—see 3.50.

3.52 HUGHES, T. H. and LAMBORN, E. H. (1923) *Towns and Town Planning, Ancient and Modern*. Oxford: Clarendon Press.
A general history of the physical aspects of planning with

much coverage of the nineteenth and twentieth centuries, though without profound analysis.

3.53 HUGO-BRUNT, Michael (1972) *The History of City Planning: A Survey.* Montreal: Harvest House.

A wide-ranging historical survey, including the nineteenth and twentieth centuries.

3.54 JELLICOE, Geoffrey and Susan (1975) *The Landscape of Man: Shaping the Environment from Prehistory to the Present Day.* London: Thames and Hudson.

Much of this ambitious survey is devoted to the creation of the urban environment, and modern urban and regional planning is fully discussed.

3.55 JENSEN, Rolf (1974) *Cities of Vision.* New York: Wiley; London: Applied Science Publishers.

Principally a qualitative analysis of various models of urban design, but with intermittent historical material and perspective.

3.56 JONAS, Stephan (1979) Du quartier au voisinage: doctrines d'urbanisme de rechange et conception d'unité de vie sociale dans l'Europe de 1900. *L'Architecture d'Aujourd'hui,* **209,** pp. 3–8.

Picks on the years 1890–1914 as the crucial period in which a number of influential reformers and planners developed a 'replacement planning' designed to master and humanize the growth of the giant, anonymous cities thrown up by industrialization. Singles out Garnier and Unwin, with particular reference to their approach to residential planning.

3.57 KING, Anthony D. (1976) *Colonial Urban Development: Culture, Social Power and Environment.* London: Routledge and Kegan Paul.

Investigates the ways in which Western ideas of urban form and life have been imposed on colonial societies, with a major case study of Delhi, 1857–1947, including some reference to the planning of its European areas.

3.58 KING, Anthony D. (1977–78) Exporting 'planning': the colonial and neo-colonial experience. *Urbanism Past and Present,* **5,** pp. 12–22.

A stimulating critique of the too easy assumption that planning ideas and methods developed in the West are appropriate to the needs of the Third World. Much perspective on the history of planning and its relationship to colonialism and neo-colonialism in the twentieth century.

3.59 KORN, Arthur (1953) *History Builds the Town.* London: Lund Humphries.
A general history of urban development which touches intermittently on urban planning.

3.60 LATINI, Antonio (1970) *Avviamenti formativi di urbanistica moderna o scientifica.* Rome: Tip. V. Ferri.
No information.

3.61 LAVEDAN, Pierre (1926) *Qu'est-ce que l'urbanisme? Introduction à l'histoire de l'urbanisme.* Paris: Henri Laurens.
More about urban studies than urban policies, and not as historical in emphasis as the title suggests. Occasional relevance to the historical development of modern town planning.

3.62 LAVEDAN, Pierre (1952) *Histoire de l'urbanisme: époque contemporaine.* Paris: Henri Laurens.
The last volume of a monumental history of urban design by the doyen of French planning historians. Like his mentor, Marcel Poëte, and his contemporary, Gaston Bardet, Lavedan does not appear to have been very interested in modern town planning and this volume is very partial in its coverage. The only sections relevant to modern town planning and its immediate antecedents are chapter 2, on ideal solutions to urban problems in the mid-nineteenth century, chapter 3 on Haussmann, chapter 4 on the history of conservation, and chapter 5 on the garden city and new towns.

3.63 MALCOLMSON, Reginald (1974) *Visionary Projects for Buildings and Cities.* Washington: International Exhibitions Foundation.
An exhibition catalogue, the contents relating mainly to twentieth-century architectural and planning schemes.

3.64 MEYERSON, Martin D. and MITCHELL, Robert B. (1945) Changing city patterns. *Annals of the American Academy of Political and Social Science*, **242**, pp. 149–62.

Includes some reference to the development of modern town planning.

3.65 MOHOLY-NAGY, Sibyl (1968) *Matrix of Man: An Illustrated History of the Urban Environment*. London: Pall Mall Press.

A general history of the urban environment, with emphasis on designed forms. An unusual interpretation, in that modern planning is not portrayed as a product of historical evolution distinct from past efforts, but as one facet of a timeless activity of urban design, which allows Brasilia, for instance, to be characterized as a reincarnation of the Roman monumental tradition.

3.66 MORINI, Mario (1963) *Atlante di storia dell'urbanistica*. Milan: Hoepli.

A comprehensive history of designed settlement forms since ancient times. The section on the modern period, though lengthy, is breathless and occasionally inaccurate, and its main value lies in its numerous plans and illustrations.

3.67 MUMFORD, Lewis (1938) *The Culture of Cities*. London: Secker and Warburg.

The forerunner of *The City in History*, covering similar ground.

3.68 MUMFORD, Lewis (1961) *The City in History*. New York: Harcourt, Brace.

The epitome of Mumford's lifelong study of the history of urban civilization. Modern planning is discussed as one aspect of urban development in the twentieth century.

3.69 MUMFORD, Lewis (1968) *The Urban Prospect*. London: Secker and Warburg.

Makes some reference to modern planning.

3.70 NEWTON, Norman T. (1971) *Design on the Land: The Development of Landscape Architecture*. Cambridge, Mass.: Harvard University Press.

Of some relevance to the history of modern planning, particularly in the United States.

3.71 OLMO, Carlo (1975) *Architettura edilizia: ipotesi per una storia*. Turin: ERI.
Some relevance to the history of modern planning.

3.72 OSTROWSKI, Waclaw (1970) *Contemporary Town Planning: From the Origins to the Athens Charter*. The Hague: International Federation for Housing and Planning.
A translation of *L'urbanisme contemporain: des origines à la Charte d'Athènes* (Paris: Centre de recherche d'urbanisme, 1968). Identifies key pioneers in the development of modern planning and outlines their ideas and best-known schemes. Includes Soria y Mata, Howard, Tony Garnier, Hénard, and Le Corbusier, among others. Numerous plans.

3.73 OSTROWSKI, Waclaw (1970) *L'urbanisme contemporain: tendances actuelles*. Paris: Centre de recherche d'urbanisme.
The sequel to the above, with the main emphasis on the evaluation of contemporary orthodoxies. However, there is some historical discussion of developments since the 1930s.

3.74 PATRICIOS, N. N. (1974) The conceptual determinants of two archetypal city forms. *Planning Outlook*, new series, 15, pp. 4–17.
A comparative study of the origins and evolution of the circular and orthogonal (gridiron) forms for planned cities.

3.75 PAULSSON, Thomas (1970) *Stadsplaneringen under 1800- och 1900-talet* Stockholm: Almqvist and Wiksell.
Briefly and somewhat superficially discusses a number of aspects of the rise of town planning in the nineteenth and twentieth centuries.

3.76 PAWLEY, Martin (1971) *Architecture versus Housing*. New York/Washington: Praeger.
Broader than the title suggests, including much that is relevant to the history of planning in Europe and the United States, particularly in the twentieth century.

3.77 PERÉNYI, Imre (1958) *Városépitéstan* (2 vols.). Budapest: Tankönyvkiado.

A general study of town planning with some historical perspective.

3.78 PERÉNYI, Imre (1970) *Die moderne Stadt: Gedanken über die Vergangenheit und Zukunft der Städteplanung*. Budapest: Akadémiai Kiadó. Also published in Hungarian as *A Korszerü Város*. A general study of town planning with some historical sections. Chapters 1 and 2 are a summary of the development of town planning until the present day, and chapter 4 discusses planning in Hungary with some historical perspective.

3.79 PETSCH, Joachim (ed.) (1974–75) *Architektur und Städtebau im 20. Jahrhundert* (2 vols.). Berlin: Verlag für das Studium der Arbeiterbewegung.
A comparative study of 'capitalist' and socialist town planning.

3.80 PIEROTTI, Piero (1972) *Urbanistica: storia e prassi*. Florence: Marchi and Bertolli.
Includes a general survey of the history of town planning.

3.81 RAGON, Michel (1971–72) *Histoire mondiale de l'architecture et de l'urbanisme moderne*. *Tome 1: Idéologies et pionniers, 1800–1910*. *Tome 2: Pratiques et méthodes, 1911–1971*. Paris: Casterman.
An ambitious survey of the history of modern urban planning, somewhat disappointing in its execution. Strong emphasis on design.

3.82 RASMUSSEN, Steen Eiler (1951) *Towns and Buildings*. Cambridge, Mass.: Harvard University Press.
First published as *Byer og Bygninger: skildret i tegninger og ord* (Copenhagen: Forlaget Fremad, 1949). Discusses aspects of the development of the built environment, and is especially informative on nineteenth-century urban modernization policies.

3.83 ROSENBERG, Franz and HRUŠKA, Emanuel (1969) *Städtebau in West und Ost*. Hanover: Niedersächsische Landeszentrale für Politische Bildung.
Sets out to compare and contrast urban planning in Eastern

and Western Europe, with much historical perspective. Rosenberg's section deals solely with Western Germany, but Hruška attempts to cover the whole of Eastern Europe, though with main emphasis on the Soviet Union.

3.84 ROWEIS, Shoukry T. (1975) *Urban Planning in Early and Late Capitalist Societies (Outline of a Theoretical Perspective)* (Papers on Planning and Design, no. 7). Toronto: Department of Urban and Regional Planning, University of Toronto.

Attempts to situate planning in the concrete context of capitalism, identifying two phases—early (up to c.1900), and late capitalism. Rather wordy Marxist argumentation.

3.85 SAARINEN, Eliel (1943) *The City: Its Growth, Its Decay, Its Future.* New York: Reinhold.

A discursive commentary on various modes of town design, of incidental historical value.

3.86 SALAZAR, Javier (1979) La logica de lo racional: notas críticas. *Comun,* 1, pp. 8–20.

Much broader than its title suggests, this article surveys the development of a number of dominant motifs in housing design and urban planning since the nineteenth century.

3.87 SAMONÀ, G. (1958) L'urbanizzazione fra le due guerre mondiali. *Urbanistica,* 24, pp. 3–8.

Discusses the contribution of planning policies to the solution of urban problems in Europe between the world wars.

3.88 SCHNEIDER, Wolf (1963) *Babylon is Everywhere: The City as Man's Fate.* London: Hodder and Stoughton.

A translation of *Überall ist Babylon: Die Stadt als Schicksal des Menschen von Ur bis Utopia* (Düsseldorf: Econ. Verlag, 1960). A wide-ranging study of the development of large cities since ancient times, in the style of Mumford, with occasional relevance to town planning, especially planned new towns of the twentieth century.

3.89 SCHULTZE, Joachim Heinrich (1952) *Stadtforschung und Stadtplanung* (2nd ed.). Bremen-Horn: W. Dorn.

Some historical perspective.

3.90 Schwan, Bruno (ed.) (1935) *Städtebau und Wohnungswesen der Welt*. Berlin: E. Wasmuth.

The product of a survey commissioned by the Deutscher Verein für Wohnungsreform. Consists of contributions by various authors on planning and housing in a number of countries, with some historical perspective.

3.91 Scott, Allen J. and Roweis, Shoukry T. (1977) *Urban Planning in Theory and Practice: A Re-appraisal* (Papers on Planning and Design, no. 14). Toronto: Department of Urban and Regional Planning, University of Toronto.

An attempt to construct a Marxist theory of planning, with some historical perspective. Argues that planning is a tool which attempts to regulate the contradictions generated by capitalist city-building processes, and so has no reform potential.

3.92 Sert, José Luis (1942) *Can Our Cities Survive?* Cambridge, Mass.: Harvard University Press; London: Oxford University Press.

This is a polemical study, but Sigfried Giedion provides a short history of the CIAM on pp. ix–xi.

3.93 Sfintescu, Cincinat I. (1933) *Urbanistica Generală* (Part 1). Bucharest: I. E. Toroutiu.

Includes a historical survey (pp. 42–208) of the world-wide development of town planning, with some reference to Rumania.

3.94 Sica, Paolo (1970) *L'immagine della città da Sparta a las Vegas*. Bari: Laterza.

A general history of ideas about cities, with modern town planning covered in chapters 6 and 7. A stimulating approach, similar to Choay's.

3.95 Sica, Paolo (1978) *Storia dell'urbanistica: il Novecento*. Bari: Laterza.

A massive study of urban environmental policies and planning in the nineteenth century.

3.96 Steinmann, M. (1972) Political standpoints in CIAM, 1928–1933. *Architectural Association Quarterly*, 4, pp. 49–55.

Relevant to the origins of the Athens Charter.

3.97 SUTCLIFFE, Anthony (1979) Environmental control and planning in European capitals 1850–1914: London, Paris and Berlin, in Hammarström, Ingrid and Hall, Thomas (eds.), *Growth and Transformation of the Modern City*. Stockholm: Swedish Council for Building Research, pp. 71–88.

Attempts to explain, on the basis of a theoretical model of the European capital city, the failure of London, Paris and Berlin to establish themselves as leaders in the movement towards urban planning in the late nineteenth and early twentieth centuries.

3.98 TAFURI, Manfredo (1976) *Architecture and Utopia: Design and Capitalist Development*. Cambridge, Mass.: MIT Press.

First published in Italian as *Progetto e Utopia* (Bari: Laterza, 1973). A wide-ranging, rambling essay on aspects of the development of urban design and architecture, with main emphasis on the nineteenth and twentieth centuries.

3.99 TAFURI, Manfredo and DAL CO, Francesco (1976) *Architettura contemporanea*. Milan: Electa.

A general survey of architectural developments since the nineteenth century, including much reference to urban design and town planning.

3.100 TOMBOLA, Giuseppe (1958) *Urbanistica: storia e tecnica*. Padua: CEDAM.

Extensively illustrated survey of urban planning practice, with historical perspective.

3.101 TRIGGS, H. Inigo (1909) *Town Planning: Past, Present and Possible*. London: Methuen.

An early planning text, with some reference to the efforts of the recent past. A second edition appeared in 1911.

3.102 TROEDSSON, Carl Birger (1964) *Architecture, Urbanism and Socio-Political Developments in Our Western Civilization*. Gothenburg: Gumperts.

Of general relevance to the history of planning.

3.103 URIBE URIBE, Leonardo (1962) *Historia del urbanismo y técnicas de planificación*. Medellín (Colombia): Universidad Pontificia Bolivariana.

A general history of urban planning.

3.104 WHITTICK, Arnold (1974) *European Architecture in the Twentieth Century*. Aylesbury: Leonard Hill.

Much consideration of urban design since the later nineteenth century, though somewhat derivative.

3.105 WILLIS, F. Roy (1973) *Western Civilization: An Urban Perspective* (2 vols.). Lexington, Mass.: D. C. Heath.

A wide-ranging history of urban development. Volume 2 includes an account of twentieth-century urban development which makes much reference to town planning.

3.106 WRÓBEL, Tadeusz (1971) *Zarys historii budowy miast*. Wrocław: Zaklad Narodowy im. Ossolińskich.

A general history of urban planning and architecture.

3.107 ZEVI, Bruno (1953) *Storia dell'architettura moderna*. Turin: Einaudi.

This has some relevance to the development of town planning in the twentieth century.

4.
Planning in individual countries

The volume of planning-history studies of individual countries is largely a function of the amount of planning activity generated by those countries. Large planning schools generate a demand for national textbooks of planning history, and a fertile planning process generates numerous monitoring studies and books aimed at the informed public. The national context is a very sensible one in which to study planning history. It avoids timid localism and allows the growth of planning theory and practice to be related to basic social changes and intellectual developments. However, it appeals to those who view planning as an administrative process rather than those who see it as an art, and there are some dreary catalogues of legislative changes and ministerial circulars. On the other hand, it is within the various national contexts that the rise of the planning profession is most usefully discussed. Given that this is by far the longest section in the whole bibliography, this introduction may seem surprisingly short, but what follows can speak for itself. Please note, by the way, that much material relating to individual countries has been located thematically elsewhere in the bibliography. It should be located by checking under the name of the country concerned in the index of names (p. 265).

Australia

4.1 GRUBB, W. Maxwell (1976) History of town planning in Victoria, 1910–1944. Unpublished dissertation (Master of Town and Regional Planning), University of Melbourne.
   A full survey of several major stages in the growth of town planning in the State of Victoria.

4.2 SANDERCOCK, L. (1975) *Cities for Sale: Property, Politics and Urban Planning in Australia.* Melbourne: Melbourne University Press.
On the 'failure' of town planning in Adelaide, Melbourne and Sydney since 1900.

4.3 SHAW, J. H. (1975) *Bibliography of Town and Regional Planning in Australia.* Sydney: New South Wales University Press.
Some historical perspective.

Austria

4.4 DOBLHAMER, Gerhard (1972) *Die Stadtplanung in Oberösterreich von 1850 bis 1938.* Vienna: Springer.
A full survey of planning developments in Upper Austria between 1850 and the *Anschluss* (Linz, Wels).

4.5 SCHWEITZER, Renate (1971) *Österreichische Bibliographie für Städtebau und Raumplanung, 1850–1918.* Vienna/New York: Springer in Komm.
A bibliography of the early history of Austrian urban and environmental planning.

Brazil

4.6 GARDNER, James A. (1973) *Urbanization in Brazil.* New York: International Urbanization Survey, Ford Foundation.
Includes some consideration of recent planning policies.

4.7 GIOJA, Rolando I. (1972) *Planeamiento urbano y regional en Brasil.* Buenos Aires: Ediciones DRUSA.
A brief study, with some historical content.

Canada

4.8 ADAMSON, Anthony (1962) Form and the twentieth-century Canadian city. *Queen's Quarterly*, **69**, pp. 49–68.
Of relevance to Canadian physical planning.

4.9 ARMSTRONG, Alan H. (1968) Thomas Adams and the Commission of Conservation, in Gertler, L. O. (ed.), *Planning the Canadian Environment*. Montreal: Harvest House, pp. 17–35.

On the creation and early work of Canada's first national planning agency, from c.1915 to the 1920s. An earlier version appeared in *Plan Canada*, 1 (1), 1959, pp. 14–32.

4.10 ARTIBISE, Alan F. J. and STELTER, Gilbert A. (1979) Planning and the realities of development: introduction, in Artibise, A. F. J. and Stelter, G. A. (eds.), *The Usable Urban Past: Planning and Politics in the Modern Canadian City*. Toronto: Macmillan Company of Canada, pp. 167–76.

A brief survey, packed with information and perceptive judgments, of the rise of urban planning in Canada since the beginning of the twentieth century.

4.11 BETTISON, David (1975) *The Politics of Canadian Urban Development*. Edmonton: University of Alberta Press.

Includes an outline of Federal housing and planning legislation since 1945 (pp. 61–104).

4.12 CARVER, Humphrey (1975) *Compassionate Landscape*. Toronto: University of Toronto Press.

An autobiography, providing an informative account of the development of Canadian urban planning since 1945.

4.13 COOPER, Ian and HULCHANSKI, J. David (1978) *Canadian Town Planning, 1900–1930: A Historical Bibliography* (3 vols.). Toronto: Centre for Urban and Community Studies, University of Toronto.

Selections of printed primary material from the years 1900–30, relevant to housing, planning and public health.

4.14 GERECKE, Kent (1976) The history of Canadian city planning. *City Magazine*, 2 (3/4), pp. 12–23.

An outline of the development of town planning in Canada since the early twentieth century, with emphasis on the growth of the planning profession.

4.15 GERTLER, Leonard O. (ed.) (1968) *Planning the Canadian Environment*. Montreal: Harvest House.

A collection of essays on the history of planning in Canada, with main emphasis on the years 1959–65.

4.16 GUNTON, Thomas I. (1979) The ideas and policies of the Canadian planning profession, 1909–1931, in Artibise, A. F. J. and Stelter, G. A. (eds.), *The Usable Urban Past: Planning and Politics in the Modern Canadian City*. Toronto: Macmillan Company of Canada, pp. 177–95.

A study of the ideas of the early Canadian planning profession, based on an analysis of the main official reports and professional journals of the period. Identifies three competing approaches—rural collectivism, urban liberalism (City Beautiful and efficiency), and urban radicalism (massive public intervention). Emphasizes Canadian dependence on planning ideas imported from Britain and the United States, and suggests that efficiency became the main objective of Canadian planning, ruling out social justice.

4.17 HULCHANSKI, J. David (1978) *Canadian Town Planning and Housing, 1930–1940: A Historical Bibliography* (Bibliographic Series, no. 10). Toronto: Centre for Urban and Community Studies, University of Toronto.

A brief chronology of Canadian planning events in the 1920s, followed by a list of printed primary material (297 items).

4.18 HULCHANSKI, J. David (1979) *Canadian Town Planning and Housing 1940–1950: A Historical Bibliography* (Bibliographic Series, no. 12). Toronto: Centre for Urban and Community Studies, University of Toronto.

This contains a brief introduction to, and chronology of, the period, followed by a list of printed primary material (478 items).

4.19 NADER, George A. (1975) *Cities of Canada, Vol. 1: Theoretical, Historical and Planning Perspectives*. Toronto: Macmillan.

Much of this is a discussion of contemporary problems but there is a general survey of the history of the Canadian town from its origins to the present, including planning aspects.

4.20 NADER, George A. (1976) *Cities of Canada, Vol. 2: Profiles of Fifteen Metropolitan Centres*. Toronto: Macmillan.

Detailed studies of fifteen Canadian cities, with some historical perspective and relevance to planning.

4.21 SMITH, P. J. (1979) The principle of utility and the origins of planning legislation in Alberta, 1912–1975, in Artibise, A. F. J. and Stelter, G. A. (eds.), *The Usable Urban Past: Planning and Politics in the Modern Canadian City*. Toronto: Macmillan Company of Canada, pp. 196–225.

Argues that the principle of utility, on which the Alberta Town Planning Act of 1913 was based, proved unworkable and converted a potentially radical institution into a reactionary one.

4.22 STELTER, Gilbert A. and ARTIBISE, Alan F. J. (eds.) (1977) *The Canadian City: Essays in Urban History*. Toronto: McClelland and Stewart.

A collection of essays reflecting the rise of urban history in Canada, with some emphasis on planning. Relevant articles are listed separately in this bibliography.

4.23 VAN NUS, Walter (1975) The plan-makers and the city: architects, engineers, surveyors and urban planning in Canada, 1890–1939. Unpublished Ph.D. thesis, University of Toronto.

Case studies of planning achievements in major Canadian cities, with emphasis on politics and the differing objectives of architects, engineers and surveyors.

4.24 VAN NUS, Walter (1976) Sources for the history of urban planning in Canada, 1890–1939. *Urban History Review*, No. 1, pp. 6–9.

A brief review of some of the issues raised in the very few published studies of the history of Canadian planning between 1912 and the Second World War.

4.25 VAN NUS, Walter (1977) The fate of City Beautiful thought in Canada, 1893–1930, in Stelter, Gilbert A. and Artibise, Alan F. J. (eds.), *The Canadian City: Essays in Urban History*. Toronto: McClelland and Stewart, pp. 162–85.

Traces and explains the rise of City Beautiful (monumental-aesthetic) ideas within the Canadian architectural, engineering and surveying professions, and their replacement from about 1910 by ideals of suburban planning. It was first published in the

Canadian Historical Association's *Historical Papers/Communications Historiques 1975*, pp. 191–210.

Chile

4.26 ROBIN, John P. and TERZO, Frederick C. (1973) *Urbanization in Chile*. New York: International Urbanization Survey, Ford Foundation.
Some reference to planning.

China

4.27 BOYD, Andrew C. H. (1962) *Chinese Architecture and Town Planning, 1500 B.C.–A.D. 1911*. London: A. Tiranti.
A general survey, concentrating on physical design and form.

4.28 BUCK, David D. (1975–76) Directions in Chinese urban planning. *Urbanism Past and Present*, **1**, pp. 24–35.
A survey of Chinese urban planning policies since 1949, based on a recent visit.

4.29 GAVINELLI, Corrado and GIBELLI, Maria Cristina (1976) *Città e territorio in Cina*. Bari: Laterza.
Much reference to the history of socialist town planning in China.

4.30 GAVINELLI, Corrado and VERCELLONI, V. (eds.) (1971) Cina: architettura e urbanistica 1949–1970. *Controspazio*, **12**, pp. 2–124.
A number of the journal entirely devoted to planning and architecture in China since the establishment of the Communist regime.

4.31 Lo, Chor-Pang, PANNELL, Clifton W. and WELCH, Roy (1977) Land use changes and city planning in Shenyang and Canton. *Geographical Review*, **67** (3), pp. 268–73.
Surveys the development of the two cities since the nineteenth century, drawing attention to the effects of socialist planning policies applied by the new regime.

Colombia

4.32 ROBIN, John P. and TERZO, Frederick C. (1973) *Urbanization in Colombia.* New York: International Urbanization Survey, Ford Foundation.
Includes some consideration of recent planning policies.

Cuba

4.33 ACOSTA, Maruja and HARDOY, Jorge E. (1971) *Politicas urbanas y reforma urbana en Cuba.* Buenos Aires: Centro de Estudios Urbanes y Regionales.
A study of the urban policies pursued in Cuba under Castro.

4.34 ACOSTA, Maruja and HARDOY, Jorge E. (1971) *Reforma urbana en Cuba revolucionaria.* Caracas: Síntesis Dosmil.
The commercially published version of the above.

4.35 BARKIN, David (1978) Confronting the separation of town and country in Cuba, in Tabb, William K. and Sawers, Larry (eds.), *Marxism and the Metropolis: New Perspectives in Urban Political Economy.* New York: Oxford University Press, pp. 317–37.
Outlines the urban and regional planning policies adopted in Cuba since the Castro revolution, from a Marxist standpoint.

Czechoslovakia

4.36 HRŮZA, Jiří (1967) Pianificazione urbana e territoriale in Cecoslovacchia. *Casabella,* 313, pp. 12–21.
This throws some light on the history of planning in Czechoslovakia since the beginnings of industrialization.

4.37 [HRŮZA, Jiří (ed.)] (1958) *Town Planning in Czechoslovakia.* Prague: Association of Czechoslovak Architects.
This amounts to a survey of the history of Czech planning in recent decades.

4.38 SHVIDKOVSKIĬ, Oleg Aleksandrovich (1966) *Urbanismus socialistického Československa.* Prague: Academia.

A discussion of the objectives and achievements of socialist urban planning in Czechoslovakia.

Denmark

4.39 BIDSTRUP, Knud (1971) *Ebenezers disciple: fra dansk byplanlaegnings pionertid.* Copenhagen: Dansk Byplanlaboratorium.

A general history of the development of town planning in modern Denmark, published for the fiftieth anniversary of the Dansk Byplanlaboratorium.

4.40 ILLERIS, Sven (1966) *Spredning af befolkning, erhverv og byggeri 1955–64.* Copenhagen: Landsplanudvalgets Sekretariat.

An assessment of recent official efforts to disperse population and employment in Denmark.

4.41 KAUFMANN, Erik (1966) *27 slags planer: oversigt over og kritisk analyse af den offentlige fysiske planlaegning i Danmark.* Copenhagen: Teknisk Vorlag.

A critical assessment of the Danish planning system.

4.42 LORENZEN, Vilhelm (1947–58) *Vore byer: studier i bybygning: fra middelalderens slutning til industrialismens gennembrud, 1536–1870* (5 vols.). Copenhagen: I Kommission hos G. E. C. Gad.

Volume V (1958) of this monumental study of Danish urban development covers the early stages of industrialization (1814–70). Includes some discussion of conscious planning and policies to regulate the urban environment.

France

4.43 AUZELLE, Robert (1957) Town planning administration in France 1945–1955. *Town Planning Review,* **28**, pp. 7–36.

A general outline of major developments in French planning since the last war.

4.44 BEAUDOUIN, Eugène (1962) La société française des urbanistes. *Urbanisme*, **77**, pp. 16–19.

Briefly outlines the history of the French association of urban planners on the fiftieth anniversary of its foundation.

4.45 BIAREZ, Sylvie (1974) *Une politique d'urbanisme: les Z.U.P.* Grenoble: Centre de recherche de l'Institut d'études politiques de Grenoble.

A study of the strengths and weaknesses of the *zone à urbaniser en priorité* as a means of controlling land speculation in areas scheduled for rapid public development.

4.46 CENTRE DE RECHERCHE D'URBANISME/INTERNATIONAL FEDERATION FOR HOUSING AND PLANNING (1968) *Urbanization and Planning in France*. Paris/The Hague: Centre de recherche d'urbanisme/ International Federation for Housing and Planning.

Some historical perspective.

4.47 FRITSCH, Adolf (1973) *Planifikation und Regionalpolitik in Frankreich*. Stuttgart: W. Kohlhammer.

A study of French urban and regional planning since the Second World War.

4.48 HOUSE, J. W. (1978) *France: An Applied Geography*. London: Methuen.

Includes a lengthy discussion of 'spatial management policies' (urban and regional), with some perspective on developments since the 1950s. The author's purpose is not primarily historical, however.

4.49 LAVEDAN, Pierre (1960) *Les villes françaises*. Paris: Vincent Fréal.

Chapter 4 deals with planned physical changes in Paris and certain provincial towns in the nineteenth century. Chapter 5 discusses post-1945 reconstruction in certain provincial towns, notably Le Havre.

4.50 ROYER, Jean (1962) A propos d'un anniversaire. *Urbanisme*, **77**, pp. 2–6.

A brief disquisition on the origins of town planning in

France, the 'anniversary' in the title being that of the *Société française des urbanistes.*

4.51   *Town Planning in France* (1972). London: Ambassade de France. Some historical perspective.

4.52   TRAVIS, A. S. (1977) *The Evolution of Town Planning in France from 1900 to 1919, with Special Reference to Tony Garnier and Planning in Lyons* (C.U.R.S. Working Paper no. 48). Birmingham: Centre for Urban and Regional Studies, Birmingham University.

A brief discussion of the state of planning (almost non-existent) in early twentieth-century France, and an outline of Garnier's theoretical and practical work in Lyons.

Germany

(For German Democratic Republic, see next heading.)

4.53   ALBERS, Gerd (1963) Das Stadt-Land-Problem im Städtebau der letzten 100 Jahren. *Studium Generale*, **16**, pp. 576–84.

Discusses the relationship between town and country in the development of German planning thought and practice since the mid-nineteenth century.

4.54   ALBERS, Gerd (1967) Vom Fluchtlinienplan zum Stadtentwicklungsplan. *Archiv für Kommunalwissenschaften*, **6** (2), pp. 192–211.

An outline of the evolution of German planning theory and practice from the Prussian building-lines law of 1875 to the perfection of comprehensive planning.

4.55   ALBERS, Gerd (1975) *Entwicklungslinien im Städtebau: Ideen, Thesen, Aussagen 1875–1945.* Berlin: Bertelsmann Fachverlag.

A study of the contribution of a number of major thinkers to German planning theory, beginning with Baumeister. Composed mainly of edited documents but introduced by a general essay on the development of planning in Germany since the mid-nineteenth century.

4.56 ALBERS, Gerd (1975) Der Städtebau des 19. Jahrhunderts im Urteil des 20. Jahrhunderts, in Schadendorf, Wulf (ed.), *Beiträge zur Rezeption der Kunst des 19. und 20. Jahrhunderts*. Munich: Prestel Verlag, pp. 63–71.

Attempts to assess the strengths and weaknesses of an older tradition of German planning which has been pilloried in recent years.

4.57 ALBERS, Gerd (1978) Wandel und Kontinuität im deutschen Städtebau. *Stadtbauwelt*, **69**, pp. 426–33.

In a paper first given to the First International Conference on the History of Urban and Regional Planning in 1977, Albers argues that ever since its emergence in the later nineteenth century, German planning's strong professional backbone has given it a continuity that has been largely impervious to political changes. For English translation, see Additional entries.

4.58 ALBRECHT, Gerhard and GUT, Albert (1930) *Handwörterbuch des Wohnungswesens*. Jena: Verlag von Gustav Fischer.

An encyclopaedia with many entries relevant to the history of German planning.

4.59 BERGER-THIMME, Dorothea (1976) *Wohnungsfrage und Sozialstaat: Untersuchungen zu den Anfängen staatlicher Wohnungspolitik in Deutschland (1873–1918)*. Frankfurt: Peter Lang; Berne: Herbert Lang.

Discusses the evolution of German housing reform, with some reference to town-planning powers and practice. Includes detailed studies of the *Verein Reichswohnungsgesetz* (a housing reform pressure group), the *Rheinische Verein zur Förderung des Wohnungswesens* (a coordinating body for cooperative building societies), and the *Bund deutscher Bodenreformer* (the main campaigner for land reform). Also studies the housing reform legislation passed, or discussed, in three German States— Hamburg, Hesse and Prussia. In the latter, the 1875 *Fluchtliniengesetz* and the *Lex Adickes* are among the measures discussed. This book is a shortened version of 'Boden und Wohnungsreform in Deutschland, 1873–1918', Freiburg University, Diss. phil., 1975.

4.60 BRIX, Joseph (1911) Aus der Geschichte des Städtebaues in den letzten 100 Jahren, in [Brix, Joseph and Genzmer, Felix (eds.)], *Städtebauliche Vorträge*, 4 (2).
A survey of developments in German planning in the nineteenth century.

4.61 COLOMBO, Loreto (1973) *Urbanistica e pianificazione in Germania 1945–1970*. Naples: Giannini Editore for Istituto di Architettura e Urbanistica, Università di Napoli.
A full survey of developments in reconstruction and planning in both German republics.

4.62 FRECOT, Janos (1976) Die Lebensreformbewegung, in Vondung, Klaus (ed.), *Das wilhelminische Bildungsbürgertum: zur Sozialgeschichte seiner Ideen*. Göttingen: Vandenhoeck und Ruprecht, pp. 138–52.
Of relevance to the generation by the German bourgeoisie of a new environmental ideal, based on nature, the family, and traditional German culture, between c.1890 and 1914.

4.63 GROTE, Ludwig (ed.) (1974) *Die deutsche Stadt im 19. Jahrhundert: Stadtplanung und Baugestaltung im industriellen Zeitalter*. Munich: Prestel.
A collection of articles principally relevant to the architectural history of the German nineteenth-century town, but with some discussion of broader questions of design and layout.

4.64 HALL, Peter (1966) Rhine-Ruhr, in Hall, Peter (ed.), *The World Cities*. London: Weidenfeld and Nicolson, pp. 122–57.
A survey of planning problems in the Ruhr region, set in historical perspective.

4.65 HARTOG, Rudolf (1962) *Stadterweiterungen im 19. Jahrhundert*. Stuttgart: Kohlhammer.
The German equivalent of Ashworth's *Genesis of Modern British Town Planning*, surveying the course of housing reform and planning up to the First World War. Includes a rather curious digression into British industrial housing conditions. This remains the most frequently cited authority on early German planning.

4.66 HEBEBRAND, W. (1963) Stadt und Umland. *Studium Generale*, 16, pp. 606–19.
Makes some reference to the growth of planning in Germany since the mid-nineteenth century.

4.67 HECKER, Hermann (1959) *Zur Geschichte der Landesplanung: über sozialen Wohnungsbau, Städtebau und Bauberatung zur Landesplanung: berufsgeschichtliche Erinnerungen eines alten Landesplaners.* Hamburg: Hammonia-Verlag.
Personal reminiscences of a long career in German planning.

4.68 HELMS, H. G. and JANSSEN, J. (eds.) (1970) *Kapitalistischer Städtebau.* Neuwied/Berlin: Hermann Luchterhand Verlag.
A collection of essays on housing and planning history in Germany since the later nineteenth century, published as a rather heavy-handed attempt to put forward a distinctively Marxist view of planning history. Now a famous book in Germany, it has appeared in more recent editions.

4.69 HOFMANN, Wolfgang (1971) Oberbürgermeister und Stadterweiterungen, in Croon, Helmuth, Hofmann, W. and von Unruh, G. C. (eds.), *Kommunale Selbstverwaltung im Zeitalter der Industrialisierung.* Stuttgart: Kohlhammer, pp. 59–85.
Discusses the new challenges by which the *Oberbürgermeister* were confronted after rapid urban growth set in in Germany after about 1860, with special reference to their part in town-extension planning.

4.70 KABEL, Erich (1949) *Baufreiheit und Raumordnung: die Verflechtung von Baurecht und Bauentwicklung im deutschen Städtebau.* Ravensburg: O. Maier.
Amounts to a general history of German town planning.

4.71 KRABBE, Wolfgang R. (1974) *Gesellschaftsveränderung durch Lebensreform: Strukturmerkmale einer sozialreformerischen Bewegung im Deutschland der Industrialisierungsperiode.* Göttingen: Vandenhoeck and Ruprecht.
Discusses land reform and the Garden City movement in the context of the German middle-class anti-industrial movement of the later nineteenth century. See especially pp. 16–37.

4.72 LANE, Barbara Miller (1968) *Architecture and Politics in Germany, 1918–1945*. Cambridge, Mass.: Harvard University Press.

Principally a study of architecture, but of some relevance to urban design and planning. Remains the outstanding authority on National Socialist design.

4.73 LEES, Andrew (1979) Critics of urban society in Germany, 1854–1914. *Journal of the History of Ideas*, **40** (1), pp. 61–83.

Throws some light on the way in which planning policy sprang out of intellectual attitudes towards large cities in Germany.

4.74 MULLIN, John R. (1978) German new towns: perspective and overview, in Golany, Gideon (ed.), *International Urban Growth Policies: New Town Contributions*. New York: John Wiley, pp. 129–46.

Reviews recent research on German 'new towns'.

4.75 MUTHESIUS, Stefan (1974) *Das englische Vorbild: eine Studie der deutschen Reformbewegungen in Architektur, Wohnbau und Kunstgewerbe im späten 19. Jahrhundert*. Munich: Prestel.

Basically a study of architectural design, but of some relevance to urban design. Stresses the extraordinary respect which British design enjoyed in Germany at the turn of the century. The author is a relative of Hermann Muthesius, author of *Das englische Haus*, the influential German study of English house-design in the early 1900s.

4.76 ORTMANN, Wolf (1956) *Städtebau früher und heute: kurze Einführung in das Wesen des Städtebaues*. Düsseldorf: Werner-Verlag.

A brief discussion of modern planning with some historical perspective, mainly relevant to Germany.

4.77 PETSCH, Joachim (1976) *Baukunst und Stadtplanung im Dritten Reich: Tradition, Bestandaufnahme, Entwicklung, Nachfolge*. Munich: Carl Hanser.

A general study of the architecture and planning of the Third Reich, with principal emphasis on physical design.

4.78 PEVSNER, Nikolaus (1974) Ein Nachwort: deutsch-englische

Wechselbeziehungen, in Grote, Ludwig (ed.), *Die deutsche Stadt im 19. Jahrhundert: Stadtplanung und Baugestaltung im industriellen Zeitalter*. Munich: Prestel Verlag, pp. 311–14.
Discusses ways in which Germany and England mutually influenced each other in architecture and planning during the nineteenth century.

4.79 PICCINATO, Giorgio (1974) *La costruzione dell'urbanistica: Germania, 1871–1914*. Rome: Officina.
Contains a lengthy essay on the development of German planning before 1914, supported by extensive extracts from contemporary planning and housing-reform texts. Extensively illustrated.

4.80 PRAGER, Stephan (1955) *Die Deutsche Akademie für Städtebau und Landesplanung: Rückblick und Ausblick, 1922–1955*. Tübingen: Wasmuth.
An official history commissioned by the Academy.

4.81 SCHULZ, Joachim (1964) Hochhäuser und Citygedanke in Deutschland 1921 bis 1923. *Deutsche Architektur*, 13 (12), pp. 750–5.
Discusses the impact of architectural projects for tower buildings on city-centre planning concepts in Germany in the early 1920s.

4.82 SCHUMACHER, Fritz (1935) *Strömungen in deutscher Baukunst seit 1800*. Leipzig: Seemann.
An architectural history of modern Germany, of some relevance to urban planning. A second edition was published in 1955.

4.83 SPEER, Albert (1970) *Inside the Third Reich*. London: Weidenfeld and Nicolson.
A translation of *Erinnerungen* (Berlin: Propyläen, 1969). An autobiography by Hitler's personal architect and later armaments minister. Describes some of the major urban design projects of the 1930s, and notably the plans for Berlin.

4.84 STÜBBEN, Joseph (1920) Die Entwicklung des deutschen Städtebaus und ihr Einfluss auf das Ausland. *Stadtbaukunst alter und neuer Zeit*, **8**, pp. 113–16; **9**, pp. 129–33; **10**, pp. 151–4.

Outlines the development of planning in Germany between the later nineteenth century and 1920, and goes on to discuss German influence on parallel developments in the other European countries and the United States. This is, for Stübben, an unusually nationalistic treatment, implying that the most important developments abroad have been the product of German influence and that, in its absence, countries such as Denmark have been seriously retarded. Its objective, however, was to boost German morale after defeat in World War I.

4.85 TAFURI, Manfredo (1971) Socialdemocrazia e città nella repubblica di Weimar. *Contropiano*, **1**, pp. 207–23.

A review article, discussing the planning initiatives of Social Democracy and the trade unions in Weimar Germany.

4.86 TAYLOR, Robert R. (1974) *The Word in Stone: The Role of Architecture in the National Socialist Ideology*. Berkeley: University of California Press.

Includes a brief chapter (pp. 250–69) on Nazi building plans for the leading German cities.

4.87 TEUT, Anna (1967) *Architektur im Dritten Reich, 1933–1945*. Berlin: Bertelsmann.

The classic German study of National Socialist architecture, with some coverage of urban design and planning.

4.88 THIES, Jochen (1976) *Architekt der Weltherrschaft: die Endziele Hitlers*. Düsseldorf: Droste.

One of the few scholars to argue that National Socialism had a distinctive approach to urban planning, Thies here presents a full survey of what he has called 'the architecture of world dominance'. He maintains that Hitler's plans for the major cities provide *prima facie* evidence of Hitler's ambition to rule the world, with Berlin as the new Rome.

4.89 THIES, Jochen (1977) *Hitlers Städte: Baupolitik im Dritten Reich: eine Dokumentation*. Cologne: Böhlau Verlag.

Pursuing his main thesis, Thies here presents a collection of primary evidence relating to Nazi reconstruction plans for German cities.

4.90 THIES, Jochen (1978) Hitler's European building programme. *Journal of Contemporary History*, **13** (3), pp. 413–32.
Discusses a number of Nazi urban schemes, inside and outside Germany, and concludes that they were partly intended to create a physical framework for world domination.

4.91 THIES, Jochen (1978) Nationalsozialistische Städteplanung: die Führerstädte. *Die alte Stadt*, **5**, pp. 23–38.
Another statement of Thies's views on urban reconstruction plans in the Third Reich.

4.92 UHLIG, Günther (1977) Stadtplanung in der Weimarer Republik: sozialistische Reformaspekte, in Neue Gesellschaft für Bildende Kunst (ed.), *Wem gehört die Welt? Kunst und Gesellschaft in der Weimarer Republik*. Berlin: Neue Gesellschaft für Bildende Kunst, pp. 50–71.
A review of the progress and disappointments of urban planning in the Weimar period.

4.93 WEDEPOHL, Edgar (1961) *Deutscher Städtebau nach 1945*. Essen: R. Bacht.
Summarizes developments in planning and reconstruction since 1945 in fifty-eight German towns, with numerous maps and illustrations.

4.94 WURZER, Rudolf (1974) Die Gestaltung der deutschen Stadt im 19. Jahrhundert, in Grote, Ludwig (ed.), *Die deutsche Stadt im 19. Jahrhundert: Stadtplanung und Baugestaltung im industriellen Zeitalter*. Munich: Prestel Verlag, pp. 9–32.
A general discussion of the development of town planning in Germany and Austria in the nineteenth century.

German Democratic Republic

4.95 SPAGNOLI, Lorenzo (1975) *Architettura e urbanistica nella Repubblica Democratica Tedesca*. Bologna: Cappelli.

An architectural and planning study with some perspective on developments since the later 1940s.

4.96 WURMS, Christopher (ed.) (1976) *Raumordnung und Territorialplanung in der DDR* (Dortmunder Beiträge zur Raumplanung, Band 2). Dortmund: Institut für Raumplanung, Universität Dortmund.

A collection of essays on urban and regional planning in the German Democratic Republic, with some post-1945 historical perspective.

Hungary

4.97 BEREND, Ivan T. (1972) Development strategy and urbanization in Hungary: 1950–1970, in Brown, Alan A., Licari, Joseph A., and Neuberger, Egon (eds.), *Urban and Social Economics in Market and Planned Economies: Policy, Planning and Development*, vol. 1. New York: Praeger, pp. 271–86.

Analyses the effect of economic planning on urban growth, problems, and planning policies.

4.98 VIRÁGH, Pál (1968) *Town Planning in Hungary*. Budapest: Ministry of Building and Urban Development.

A brief text, with numerous illustrations. Some recent historical perspective.

India

4.99 BHARDWAJ, R. K. (1974) *Urban Development in India*. Delhi: National Publishing House.

Includes some discussion of recent planning policies.

Israel

4.100 ASSOCIATION OF ENGINEERS AND ARCHITECTS IN ISRAEL (1964) *A Bibliography on Town and Country Planning in Israel, 1949–1964*. Haifa: Building Centre.

Includes much historical material.

Italy

4.101 ANTONINI, Ezio (1976) Le 'regole del gioco' della crescita urbana in Italia: la normativa urbanistica del 1865 al 1942, in Mioni, Alberto (ed.), *Sulla crescita urbana in Italia*. Milan: Franco Angeli, pp. 145–54.
A brief outline of the development of legislation and regulations controlling and directing the urban environment in Italy, 1865–1942.

4.102 BOATO, A. (1967) L'esperienza urbanistica del Trentino. *Città e Società*, 3, pp. 81–98.
Outlines the progress of town planning in the Trentino up to the new provincial plan of 1964.

4.103 BORALEVI, Alberto (1979) Le 'città dell'impero': urbanistica fascista in Etiopia, 1936–1941. *Storia Urbana*, 3 (8), pp. 65–116.
Studies the urban and regional development policies pursued by the Italian occupiers of Ethiopia. Includes detailed analysis of the regulating plans applied to Addis Abeba and smaller towns.

4.104 CAROZZI, Carlo and MIONI, Alberto (1970) *L'Italia in formazione: ricerche e saggi sullo sviluppo urbanistico del territorio nazionale*. Bari: De Donato.
Includes a section (pp. 417–80) on public intervention in the development of the environment between the mid-nineteenth and early twentieth centuries, including town planning, followed by documents (pp. 481–539).

4.105 DE SETA, Cesare (1966) Parabole della legge urbanistica. *Ponte*, 2, pp. 172–81.
Outlines developments in Italian town planning legislation since 1942.

4.106 DE SETA, Cesare (1972) *La cultura architettonica fra le due guerre*. Bari: Laterza.
Throws some light on urban planning in Italy between the wars.

4.107 DE SETA, Cesare (1977) *Città, territorio e Mezzogiorno in Italia*. Turin: Einaudi.

A collection of essays published over a number of years on aspects of urban and regional planning in Italy since the Second World War. Includes studies relating to Urbino, Florence and Venice. The main emphasis, however, is on the planned development of the South.

4.108 DEAN, Elena Papani (1979) La dominazione italiana e l'attività urbanistica ed edilizia nel Dodecaneso, 1912–1943. *Storia Urbana*, **3** (8), pp. 3–48.
Outlines the town and regional planning undertaken during thirty years of Italian domination of the Greek islands in the Aegean.

4.109 ISTITUTO NAZIONALE DI URBANISTICA (1952) *Esperienze urbanistiche in Italia*. Rome: Istituto Nazionale di Urbanistica.
Discusses various aspects of the development of urban planning in Italy.

4.110 La legislazione urbanistica dal 1942 al 1956: testi e proposte (1956). *Urbanistica*, **20**, pp. 29–76.
Reprints the major Italian planning bills and statutes 1942–56, with a commentary.

4.111 MERCANDINO, Cesare and Augusto (1976) *Storia de territorio e delle città d'Italia: dal 1800 ai giorni nostri*. Milan: Mazzotta.
A general survey of urban development in Italy, with much consideration of town planning and its effects.

4.112 MIONI, Alberto (1976) *Le trasformazioni territoriali in Italia nella prima età industriale*. Venice: Marsilio.
A study of the spatial development of Italy between the mid-nineteenth century and the Second World War, with much reference to the evolution of public policy in urban, rural and regional planning.

4.113 PICCINATO, Luigi (1976) Le origini degli studi di storia urbanistica in Italia, in Martinelli, Roberta, and Nuti, Lucia (eds.), *La storiografia urbanistica*. Lucca: CISCU, pp. 97–103.
Briefly outlines the development of town planning in Italy since the late nineteenth century, claiming that enlightened

policies did not begin to emerge until the FIHUAT congress of 1929.

4.114 PICCINATO, Luigi (1976) Urbanistica e storia in Italia negli anni Trenta. *Storia della Città*, 1, pp. 35–9.

A brief discussion of general developments in Italian town planning in the interwar years.

4.115 PIRODDI, Elio (1971) *Cento anni di pianificazione urbana in Italia*. L'Aquila: L. U. Japadre.

A general survey of the development of urban planning in modern Italy.

4.116 REITANI, Giuseppe (1979) Politica territoriale ed urbanistica in Tripolitania, 1920–1940. *Storia Urbana*, 3 (8), pp. 49–64.

On Italian urban and rural planning in Libya. Concentrates on the foundation of planned villages and the regulating plan for Tripoli.

4.117 SERNINI, Michele (1978) Le circoscrizioni amministrative nella politica di controllo degli insediamenti in Italia, dal 1925 ad oggi. *Storia Urbana*, 2 (6), pp. 209–39.

Outlines the development of central control of local government in Italy from the beginning of the Fascist period to the 1970s, with some reference to urban and regional planning.

4.118 SORI, Ercole (1976) Aspetti sociopolitici della crescita urbana in Italia: urbanesimo, disagio sociale, fermenti culturali e lotte politiche intorno alla questione delle abitazioni tra '800 e '900, in Mioni, Alberto (ed.), *Sulla crescita urbana in Italia*. Milan: Franco Angeli, pp. 165–205.

Deals principally with the development of the housing question and housing policies in Italy since the nineteenth century, but considers town planning as one element in this evolution.

Japan

4.119 BIGWOOD, Richard (1978) Pluralistic planning and a back-drop of history. *Built Environment*, 4 (1), pp. 20–3.

A brief introduction to Japanese planning, with some historical perspective.

4.120 HONJO, Masahiko (1968) Urban development administration: the case of Japan, in Herbert, John D., and Van Huyck, Alfred P. (eds.), *Urban Planning in the Developing Countries*. New York: Praeger, pp. 35–63.

Includes a historical survey of the development of planning in Japan since the nineteenth century.

4.121 ITŌ, Mitsuharu, *et al.* (eds.) (1972–73) *Gendai toshi seisaku* (11 vols. and 1 supp.). Tokyo: Iwanami Shoten.

A general study of the development of urban policy in modern times, this includes a discussion of the evolution of town planning in Japan.

4.122 *Kindai Nihon Kenchikugaku Hattatsushi* (1972). Tokyo: Maruzen.

Edited by *Nihon Kenchiku Gakkai*, Part 6 of this compilation (pp. 975–1114) briefly outlines the history of Japanese town planning.

4.123 TAJIMA, M. (1963) I quattro periodi dell'urbanistica giaponnese. *Casabella*, **273**, pp. 16–23.

A brief essay on Japanese planning, including an outline of its development since the Middle Ages.

Mexico

4.124 *Arquitectura y urbanismo en Mexico* (1961). Mexico City: U.N.A.M.

An official handbook published by the Mexican Union of Architects. One chapter is devoted to the history of architecture and planning in Mexico.

The Netherlands

4.125 BLIJSTRA, Reinder (1963) *Town Planning in the Netherlands since 1900*. Amsterdam: Van Kampen.

A brief and discursive essay (73 pp.) followed by numerous illustrations.

126 HALL, Peter (1966) Randstad Holland, in Hall, Peter (ed.), *The World Cities*. London: Weidenfeld and Nicolson, pp. 95–121.
A brief but lively discussion of the problems facing the urban areas of the Netherlands and the policies designed to meet them, with much historical perspective on growth-control and decentralization policies since 1945.

127 LANGE, Gerd (1966) Landesplanung in den Niederlanden: die Karte Hollands ändert sich, in [†Eggeling, Fritz (ed.)], *Städtebau im Ausland*. Berlin: Zentralinstitut für Städtebau, Technische Universität Berlin, pp. 53–64.
A brief survey of the development of urban planning in the Netherlands.

Norway

128 PEDERSEN, Sverre (1928) Litt om byregulering i de norske byer, in *Minneskrift for 25 års bymøter 16. juni 1903–16. juni 1928*. Oslo: Ed. Norges Byforbund.
Discusses aspects of the early development of urban regulation in Norway.

Poland

129 CIBOROWSKI, Adolf (1956) *Town Planning in Poland, 1945–1955*. Warsaw: Polonia Publishing House.
An official handbook, with much emphasis on postwar reconstruction.

130 FALLENBUCHL, Zbigniew M. (1972) The impact of the development strategy on urbanization: Poland 1950–1970, in Brown, Alan A., Licari, Joseph A. and Neuberger, Egon (eds.), *Urban and Social Economics in Market and Planned Economies: Policy, Planning and Development*, vol. 1. New York: Praeger, pp. 287–318.
Discusses the impact of economic planning on population growth in Polish towns since World War II.

4.131 FISHER, Jack C. (ed.) (1966) *City and Regional Planning in Poland*. Ithaca: Cornell University Press.
Includes a survey of the growth of urban planning in Poland, and case-studies of post-1945 reconstruction, notably in Warsaw (chapters 1–3).

4.132 KOTARBIŃSKI, Adam (1967) *Rozwój urbanistyki i architetury polskiej w latach 1944–1964: próba charakterystyki krytycznej*. Warsaw: Pánstwowe Wydawn Naukowe.
A survey of the development of Polish planning and architecture, 1944–64.

South Africa

4.133 FLOYD, Thomas Berry (1960) *Town Planning in South Africa*. Pietermaritzburg: Shuter and Shooter.
A general handbook, with some historical material.

4.134 FLOYD, Thomas Berry (1966) *More About Town Planning in South Africa*. Pietermaritzburg: Shuter and Shooter.
A supplement to the above.

Spain

4.135 BIDAGOR LASARTE, Pedro (1964) *Proceso evolutivo y situación actual del urbanismo en España*. Madrid: Ministerio de la Vivienda.
An official survey of the development and present condition of planning in Spain.

4.136 BOHIGAS, Oriol (1970) *Arquitectura i urbanisme durant la República*. Barcelona: Tusquets.
An illustrated study of architecture and planning in Catalonia in the 1930s, with much emphasis on housing. Barcelona is naturally prominent but proper attention is given to other towns in the province.

4.137 JÜRGENS, Oskar (1926) *Spanische Städte: ihre bauliche Entwicklung und Ausgestaltung*. Hamburg: Wilhelm Giese.

A general history of the physical development of Spanish towns.

138 RIBAS Y PIERA, Manuel (1964) Historia recent de la urbanistica als paisas catalans, in Bardet, Gaston, *El urbanismo*. Barcelona: Edicios 62.

This chapter on recent town-planning developments in Catalonia was added to the Spanish edition of Bardet's *L'urbanisme*.

139 RIBAS Y PIERA, Manuel (1965) La planificación urbanistica en España. *Zodiac*, 15, pp. 212–20.

A brief survey of the recent history of urban planning in Spain.

140 TORRES BALBÁS, Leopoldo, *et al.* (1954) *Resumen historico del urbanismo en España*. Madrid: Istituto de Estudios de Administración Local.

Nineteenth-century planning is discussed in chapter 4. Particularly interesting are the sections on town-planning legislation, and on the extension plans of four of the biggest cities.

Sweden

141 ÅSTRÖM, Kell (1969) *City Planning in Sweden*. Stockholm: Swedish Institute.

A translation of *Svensk stadsplanering* (Stockholm: A. B. Byggmästerens, 1967). The early pages provide a brief historical account.

142 LINDEN, G. (1924) Town planning in Sweden after 1850. *Town Planning Review*, 10, pp. 269–74.

A brief account of town-extension and other planning policies pursued in Sweden during its early industrialization period.

143 ÖDMANN, Ella (1973) Some views on land ownership in urban planning and housing production in Sweden. *Geoforum*, 13, pp. 31–41.

Outlines developments in planning, municipal land purchase and housing in three towns since 1950.

4.144 PAULSSON, Gregor (1950, 1953) *Svensk stad* (2 vols.). Stockholm: Albert Bonniers.
A comprehensive study of the urban development of Sweden since the Middle Ages, with much emphasis on physical form. Some discussion of nineteenth-century planning in volume 1, pp. 413 ff, and volume 2.

4.145 PAULSSON, Thomas (1959) *Den glömda staden: svensk stadsplanering under 1900-talets början med särskild hänsyn till Stockholm: Idéhistoria, teori och praktik.* Stockholm: Kommunalförveltning.
A discussion of the development of modern town planning in Sweden, c.1890–c.1930, emphasizing the interplay between influences from various foreign countries. Much attention paid to the work of the pioneer planner, Per Olof Hallman. Despite the title, this book is by no means limited to Stockholm. English summary.

4.146 WESTERMAN, Allan (1965) *Swedish Planning of Town Centres.* Stockholm: Swedish Institute.
Some historical perspective.

Union of Soviet Socialist Republics

4.147 AKADEMIIA ARKHITEKTURY S.S.S.R. (1944) *10 Let Arkhitektury S.S.S.R.* Moscow: Izdatel'stvo Akademii Arkhitektury S.S.S.R.
A general history of a decade of Russian architecture, this includes coverage of urban design and planning, 1934–44.

4.148 BARANOV, Nikolai Varfolomeevich (1962) *Sovremennoe gradostroitel'stvo: glavn'ye problemy.* Moscow: Gosstroiizdat.
A general study of Russian planning with some recent historical perspective.

4.149 BATER, James H. (1977) Soviet town planning: theory and practice in the 1970s. *Progress in Human Geography*, 1 (2), pp. 177–207.
Surveys Soviet planning theory and practice since 1945,

emphasizing discrepancies between the two, and suggesting a convergence of socialist and capitalist planning.

4.150 BLIZNAKOV, Milka (1976) Urban planning in the U.S.S.R.: integrative theories, in Hamm, Michael F. (ed.), *The City in Russian History*. Lexington: University of Kentucky Press, pp. 243–56.

A survey of Russian planning debates in the interwar years, concentrating on the conflict of 'urbanist' and 'disurbanist' theories.

4.151 BLUMENFELD, Hans (1942) Regional and city planning in the Soviet Union. *Task* (Cambridge, Mass.), **3**, pp. 33–52.

Outlines the Soviet experience in planning up to 1941.

4.152 CECCARELLI, Paolo (ed.) (1970) *La costruzione della città sovietica 1929–31*. Padua: Marsilio.

A collection of contemporary texts with an introduction by the editor. A later edition is available.

4.153 COOKE, Catherine (1974) The town of socialism. Unpublished Ph.D. thesis, Department of Architecture, University of Cambridge.

Concentrates on the Russian planning debate of 1929–31, and its influence on the subsequent development of the planned Soviet city.

4.154 COOKE, Catherine (1977) Activities of the garden city movement in Russia. *Transactions of the Martin Centre for Architectural and Urban Studies*, **1**, pp. 225–49.

Similar to the author's later article in the *Architectural Review*, this argues that the ideas of Ebenezer Howard had a substantial influence in Russia.

4.155 COOKE, Catherine (1978) Russian responses to the garden city idea. *Architectural Review*, **163** (976), pp. 355–63.

Discusses the application, and adaptation, of the Garden City idea in Russia between the early 1900s and the early 1930s, in the context of the general development of planning theory and practice.

4.156 DE MICHELIS, Marco and PASINI, Ernesto (1976) *La città sovietica, 1925–1937*. Venice: Marsilio.
A well-researched but uncritical account of the development of town-planning policies in the U.S.S.R. between the wars.

4.157 DIACONOFF, P. A. (1973) Gosplan and the politics of Soviet planning, 1929–1932. Unpublished Ph.D. thesis, University of Indiana.
A discussion of a crucial period in the development of Soviet planning.

4.158 FRAMPTON, Kenneth (1968) Note on Soviet urbanism, 1917–1932. *Architects' Yearbook*, **12**, pp. 238–52.
Analysis of eight characteristic planning schemes of the period.

4.159 FROLIC, B. Michael (1963–64) The Soviet city. *Town Planning Review*, **34** (4), pp. 285–306.
Brings out the distinctive features of Soviet planning, with special emphasis on the microdistrict. Some historical perspective.

4.160 *Gradostroitel'stvo CCCP* (1967). Moscow: Stroiizdat.
A lengthy survey of Soviet urban planning, 1917–67.

4.161 *Istoria sovetskoy arkhitectoury 1917–1958* (1962). Moscow: Gosstroiizdat.
A general history of Soviet architecture, covering urban design and planning.

4.162 IVANITSKII, A. (1941) The development of city planning in the Soviet Union. *American City*, **56** (8), pp. 44–6, 81.
A survey of the development of Soviet town planning up to 1941.

4.163 KOPP, Anatole (1970) *Town and Revolution: Soviet Architecture and City Planning, 1917–35*. London: Thames and Hudson.
First published as *Ville et révolution: architecture et urbanisme soviétiques dans les années vingt* (Paris: Anthropos, 1967). A study of Soviet planning theory and practice in the crucial post-

Revolution period. This remains the outstanding study of early Soviet planning in English, though much of the emphasis is on architecture.

4.164 KOPP, Anatole (1975) *Changer la vie, changer la ville: de la vie nouvelle aux problèmes urbains, U.R.S.S. 1917–1932*. Paris: Union générale d'éditions.
Includes full discussion of developments in Soviet urban planning between 1917 and 1932.

4.165 LISSITZKY, El (1930) *Russland: die Rekonstruktion der Architektur in der Sowjetunion*. Vienna: Schroll.
This throws some light on the development of early Soviet planning.

4.166 LISSITZKY, El (1965) *Russland: Architektur für eine Weltrevolution*. Berlin: Ullstein.
A new edition of Lissitzky's tract of 1930, supplemented by other contemporary texts on architecture and town planning.

4.167 MARIENBACH, J. A. (1962) V. I. Lenin i pervyje gradostrojitelnyje meroprijatija sovetskoj vlasti. *Voprosy sovremennoj architektury*, Sbornik 1, pp. 155–81.
Discusses Lenin's influence on early Soviet urban planning.

4.168 MAY, Ernst (1961) Cities of the future. *Survey*, **38**, pp. 179–85.
A brief discussion of the strengths and weaknesses of Soviet planning by the former Frankfurt planner who moved to Russia in the early 1930s.

4.169 MILIUTIN, N. A. (1974) *Sotsgorod: The Problem of Building Socialist Cities*. Cambridge, Mass./London: MIT Press.
A translation of Miliutin's 1930 essay on the linear city and other planning schemes, with extensive commentary and notes by George R. Collins and William Alex.

4.170 *Osnovy sovetskogo gradostroitel'stva* (3 vols.) (1966–67). Moscow: Stroiizdat.
A full study of Soviet urban development, including much discussion of planning.

4.171 PARKER, J. A., PARKINS, M. F. *et al.* (1952) *An Examination of Soviet Theory and Practice in City and Regional Planning.* Chapel Hill, North Carolina: Institute for Research in Social Science, University of North Carolina.

A full study of Soviet urban and regional planning from the Revolution to 1950. Includes a case-study of the pre-war planning of Leningrad and its subsequent reconstruction.

4.172 PARKINS, Maurice Frank (1949) *City Planning in Soviet Russia: An Interpretative Bibliography.* Cambridge, Mass.: Russian Research Center, Harvard University.

A first draft of the ambitious bibliography published in 1953 (see 4.173).

4.173 PARKINS, Maurice Frank (1953) *City Planning in Soviet Russia: With an Interpretative Bibliography.* Chicago: University of Chicago Press.

A very full historical survey of Soviet planning from 1922 to 1952. Extensive bibliography.

4.174 PERÉNYI, Imre (1947) *Városépités a Szovjetunióban.* Budapest: Új Magyar Könyvkiado.

A general study of Soviet urban planning, with some historical perspective.

4.175 QUILICI, Vieri (1976) *Città russa e città sovietica: caratteri della struttura storica: ideologia e pratica della trasformazione socialista.* Milan: Mazzotta.

A general study of the history of urban development and town planning in the Soviet Union.

4.176 SAWERS, Larry (1978) Cities and countryside in the Soviet Union and China, in Tabb, William K., and Sawers, Larry (eds.), *Marxism and the Metropolis: New Perspectives in Urban Political Economy.* New York: Oxford University Press, pp. 338–64.

Compares from a Marxist standpoint, urban and regional planning in the two socialist societies since their establishment. Concludes that the goal of Soviet planning has come to be efficiency; that of Chinese planning is 'engagement'—the incorporation of disparate elements into a single community.

4.177 SHKVARIKOV, V. A. (ed.) (1940) *Russkaia Arkhitektura*. Moscow: Gosudarstvennoe Arkhitekturnoe Izdatel'stvo Akademii Arkhitektury S.S.S.R.

A general history of Russian architecture, this covers the history of town planning in Russia up to the twentieth century.

4.178 SHKVARIKOV, V. A. (1954) *Ocherk istorii planirovki i zastroyki russkikh gorodov*. Moscow: Gos. izd-vo lit-r'y po stroitel'stvu i arkhitektury.

A study of the history of the planning and building of Russian towns.

4.179 *Socialismo, città, architettura: URSS 1917–37: il contributo degli architetti europei* (2 vols.) (1971–72). Rome: Officina.

Discusses the contribution of European architects to the evolution of socialist design in the Soviet Union until Stalinism closed off such influences.

4.180 SOSNOVY, T. (1961) Town planning and housing. *Survey*, 38, pp. 170–8.

Includes discussion of Russian planning debates in the 1920s.

4.181 STARR, S. Frederick (1976) The revival and schism of urban planning in twentieth century Russia, in Hamm, Michael F. (ed.), *The City in Russian History*. Lexington: University of Kentucky Press, pp. 222–42.

Briefly surveys developments in Russian town planning in the interwar years.

4.182 STARR, S. Frederick (1971) Writings from the 1960s on the Modern Movement in Russia. *Journal of the Society of Architectural Historians*, 30 (2), pp. 170–8.

A lengthy review of changing views, both inside and outside the Soviet Union, on the Russian branch of the Modern Movement. Includes some discussion of planning.

4.183 STARR, S. Frederick (1977) L'urbanisme utopique pendant la révolution culturelle soviétique. *Annales E.S.C.*, 32 (1), pp. 87–105.

Deals mainly with the anti-urban movements of the 1920s.

4.184 ŠVIDKOVSKIJ, O. A. and CHAN-MAGOMEDOV, S. (1964) *Sovetskoje*

gradostroitel'stvo 1920-ch–nachala 1930-ch godov. Moscow: Rukopis.
A study of Soviet urban planning in the 1920s and 1930s.

4.185 TAFURI, Manfredo (1975) Verso la 'città socialista': richerche e
realizzazioni nell'Unione Sovietica tra la NEP e il primo piano
quinquennale. *Lotus*, **9**, pp. 76–93.
On developments in Soviet urban planning in the 1920s.

4.186 WHITE, Paul M. (1978) *Soviet Town Planning: A Bibliographic Guide to
English Language References* (C.U.R.S. Working Paper no. 58).
Birmingham: Centre for Urban and Regional Studies,
Birmingham University.
Includes a number of historical items.

4.187 WHITE, Paul M. (1979) *Urban Planning in Britain and the Soviet Union:
A Comparative Analysis* (C.U.R.S. Research Memorandum no. 70).
Birmingham: Centre for Urban and Regional Studies,
Birmingham University.
Includes a discussion of the theory and practice of Soviet
planning since the 1920s, pointing out some of its weaknesses
and contradictions. Goes on to compare the practice of Soviet
and British planning since 1945, with special reference to
Moscow and London. Throughout, White identifies a
convergence of planning in the two countries.

4.188 ZILE, Zigurd L. (1963) Programs and problems of city planning in
the Soviet Union. *Washington University Law Quarterly*, **1**, pp. 19–59.
A general survey of the development of town planning in the
Soviet Union since the Revolution.

United Kingdom

4.189 ADAMS, Ian H. (1978) *The Making of Urban Scotland.* London: Croom
Helm.
Makes full reference to the role of urban and regional
planning in the development of urban Scotland since the turn of
the century.

4.190 ADAMS, James W. R. (1952) *Modern Town and Country Planning: A*

History of and Introduction to the Study of the Law and Practice of Modern Town and Country Planning in Great Britain. London: J. and A. Churchill.

An updated version of Thomas Adams, *Recent Advances in Town Planning* (1932). Strong historical perspective.

4.191 ADAMS, James W. R. (1959) *Report of the Work of the Planning Department from 1948–1959 with Some Reference to Earlier Town and Country Planning Activities in Kent.* Maidstone: Kent County Council.

An 'official' report by the Chief Officer, but with a strong sense of history. This remains one of the few historical studies of planning at county level.

4.192 ALESSANDRI, Giovanni (1965) Urbanistica inglese. *Aggiornamenti Sociali,* **16** (3, 5, 6).

A survey of British planning policies since the Second World War. This study was reprinted as a pamphlet by Centro Studi Sociali, Milan (n.d.).

4.193 ASHWORTH, William (1954) *The Genesis of Modern British Town Planning.* London: Routledge and Kegan Paul.

The first general history of British planning by a professional historian and still unsurpassed. Based on a Ph.D. thesis, it portrays planning as a cumulative development from the public health agitation of the 1830s to the 1947 Act.

4.194 BATTY, Michael (1976) Models, methods and rationality in urban and regional planning: developments since 1960. *Area,* **8** (2), pp. 93–7.

Discusses the influence of systems analysis on British planning since 1960.

4.195 BELL, Colin and Rose (1969) *City Fathers: The Early History of Town Planning in Britain.* London: Cresset Press.

This is principally a study of the small, planned community tradition in British urban design up to the end of the nineteenth century.

4.196 BOR, Walter (1974) The Town and Country Planning Act, 1968. *The Planner,* **60** (5), pp. 696–702.

One of a series of articles on major British statutes, this has some historical perspective but is mainly a discussion of the Act's qualities.

4.197 BUCHANAN, Colin (1972) *The State of Britain.* London: Faber.
Part of this is a historical appraisal of the antecedents and results of the Town and Country Planning Act of 1947.

4.198 BURKE, Gerald L. (1971) *Towns in the Making.* London: Edward Arnold.
An introduction to the history of 'town-making' for the student. Chapters 7 and 8 provide a brief outline of the development of British town planning on the lines pioneered by Ashworth.

4.199 CALABI, Donatella (1979) *Il 'male' città: diagnosi e terapia: didattica e istituzioni nell'urbanistica inglese del primo '900.* Rome: Officina Edizioni.
A study of the first efforts to teach town planning in Britain in the early 1900s (at Liverpool, London and Birmingham), and the rise of the planning profession before 1914. Most of the book consists of documents relating to these two themes.

4.200 CENTRE FOR URBAN STUDIES (1964) *Land Use Planning and the Social Sciences: A Selected Bibliography.* London: Centre for Urban Studies.
An extensive bibliography of British planning, with some historical references. Supplements have appeared since 1964.

4.201 CHERRY, Gordon E. (1969) Influences on the development of town planning in Britain. *Journal of Contemporary History,* 4 (3), pp. 43–59.
A survey of the evolution of urban and regional planning in Britain since the later nineteenth century.

4.202 CHERRY, Gordon E. (1970) *Town Planning in its Social Context.* London: Leonard Hill.
Relates British planning to general developments in society and social policy, including some historical material.

4.203 CHERRY, Gordon E. (1972) *Urban Change and Planning: A History of Urban Development in Britain since 1750.* Henley-on-Thames: Foulis.

A study of the development of urban environmental policies and planning from the beginnings of industrialization to the present day, in the context of social and economic development and the urbanization process.

4.204 CHERRY, Gordon E. (1974) The development of planning thought, in Bruton, Michael J. (ed.), *The Spirit and Purpose of Planning*. London: Hutchinson, pp. 66–84.

A summary of the history of major currents in British planning ideas since the turn of the century.

4.205 CHERRY, Gordon E. (1974) *The Evolution of British Town Planning*. Heath and Reach: Leonard Hill.

A commemorative volume on the history of the planning profession in general, and of the R.T.P.I. in particular, placed in the context of the broader development of British planning theory and practice.

4.206 CHERRY, Gordon E. (1974) The Housing, Town Planning etc. Act, 1919. *The Planner*, 60 (5), pp. 681–4.

Mainly a survey of the parliamentary proceedings.

4.207 CHERRY, Gordon E. (1975) Factors in the origins of town planning in Britain: the example of Birmingham, 1905–1914 (C.U.R.S. Working Paper no. 36). Birmingham: Centre for Urban and Regional Studies, Birmingham University.

Argues that the City of Birmingham played a big role in promoting the idea of town planning in England. Throws much light on the career of J. S. Nettlefold, municipal councillor and early advocate of planning.

4.208 CHERRY, Gordon E. (1979) The town planning movement and the late Victorian city. *Institute of British Geographers Transactions*, new series, 4 (2), pp. 306–19.

Attempts to account for the emergence of town planning in Britain at the turn of the century in terms of the convergence of a number of strands of development. Identifies a fulcrum period, 1885–1905.

4.209 CREESE, Walter L. (1966) *The Search for Environment: The Garden City Before and After*. New Haven: Yale University Press.

A detailed study of the British new communities tradition, from the early model industrial villages to the new towns, concentrating on the physical environment.

4.210 CULLINGWORTH, J. B. (1975) *Environmental Planning 1939–1969. Vol. 1, Reconstruction and Land Use Planning.* London: HMSO.

The first of an official series of peacetime histories covering post-1945 developments in central government policy and administration. Mainly a blow-by-blow account of Whitehall committee proceedings during and immediately after the Second World War.

4.211 CULLINGWORTH, J. B. (1964) *Town and Country Planning in England and Wales.* London: Allen and Unwin.

Chapter 1 is a brief survey of the development of town and country planning since the early nineteenth century, with the main emphasis on legislation. New editions have continued to appear at intervals of three or four years since 1964.

4.212 DANIELS, R. W. (1977) Planning and motorways 1929–74, in Marshall, J. D. (ed.), *The History of Lancashire County Council, 1889 to 1974.* London: Martin Robertson, pp. 306–60.

A thorough study of the planning work of the Lancashire County Council between the Second World War and the early 1970s. Includes a long discussion of motorway planning.

4.213 DARLEY, Gillian (1975) *Villages of Vision.* London: Architectural Press.

A study of the development of Arcadian design in Britain from the eighteenth century to the present day, but concentrating on the nineteenth and early twentieth centuries. Includes estate villages, industrial settlements, and garden cities.

4.214 DE CASSERES, J. M. (1927) *Stedebouw.* Amsterdam: S. L. Van Looy.

A study of British town planning with much historical perspective. Foreword by Patrick Abercrombie.

4.215 DIAMOND, D. R. (1975) Planning the urban environment. *Geography,* **60,** pp. 189–93.

A brief outline of the history of British planning.

4.216 DONNELLY, Desmond (1949) The Town and Country Planning Association. *Town and Country Planning*, **17** (65), pp. 13–18.

A brief survey of the Association's history to mark the fiftieth anniversary of the Garden City Association.

4.217 EVERSLEY, David E. C. (1973) *The Planner and Society: The Changing Role of a Profession*. London: Faber.

Includes a lengthy account of the origins and development of the practice and profession of town planning in Britain since the early nineteenth century.

4.218 FOGARTY, M. P. (1948) *Town and Country Planning*. London: Hutchinson.

Contains quite a lengthy survey (pp. 1–71) of the origins of planning and its progress. Of particular interest is the account of the interwar years, in which special reference is made to Birmingham.

4.219 FOLEY, Donald L. (1960) British town planning: one ideology or three? *British Journal of Sociology*, **11**, pp. 211–31.

A stimulating attempt to discover the essence of British planning, with some historical relevance.

4.220 FOLEY, Donald L. (1962) Idea and influence: the Town and Country Planning Association. *Journal of the American Institute of Planners*, **28** (1), pp. 10–17.

Outlines the history of the T.C.P.A. and evaluates its achievement.

4.221 GLADSTONE, Francis (1976) *The Politics of Planning*. London: Temple Smith.

A critical account of recent British urban planning policies, with vignettes of Sheffield, Middlesbrough, South Hampshire, and Liverpool.

4.222 HAWTREE, Martin (1974) The origins of the modern town planner: a study in professional ideology. Unpublished Ph.D. thesis, Liverpool University.

Analyses the various strands of professional and reform

activity which, with some difficulty, coalesced in the early 1900s
to form the British planning profession.

4.223 HUMPHRIES, Herbert H. (1934–35) The history of town planning in
Birmingham and the Midland region. *Journal of the Town Planning
Institute*, **21**, pp. 4–18.
Surveys early developments in planning in the West Midlands,
between the early 1900s and the early 1930s.

4.224 IKONNIKOV, Andrei Vladimirovich (1958) Sovremennaia
arkhitektura Anglii: planirovka gorodov i zhilisnoe stroitel'stvo.
Leningrad: Gos. izd-vo litr'i po stroitel'stvu, arkhitekture i stroit.
materialam.
A study of British town planning, with some historical
perspective.

4.225 KEABLE, Gladys (1963) *Tomorrow Slowly Comes: A Brief Account of Sixty
Years of Work for Better Towns in an Unspoiled Countryside.* London:
Town and Country Planning Association.
A personal account of the development of the Garden City
Association, Garden Cities and Town Planning Association, and
Town and Country Planning Association, from 1899 to 1959.

4.226 KEEBLE, David (1976) *Industrial Location and Planning in the United
Kingdom.* London: Methuen.
This has much bearing on the history of planned industrial
location in Britain since the last war.

4.227 KEEBLE, Lewis (1961) *Town Planning at the Crossroads.* London:
Estates Gazette.
Includes a long historical introduction on British planning.

4.228 LEWIS, D. (1961) Architettura e urbanistica in Gran Bretagna.
Casabella, **250**, pp. 29–47.
Includes discussion of planning developments in Britain since
the Second World War.

4.229 McALLISTER, Gilbert and Elizabeth G. (1941) *Town and Country
Planning: A Study of Physical Environment: The Prelude to Post-War
Reconstruction.* London: Faber.

Much historical material, including an outline of developments in British planning since 1909 and its effects between the wars.

4.230 McKAY, David H. and Cox, Andrew W. (1979) *Politics and Urban Change*. London: Croom Helm.
Discusses a number of developments in British planning policy since 1945.

4.231 MANN, Peter H. (1965) *An Approach to Urban Sociology*. London: Routledge and Kegan Paul.
Includes an account (pp. 115–48) of the growth of environmental controls and planning in Britain, 1800–1970.

4.232 MELLER, Helen E. (ed.) (1979) *The Ideal City*. Leicester: Leicester University Press.
A reprint of Canon Samuel Barnett's *The Ideal City*, and Patrick Geddes's lectures, 'Civics as applied sociology', together with an introduction by the editor.

4.233 MELLOR, J. R. (1977) *Urban Sociology in an Urbanised Society*. London: Routledge and Kegan Paul.
Deals in part with the development of the British town planning movement.

4.234 MINETT, M. John (1974) The Housing, Town Planning etc. Act, 1909. *The Planner*, **60** (5), pp. 676–80.
This is mainly a survey of the parliamentary proceedings which put the pioneer British planning Act on the statute book.

4.235 MINETT, M. John (1975) 'Community' as an ideal in British town planning: an exploration into the relationship between planning and politics 1900–1940 with particular reference to the work of Raymond Unwin. Unpublished B.Litt. thesis, Oxford University.
Traces the influence on British town planning of the attractive notion of the designed 'community', seeing Raymond Unwin as the major creator and promoter of the idea. Also argues that the broader interests of politicians have always made

their idea of town planning differ from that of the professional town planners.

4.236 MURIE, Alan (1973) Planning in Northern Ireland: a survey. *Town Planning Review*, **44**, pp. 337–58.

Outlines and assesses the history of planning and its achievement in Northern Ireland since its beginnings in 1931.

4.237 MURPHY, Lawrence R. (1970) Rebuilding Britain: the Government's role in housing and town planning, 1945–57. *The Historian*, **32** (3), pp. 410–27.

A brief outline of changes in national housing and planning policies over the period, not achieving great depth.

4.238 NUTTGENS, Patrick (1972) *The Landscape of Ideas*. London: Faber.

Chapter 5 discusses the nineteenth-century origins of planning in Britain, in the context of the history of ideas, with prominence given to thinkers on the fringes of planning such as Pugin.

4.239 *An Outline of Planning in the United Kingdom* (1976). London: HMSO.

An official handbook, employing a historical treatment.

4.240 PEPLER, George Lionel (1931) Twenty-one years of town planning in England and Wales. *Journal of the Town Planning Institute*, **17** (3), pp. 49–72.

An account of British planning developments since the 1909 Act. This article was republished as a pamphlet under the same title by the Town Planning Institute, London, in 1931.

4.241 PEPLER, George Lionel (1949) Forty years of statutory town planning. *Town Planning Review*, **20**, pp. 103–8.

A brief survey of developments since 1909 by a prominent participant.

4.242 *Planning in the United Kingdom, Habitat Vancouver 1976* (1976). London: Department of the Environment.

An official survey of British urban and regional planning, historical in approach.

.243 POOLEY, Beverley J. (1960) *The Evolution of British Planning Legislation*. Ann Arbor: Michigan University Law School.
A full study of the development of planning powers in Britain by an American jurist.

.244 PRESTHUS, Robert Vance (1951) British town and country planning: local participation. *American Political Science Review*, **45**, pp. 756–69.
Incorporates some historical perspective.

.245 RATCLIFFE, John (1976) *Land Policy: An Exploration of the Nature of Land in Society, the Problem of Community Created Land Values and the Twin Processes of Planning and Development*. London: Hutchinson.
Includes much coverage of British planning history, particularly in respect of compensation and betterment.

.246 RAVETZ, Alison (1979) The planning patchwork: an overview of post-war urban development. *Built Environment*, **5** (1), pp. 5–11.
A critique of the products of physical planning in British towns since 1945, favouring a more organic process of development.

.247 SCHAFFER, Frank (1974) The Town and Country Planning Act, 1947. *The Planner*, **60** (5), pp. 690–5.
Discusses the origins and consequences of this foundation stone of British postwar planning.

.248 SOLESBURY, William (1975) Ideas about structure plans: past, present and future. *Town Planning Review*, **46** (3), pp. 245–54.
The historical element in this article covers the development of the ideas and practice of structure planning in Britain.

.249 SPYER, Geoffrey (1971) *Architect and Community: Environmental Design in an Urban Society*. London: Peter Owen.
The early chapters contain a history of planning since the nineteenth century, principally in Britain.

.250 STEWART, Cecil (1952) *A Prospect of Cities, Being Studies Towards a History of Town Planning*. London: Longman.
Chapters 7–9 deal with modern British planning in the form

of studies of planned communities and their creators from Robert Owen to the new towns. Main emphasis is on physical form.

4.251 TARN, John Nelson (1973) *Five Per Cent Philanthropy: An Account of Housing in Urban Areas Between 1840 and 1914*. Cambridge: Cambridge University Press.
Mainly a thorough comparison of speculative and philanthropic housing, but very informative on the strong housing-reform strand in the development of British town planning.

4.252 TAYLOR, Nicholas (1973) *The Village in the City*. London: Temple Smith.
A history of the suburb from the Middle Ages to the present day. Includes a discussion of planned housing densities and the resulting British house-types. Objectivity marred by polemical tone.

4.253 TAYLOR, Ray, COX, Margaret and DICKINS, Ian (eds.) (1975) *Britain's Planning Heritage*. London: Croom Helm.
A tourist's guide to some of the most interesting and distinguished products of British urban design, including some examples of modern town planning.

4.254 TEODORI, Massimo (1967) *Architettura e città in Gran Bretagna: pianificazione urbanistica e interventi edilizi nelle città inglesi degli ultimi cento anni*. Bologna: Cappelli.
A study of British urban architecture and planning since the mid-nineteenth century. Comprehensive though somewhat derivative, with strong emphasis on physical design.

4.255 VEAL, Anthony J. (1975) *Recreation Planning in New Communities: A Review of British Experience* (C.U.R.S. Research Memorandum no. 46). Birmingham: Centre for Urban and Regional Studies, Birmingham University.
A comprehensive bibliography containing much material of historical interest, with an informative introduction.

4.256 WARD, Colin (1974) 'Say it again, Ben!': an evocation of the first seventy-five years of the Town and Country Planning Association. *Bulletin of Environmental Education*, **43**, pp. 5–19.

Sketches the development of the T.C.P.A. within the context of British planning, with an element of polemic.

4.257 WARD, Stephen V. (1974) The Town and Country Planning Act 1932. *The Planner*, **60** (5), pp. 685–9.

Discusses the background and significance of the Act, and studies its progress through Parliament.

4.258 WARD, Stephen V. (1975) *Planning, Politics and Social Change, 1939–45* (Department of Town Planning Working Papers). London: Department of Town Planning, Polytechnic of the South Bank.

Sets official wartime discussions of planning reforms in the context of changes in public opinion.

4.259 WESTERGAARD, John H. (1964) Land use planning since 1951: the legislative and administrative framework. *Town Planning Review*, **35** (3), pp. 219–37.

A comprehensive survey of legislative changes.

4.260 WOODFORD, G. P. and FAWCETT, A. (1962) La pianificazione territoriale in Gran Bretagna. *Urbanistica*, **36**, pp. 19–50.

A survey of the postwar system of planning in Britain.

4.261 WRIGHT, H. M. (1955) The first ten years: post-war planning and development in England. *Town Planning Review*, **26** (2), pp. 73–91.

A progress report on the impact of post-1945 legislation.

United States

4.262 ADAMS, Frederick J. and HODGE, Gerald (1965) City planning instruction in the United States: the pioneering days, 1900–1930. *Journal of the American Institute of Planners*, **31** (1), pp. 43–51.

Discusses the growth of the specialized training of city planners in the United States between the late nineteenth century and the 1920s, with James Sturgis Pray's Harvard course (founded 1909) and the full Harvard planning degree programme (1929) as the main milestones.

4.263 ALONSO, William (1967) Cities and city planners, in Eldredge, H. Wentworth (ed.), *Taming Megalopolis, vol. II: How to Manage an Urbanized World.* New York: Praeger, pp. 580–96.

Includes an outline of the growth of city planning in the United States as a prelude to discussion of contemporary urban problems and policies. An earlier version appeared under the same title in *Daedalus,* 92 (4), 1963, pp. 824–39.

4.264 BLACK, Russell Van Nest (1967) *Planning and the Planning Profession: The Past Fifty Years, 1917–1967.* Washington: American Institute of Planners.

An official history of U.S. urban and regional planning, with special emphasis on the American Institute of Planners.

4.265 BURG, David F. (1976) *Chicago's White City of 1893.* Lexington: Kentucky University Press.

A history of the World's Columbian Exposition in Chicago in 1893, with some reference to its planning and architecture.

4.266 CADY, David Barry (1970) The influence of the garden city ideal on American housing and planning reform, 1900–1940. Unpublished Ph.D. thesis, University of Wisconsin.

Argues that the Garden City idea was very influential in the United States between the wars, even though no pure garden cities were built. Much emphasis on the propaganda work of the Regional Planning Association.

4.267 CIUCCI, Giorgio, DAL CO, Francesco, MANIERI-ELIA, Mario and TAFURI, Manfredo (1973) *La città americana dalla guerra civile al New Deal.* Bari: Laterza.

Relevant to town planning are the essays on Burnham and the City Beautiful movement (Manieri-Elia), the development of park and regional planning (Dal Co), and Broadacre City (Ciucci).

4.268 COMMITTEE ON TOWN PLANNING OF THE AMERICAN INSTITUTE OF ARCHITECTS (ed. George B. Ford) (1917) *City Planning Progress in the United States, 1917.* Washington: Journal of the American Institute of Architects.

The product of a coordinated effort, based on a questionnaire survey, to record what had been achieved in city planning in every U.S. city to have engaged in it. Briefly covers over 330 towns. Illustrated.

4.269 CONKIN, Paul K. (1959) *Tomorrow a New World: The New Deal Community Program.* Ithaca: Cornell University Press.
A study of community planning in the 1930s, including the greenbelt towns.

4.270 CROSTA, Pierluigi, FOLIN, Marino, CALABI, Donatella, MANCUSO, Franco and POTENZA, Stefania (1975) *L'urbanistica del riformismo: U.S.A. 1890–1940.* Milan: Gabriele Mazzotta.
A collection of essays, covering U.S. urban development and policies as a capitalist phenomenon, growth of zoning in New York, public housing, the TVA, and the Chicago School of Sociology.

4.271 DORSETT, Lyle W. (1968) *The Challenge of the City, 1860–1910.* Lexington: D. C. Heath.
A collection of documents of U.S. urban history, including some of relevance to the City Beautiful movement.

4.272 ESKEW, Garnett Laidlaw (1959) *Of Land and Men: The Birth and Growth of an Idea.* Washington: Urban Land Institute.
Some relevance to the history of urban and regional planning in the United States.

4.273 FAGIN, Henry (1967) Sprawl and planning, in Gottman, Jean and Harper, Robert A. (eds.), *Metropolis on the Move: Geographers Look at Urban Sprawl.* New York: John Wiley, pp. 153–73.
Outlines the reaction of U.S. planners to suburbanization since the 1920s, concentrating on influential studies and surveys.

4.274 FUNIGIELLO, Philip J. (1972) City planning in World War II: the experience of the National Resources Planning Board. *Social Science Quarterly*, 53 (1), pp. 91–104.
On the largely unsuccessful efforts of the Board to stimulate enlightened city planning during the war years, until its abolition in 1943.

4.275 GELFAND, Mark I. (1975) *A Nation of Cities: The Federal Government and*

Urban America, 1933–1965. New York: Oxford University Press.

Studies the slow evolution of a national urban policy in the United States from the New Deal to Johnson. Includes some discussion of planning.

4.276 GILLETTE, Howard, Jr. (1977) Film as artifact: *The City* (1939). *American Studies*, **18** (2), pp. 71–85.

Well-researched study of the background to the production, by Clarence Stein, of one of the most effective planning propaganda films ever made. Throws much light on the conflicts between the professional film-makers and the urban reformers, who used the film to stress the virtues of the greenbelt towns programme.

4.277 GOIST, Park Dixon (1967) The city as organism: two recent theories of the city. Unpublished Ph.D. thesis, University of Rochester.

Compares the two main tendencies in American urban thinking in the interwar years—the Chicago school sociologists and the Garden City/regionalist planners and architects. Concludes that both were firmly rooted in nineteenth- and twentieth-century social theorizing, and explains their 'organic' approaches as a natural response to the phenomenon of the city as understood at the time.

4.278 GOIST, Park Dixon (1977) *From Main Street to State Street: Town, City, and Community in America*. Port Washington, N.Y.: Kennikat Press.

Includes some discussion of aspects of the development of planning in the United States.

4.279 GOODMAN, Robert (1972) *After the Planners*. Harmondsworth: Penguin.

A polemic, but throws much light on the recent history of American city planning.

4.280 GUTTENBERG, Albert S. (1969) *Environmental Reform in the United States: The Populist-Progressive Era and the New Deal* (Council of Planning Librarians, Exchange Bibliography no. 85). Monticello, Ill.: Council of Planning Librarians.

A collection of both primary and secondary printed material.

4.281   HANCOCK, John L. (1967) Planners in the changing American city,
        1900–1940. *Journal of the American Institute of Planners*, **33** (5),
        pp. 290–304.
        Outlines the growth of, and changes in, the planning
        profession in the United States.

4.282   HEGEMANN, Werner (1925) *Amerikanische Architektur und
        Stadtbaukunst: ein Überblick über den heutigen Stand der amerikanischen
        Baukunst in ihrer Beziehung zum Städtebau.* Berlin: E. Wasmuth.
        Contains some historical perspective on the development of
        urban design in the United States. A second edition appeared in
        1927.

4.283   HEGEMANN, Werner (1936–38) *City Planning, Housing* (3 vols.). New
        York: Architectural Book Publishing Co.
        Hegemann planned this book as a companion to *The American
        Vitruvius*. The last two volumes were published posthumously (the
        author died in 1936). The main emphasis in volume I is on the
        history of housing reform since the nineteenth century, mainly
        in the United States, with a polemical tone. Volume II deals with
        urban design (civic art). Volume III consists of plates and
        drawings.

4.284   HEGEMANN, Werner and PEETS, Elbert (1922) *The American
        Vitruvius: An Architect's Handbook of Civic Art.* New York:
        Architectural Book Publishing Co.
        A review of the recent revival of urban design, particularly in
        the United States.

4.285   HEIFETZ, R. (1969) *Annotated Bibliography on the Changing Scope of
        Urban Planning in the U.S.A.* (Council of Planning Librarians,
        Exchange Bibliography no. 86). Monticello, Ill.: Council of
        Planning Librarians.
        A collection of references of relevance to U.S. planning since
        the turn of the century.

4.286   HUBBARD, Theodora Kimball (1920) *Municipal Accomplishment in City
        Planning and Published City Plan Reports in the United States.* Boston,
        Mass.: National Conference on City Planning.
        The product of an inquiry by the Detroit City Plan

Commission, this outlines city planning progress in U.S. cities since the early 1900s.

4.287 HUBBARD, Theodora Kimball and HUBBARD, Henry Vincent (1929) *Our Cities, Today and Tomorrow: A Survey of Planning and Zoning Progress in the United States.* Cambridge, Mass.: Harvard University Press.

An extensive study of recent developments in city and regional planning in the United States.

4.288 HUBBARD, Theodora Kimball and McNAMARA, Katherine (1928) *Planning Information Up-to-date: A Supplement, 1923–1928, to Kimball's Manual of Information on City Planning and Zoning.* Cambridge, Mass.: Harvard University Press.

A full review of planning progress in the United States in the mid-1920s.

4.289 HUGGINS, K. A. H. (1967) The evolution of city and regional planning in North Carolina, 1900–1950. Unpublished Ph.D. thesis, Duke University.

No information.

4.290 JOHNSTON, Norman J. (1965) A preface to the Institute. *Journal of the American Institute of Planners,* **31** (3), pp. 198–209.

Discusses the background to the foundation of the American Institute of Planners in 1917.

4.291 KIMBALL, Theodora (1923) *Manual of Information on City Planning and Zoning.* Cambridge, Mass.: Harvard University Press.

The vademecum of the early American planning movement. An ambitious and successful attempt to encapsulate the condition and recent achievement of U.S. planning in one volume.

4.292 KULSKI, Julian Eugene (1967) *Land of Urban Promise: Continuing the Great Tradition: A Search for Significant Urban Space in the Urbanized North-east.* Notre Dame/London: University of Notre Dame Press.

A history of the classical tradition in U.S. urban design, from its origins until the present, but with much of the tone of a polemical tract, lamenting the prevalence of bad design.

.293 LEPAWSKY, Albert (1976) The planning apparatus: a vignette of the New Deal. *Journal of the American Institute of Planners,* 42 (1), pp. 16–32.

A global analysis and assessment of the whole New Deal approach to a planned society and economy, including some reference to environmental planning. A friendly approach, identifying the New Deal as the high watermark of planning in the United States.

.294 LUBOVE, Roy (1952) New cities for old: the urban reconstruction program of the 1930s. *Social Studies,* 53, pp. 203–13.

On the housing and urban renewal policies of the Roosevelt administration.

.295 LUBOVE, Roy (1962) *The Progressives and the Slums: Tenement House Reform in New York City, 1890–1917.* Pittsburgh: Pittsburgh University Press.

A study of the housing-reform movement in New York during the period in which it helped create, and then largely separated from, the American city planning movement. Based on a Ph.D. thesis presented at Cornell University in 1960.

.296 LUBOVE, Roy (1963) *Community Planning in the 1920s: The Contribution of the Regional Planning Association of America.* Pittsburgh: Pittsburgh University Press.

A study of the work and influence of the leading American planning pressure group of the interwar years.

.297 LUBOVE, Roy (1967) *The Urban Community: Housing and Planning in the Progressive Era.* Englewood Cliffs: Prentice Hall.

A collection of documents with an introduction by Lubove. Deals in part with city planning in the United States in the late nineteenth and early twentieth centuries.

.298 McNAMARA, Katherine (1936) *Bibliography of Planning, 1828–1935: A Supplement to Manual of Planning Information, 1928, by Theodora Kimball Hubbard and Katherine McNamara.* Cambridge, Mass.: Harvard University Press.

The third in the series established by Theodora Kimball in 1923.

4.299 MERRIAM, C. E. (1944) The National Resources Planning Board: a chapter in American planning experience. *American Political Science Review*, **38** (6), pp. 1075–88.

An outline of the activities of the Board in land conservation, reclamation, river control, and regional planning.

4.300 MOLLENKOFF, John H. (1978) The post-war politics of urban development, in Tabb, William K. and Sawers, Larry (eds.), *Marxism and the Metropolis: New Perspectives in Urban Political Economy*. New York: Oxford University Press, pp. 117–52.

This Marxist critique has some bearing on U.S. urban and regional planning policies since the last war.

4.301 MULLIN, John R. (1976–77) American perceptions of German city planning at the turn of the century. *Urbanism Past and Present*, **3**, pp. 5–15.

A brief discussion of the strong influence of German town planning on the development of American city planning after the City Beautiful phase. Concentrates on a number of innovations in planning powers adopted in Frankfurt under Adickes and much admired by Americans.

4.302 NATIONAL CONFERENCE ON CITY PLANNING (1927) *Planning Problems of Town, City and Region*. Philadelphia: National Conference on City Planning.

Includes an outline of the growth of city planning in the United States.

4.303 NEUFIELD, Maurice Frank (1935) The contributions of the World's Columbian Exposition to the idea of a planned society in the United States. Unpublished Ph.D. thesis, University of Wisconsin.

No information.

4.304 NOLEN, John (1966) Twenty years of city planning progress in the United States, 1907–1927 (Parts I and II). *American Society of Planning Officials Newsletter*, **32** (6), pp. 69–70; **32** (7), pp. 90–3.

A brief outline of major developments in the early years of American planning by a key participant.

4.305 PEISCH, Mark L. (1964) *The Chicago School of Architecture: Early*

Followers of Sullivan and Wright. London: Phaidon Press.

Discusses the work of the Chicago School in landscape architecture and town planning (pp. 86–104) and Griffin's plan for Canberra (pp. 105–24), with very strong emphasis on design. Pages 125–40 include some information on Griffin's postwar activities in town planning.

4.306 PERLOFF, Harvey S. (1956) Education of city planners: past, present and future. *Journal of the American Institute of Planners*, **22**, pp. 186–217.

Basically a contribution to current debate, but most of the article is a very informative survey of the development of planning education in the United States since the early 1900s, in the context of the developing theory and practice of town planning.

4.307 PETERSON, Jon Alvah (1967) The origins of the comprehensive city planning ideal in the United States, 1840–1911. Unpublished Ph.D. thesis, Harvard University.

Attempts to trace back the idea of city planning to its roots in art and architecture, and as a result lays strong emphasis on the City Beautiful movement.

4.308 PETERSON, Jon Alvah (1976) The City Beautiful movement: forgotten origins and lost meanings. *Journal of Urban History*, **2** (4), pp. 415–34.

Tries to establish broader and deeper origins for the movement than those provided by the traditional 1893-exhibition interpretation. Identifies three main roots— municipal art, civic improvement, and outdoor art. Sees the key period of gestation as 1897–1902, and the main prophet of the movement as Charles Mulford Robinson.

4.309 QUANDT, Jean Briggs (1970) From the small town to the great community: the idea of community in the Progressive period. Unpublished Ph.D. thesis, Rutgers University.

Analyses the ideas on community of a cohort of intellectuals, born 1855–68, during the Progressive era. Includes Robert Park, Jane Addams, and Frederic Howe. Discusses their efforts to revive the community through the settlement house, the community centre, and the neighbourhood.

4.310 QUEEN, Stuart A. and THOMAS, Lewis F. (1939) *The City: A Study of Urbanism in the United States.* New York: McGraw-Hill.

Includes a brief summary (pp. 458–73) of the development of physical planning in American cities.

4.311 REPS, John W. (1965) *The Making of Urban America: A History of City Planning in the United States.* Princeton, N.J.: Princeton University Press.

A comprehensive study of the planned forms of American cities from the beginnings of settlement until the First World War.

4.312 REPS, John W. (1969) *Town Planning in Frontier America.* Princeton, N.J.: Princeton University Press.

A study of planned towns founded during the nineteenth-century expansion of the United States, concentrating mainly on layout.

4.313 REPS, John W. (1973) Public land, urban development policy, and the American planning tradition, in Clawson, Marion (ed.), *Modernizing Urban Land Policy.* Baltimore: Johns Hopkins University Press, pp. 15–48.

A historical treatment of the planned extensions of towns onto common land in the United States up to about 1850.

4.314 REPS, John W. (1975) Bonanza towns: urban planning on the Western mining frontier, in Ehrenberg, R. E. (ed.), *Pattern and Process: Research in Historical Geography.* Washington, D.C.: Howard University Press, pp. 272–89.

Describes and analyses the planning of a number of mining towns in the western United States between the 1840s and the 1860s.

4.315 REPS, John W. (1979) *Cities of the American West: A History of Frontier Urban Planning.* Princeton, N.J.: Princeton University Press.

A massive study of town foundation in the American West between the late eighteenth and late nineteenth centuries. Much concentration on layout and physical form, as is normal with this author. Profusely illustrated.

4.316 RODGERS, Cleveland (1947) *American Planning: Past, Present and Future.* New York: Harper Bros.

A general commentary with some historical perspective.

4.317 SCHULTZ, Stanley K. and McSHANE, Clay (1978) To engineer the metropolis: sewers, sanitation and city planning in late-nineteenth-century America. *Journal of American History*, **65** (2), pp. 389–411.

Emphasizes the important advances made in public health and sanitary engineering in the late nineteenth and early twentieth centuries, and argues that the engineer's role in the development of American urban planning has been underestimated.

4.318 SCOTT, Mel (1969) *American City Planning Since 1890: A History Commemorating the Fiftieth Anniversary of the American Institute of Planners.* Berkeley: University of California Press.

A commemorative study commissioned by the American Institute of Planners. Sober, comprehensive and authoritative, this remains the outstanding survey of American twentieth-century planning.

4.319 SCULLY, Vincent Joseph (1969) *American Architecture and Urbanism.* London: Thames and Hudson.

A general history of the development of urban form in the United States.

4.320 SHURTLEFF, Flavell (1926) City and regional planning since 1876. *American Architect*, **129**, pp. 57–60.

A brief note by an American planning pioneer.

.321 SIMPSON, Michael A. (1969) *People and Planning.* Cleveland: Ohio Planning Conference.

A history of the Ohio Planning Conference, 1919–65.

.322 SIMPSON, Michael A. (1976) Two traditions of American planning: Olmsted and Burnham. *Town Planning Review*, **47** (2), pp. 174–9.

A review article based on the biographies by Roper and Hines.

4.323 TUNNARD, Christopher (1953) *The City of Man*. London: Architectural Press.

A general history of urban design, but principally relevant to the United States. Strong emphasis on physical and aesthetic elements, with a polemical tone.

4.324 TUNNARD, Christopher (1968) *The Modern American City*. Princeton, N.J.: Van Nostrand.

A substantial survey of the development of U.S. planning, followed by a selection of documents.

4.325 TUNNARD, Christopher and REED, Henry H. (1955) *American Skyline: The Growth and Form of Our Cities and Towns*. Boston: Houghton Mifflin.

A study of the growth of urban form in the United States from its origins to the present, including much reference to the effects of city planning.

4.326 WEIMER, David R. (ed.)(1962) *City and Country in America*. New York: Appleton-Century-Crofts.

A wide-ranging survey of the development of planning ideas in the United States from the eighteenth century to the present.

4.327 WILSON, William H. (1974) *Coming of Age: Urban America, 1915–1945*. New York: John Wiley.

An urban history of twentieth-century America, with main emphasis on physical form. Includes much consideration of urban planning and its political context.

4.328 WORSTER, Donald (ed.) (1973) *American Environmentalism: The Formative Period, 1860–1915*. New York: John Wiley.

A collection of contemporary documents, some of relevance to the history of urban planning, with a brief introduction.

Yugoslavia

4.329 MAKSIMOVIĆ, Branko (1962) *Urbanizam u Srbiji: osnivanje i rekonstrukcija varosi u 19. veku* (2nd ed.). Belgrade: Gradevinska knj.

A study of nineteenth-century urban development in Serbia,

with special reference to the reconstruction of existing towns and the foundation of new ones.

4.330 Mušič, Vladimir Braco (1972) The response of Yugoslav urban planning to development of the country, in Brown, Alan A., Licari, Joseph A. and Neuberger, Egon (eds.), *Urban and Social Economics in Market and Planned Economies: Policy, Planning and Development*, vol. 1. New York: Praeger, pp. 319–34.

A brief discussion of Yugoslav urban planning policies since the Second World War.

For country references in the 'Additional entries' section, see: Brazil, 9.32; Canada, 9.9, 9.102; China, 9.80; Germany, 9.3–4, 9.37, 9.58, 9.96, 9.130; India, 9.128; Italy, 9.22; Japan, 9.1, 9.47, 9.55, 9.67, 9.69, 9.76, 9.80, 9.95, 9.133; The Netherlands, 9.41; Poland, 9.60; Union of Soviet Socialist Republics, 9.12, 9.45, 9.114, 9.136–7; United Kingdom, 9.13, 9.25, 9.36, 9.53, 9.61, 9.107, 9.115–6, 9.127, 9.137; United States, 9.20, 9.27–8, 9.54, 9.88–90, 9.103, 9.139.

5.
Planning in individual
towns and cities

This section has been decimated by the inclusion of many local studies in Section 8, Aspects of Urban and Regional Planning, from which they can be retrieved by consulting the index of names. However, enough remains to indicate the great volume of local case studies of planning. This genre seems to be on an exponential curve of growth. The high proportion of Italian studies is partly a function of the excellence of the bibliographies which have appeared in *Storia Urbana* in the last few years, but there is no doubt that Italy shines in this area. Her architects and planners have a strong historical sense, several Italian journals are interested in planning history, and, with many towns preparing regulating plans as early as the mid-nineteenth century, there is plenty to study. Indeed, *Storia Urbana* currently publishes more planning history than any other journal in the world. The Italian story, as depicted by Italian scholars, is partly one of muddle and failure, but there is clearly a strong link here between planning activity and the writing of planning history.

In view of the inevitable variations in coverage from continent to continent and from country to country, it would be dangerous to draw any other conclusions from the distribution of studies in this section. In many towns and countries, it may be difficult to study recent planning because of difficulties of access to the necessary documents. In others, on the contrary, the frequency of planning-history studies may reflect the openness of the planning process, as for instance in Canada. Some of these studies are expressions of local pride, but rather more adopt the critical approach to which most local activities are so vulnerable. However, one can at least say that these city-studies are the stuff of planning history. In showing how general powers are put into effect, and general principles applied to specific problems, they maintain an essential link with reality which is often lost in more general writing.

Adelaide

5.1 WILLIAMS, Michael (1974) *The Making of the South Australian Landscape.* London/New York: Academic Press.

   Includes a full account of the planning of Adelaide since the nineteenth century, tracing the influence of the green-belt concept of the original planner, Colonel Light, on later growth.

Atlanta

5.2 BROWNELL, Blaine A. (1975) The commercial-civic elite and city planning in Atlanta, Memphis and New Orleans in the 1920s. *Journal of Southern History*, 41 (3), pp. 339–68.

   Traces planning developments in the three southern cities in the 1920s, arguing that they were largely a response to the demands and initiatives of business leaders.

5.3 MARSHALL KAPLAN, GANS, and KAHN (1969) *The Model Cities Program: A History and Analysis of the Planning Process in Three Cities: Atlanta, Georgia; Seattle, Washington; Dayton, Ohio.* Washington: Department of Housing and Urban Development.

   An official report, on a 1960s initiative, by a private planning partnership.

5.4 MARSHALL KAPLAN, GANS, and KAHN (1970) *The Model Cities Program: The Planning Process in Atlanta, Seattle, and Dayton.* New York: Praeger.

   The commercially published version of the previous item.

Autun

5.5 VUILLEMOT, Gustave (1971) *Regards sur 19 siècles d'urbanisme autunois* ... Autun: Musée Rollin.

The catalogue of an exhibition tracing the building and planning development of Autun in Saône-et-Loire from its Roman foundation until the present day.

Baden

5.6 KUNZE, Eduard, etc. (1972) *Stadtplanung Baden: Entwicklung, Ziele, Massnahmen.* Vienna/New York: Springer in Komm.
A survey of planning in Baden with some historical perspective.

Barcelona

5.7 BAREY, André (1976) L'évolution de Barcelone et le phénomène catalan (1860–1970). *Archives d'Architecture Moderne*, 13, pp. 4–38.
Inter alia, this discusses the development of planning policies for Barcelona from the Cerdà plan to 1970. Uses material from the exhibition organized on the centenary of Cerdà's death, in 1976.

5.8 BOHIGAS, Oriol (1963) *Barcelona entre el Pla Cerdà i el Barraquisme.* Barcelona: Edicios 62.
A history of the planning of Barcelona and its relationship to housing conditions between the mid-nineteenth century and the present day. Highly polemical tone.

5.9 CIRCULO DE ECONOMIA (1973) *Gestion o Caos, el Área metropolitana de Barcelona.* Barcelona: Ediciones Ariel.
Includes some perspective on the planning of Barcelona since Cerdà.

5.10 FERRAS, Robert (1977) *Barcelone: croissance d'une métropole.* Paris: Editions Anthropos.
A lengthy study of the city's current structure and problems, this has much relevance to the history of planning, particularly in pp. 319–66, where the Cerdà plan and the GATCPAC are discussed, together with other initiatives.

5.11 MARTORELL PORTAS, V. *et al.* (1970) *Historia del urbanismo en Barcelona, del Plan Cerdà al Area Metropolitana.* Barcelona: Editorial Labor.
A planning history of Barcelona since Cerdà.

5.12 RODRÍGUEZ-LORES, Juan, BAUMGARTEN, Ilse and FRANKE, Thomas (1979?) *Katalog zur Ausstellung 'Politische Stadtplanung in Barcelona ab 1859'.* Aachen: Lehrstuhl für Planungstheorie, R–W Technische Hochschule, Aachen.
An exhibition catalogue designed to accompany the comprehensive Barcelonese Cerdà exhibition on its appearance in Germany. Discussion of the Cerdà plan is followed by briefer remarks on subsequent planning in Barcelona (Jaussely and GATCPAC).

5.13 WYNN, Martin (1979) Barcelona: planning and change 1854–1977. *Town Planning Review*, **50** (2), pp. 185–203.
A review of the history of the planning of Barcelona since Cerdà, based on extensive reading of Spanish secondary sources.

Basle

5.14 KAUFMANN, R. (1948–49) *Die bauliche Entwicklung der Stadt Basel* (2 vols.). Basle: Helbing und Lichtenhahn.
A full history of the physical development of Basle, including some reference to planning.

Belfast

5.15 BECKETT, J. C. and GLASSCOCK, R. E. (1967) *Belfast: The Origin and Growth of an Industrial City.* London: British Broadcasting Corporation.
The texts of a series of radio talks on the history of Belfast, including some references to planning.

Berlin

5.16 *Berlin und seine Bauten. Teil II: Rechtsgrundlagen und Stadtentwicklung* (1964). Berlin/Munich: Ernst und Sohn.

Part of a multi-volume survey of Berlin architecture undertaken by the Architekten- und Ingenieurverein zu Berlin, this volume covers modern planning.

5.17 Berlino (1964). *Casabella*, **288**, pp. 1–55.

A number entirely devoted to Berlin, with articles of historical relevance by U. Conrads, K. J. Thiele, A. Rossi, and K. Liebknecht. Main emphasis is on postwar reconstruction of both halves of the city, but there is some discussion of planning policies pursued since the nineteenth century.

5.18 HEGEMANN, Werner (1930) *Das steinerne Berlin: Geschichte der grössten Mietskasernenstadt der Welt*. Berlin: G. Kiepenheuer.

An architectural, housing and planning history of Berlin from its origins until the 1920s, and a bitter critique of 'Absolutist' planning, on which the author blames the extreme overcrowding of Berlin dwellings. One of the most influential pieces of planning history ever written, it was republished by Ullstein of Berlin in 1963. It has recently been translated into Italian.

5.19 HEINRICH, Ernst (1960) Die städtebauliche Entwicklung Berlins seit dem Ende des 18. Jahrhunderts, in Dietrich, Richard (ed.), *Berlin: Neun Kapitel seiner Geschichte*. Berlin: Walter de Gruyter, pp. 199–237.

A general survey of the building and planning of Berlin since the later eighteenth century.

5.20 KRAUSE, Rudolf (1958) *Die Berliner City: frühere Entwicklung, gegenwärtige Situation, mögliche Perspektiven*. Berlin: Duncker und Humboldt.

A study of the development of the business and administrative centre of Berlin.

5.21 LARSSON, Lars Olof (1978) *Die Neugestaltung der Reichshauptstadt: Albert Speers Generalbebauungsplan für Berlin*. Stockholm: University of Stockholm (distributed by Almqvist and Wiksell).

A detailed study of both the planning and architectural aspects of the Berlin plans of the 1930s and early 1940s, based on previously unused papers from Speer's office. Fully illustrated.

5.22 MATZERATH, Horst and THIENEL, Ingrid (1977) Stadtentwicklung, Stadtplanung, Stadtentwicklungsplanung: Probleme im 19. und im 20. Jahrhundert am Beispiel der Stadt Berlin. *Die Verwaltung*, 10 (2), pp. 173–96.

A general outline of major developments in the planning of Berlin from the mid-nineteenth century until the present day.

5.23 SCHINZ, Alfred (1964) *Berlin, Stadtschicksal und Städtebau*. Brunswick: G. Westermann.

Analyses a number of Berlin planning episodes.

5.24 THIENEL, Ingrid (1973) *Städtewachstum im Industrialisierungsprozess des 19. Jahrhunderts: das Berliner Beispiel*. Berlin/New York: Walter de Gruyter.

A study of the development of the physical, social and economic structure of Berlin during the nineteenth century, with detailed analysis of two suburbs, Moabit and Rixdorf. It includes some discussion of town-extension planning and the development of building regulations, in Berlin as a whole (see especially pp. 21–44, 131–74), and in the two suburbs.

5.25 WERMUTH, Adolf (1922) *Ein Beamtenleben: Erinnerungen von Adolf Wermuth*. Berlin: A. Scherl.

Throws some light on the pre-1914 planning of Berlin.

5.26 WERNER, Frank (1969) *Stadtplanung Berlin 1900–1950*. Berlin: Kiepert.

A full study of planning developments in the city, emphasizing physical design. Generally critical of official policies. A second edition appeared in 1972.

5.27 WERNER, Frank (1969) *Städtebau Berlin-Ost*. Berlin: Kiepert.

On planning developments in East Berlin since the Second World War.

5.28 WERNER, Frank (1976) *Stadtplanung Berlin: Theorie und Realität. Teil 1, 1900–1960*. Berlin: Kiepert.

A comprehensive study of planning developments in Berlin from the close of the nineteenth century to 1960, including a full consideration of the planning of East Berlin since 1948. Ends with an attempt to construct a theory of planning on the basis of the Berlin experience. Marred by somewhat breathless treatment and poor presentation. A second edition, greatly enlarged, appeared in 1978.

5.29 WOLTERS, Rudolf (1978) *Stadtmitte Berlin: stadtbauliche Entwicklungsphasen von den Anfängen bis zur Gegenwart.* Tübingen: Wasmuth.
A planning history of the centre of Berlin.

Bielefeld

5.30 [STADT BIELEFELD] (1967) *Bielefeld, bauen und planen: Bauten und Planungen der letzten 20 Jahre.* Berlin-Steglitz: Länderdienst Verlag.
Surveys reconstruction and new planning departures in Bielefeld, North-Rhine–Westphalia, since the Second World War.

Bilbao

5.31 FULLAONDO, Juan Daniel (1969) *La arquitectura y el urbanismo de la región y el entorno de Bilbao.* Madrid: Ediciones Alfaguara.
Some historical perspective on planning in Bilbao and its region.

5.32 SALAZAR, Javier (1979) El planteamiento urbanistico y la estructura urbana del Gran Bilbao. *Comun*, **2**, pp. 78–92.
A survey of the growth and planning of metropolitan Bilbao, with much discussion of the evolution of planning policy, particularly since the early 1940s.

Birmingham

5.33 BORG, Neville (1974) Birmingham, in Holliday, John (ed.), *City Centre Redevelopment: A Study of British City Centre Planning and Case Studies of Five English City Centres.* London: Charles Knight, pp. 30–77.
A survey of the postwar replanning and redevelopment of

central Birmingham by the then City Engineer. Uncritical but
informative.

5.34 BRIGGS, Asa (1952) *History of Birmingham, vol. II.* London: Oxford
University Press.
The second volume of the official history of Birmingham
covering 1864–1938. Includes some discussion of planning issues
and policies.

5.35 MACMORRAN, James L. (1973) *Municipal Public Works and Planning in
Birmingham: A Record of the Administration and Achievements of the Public
Works Committee and Department of the Borough and City of Birmingham,
1852–1972.* Birmingham: City of Birmingham Public Works
Committee.
An 'official' account by a former senior officer. At the end of
the period studied, planning still remained under the control of
the Public Works Committee in Birmingham.

5.36 SMITH, Roger (1974) Post-war Birmingham: planning and
development. *Town Planning Review,* 45, pp. 189–206.
A succinct but comprehensive survey of the post-1945
planning history of Birmingham, covering developments within
the boundaries and the city's relations with other authorities,
sometimes sorely tried by its efforts to house its massive overspill
population.

5.37 SUTCLIFFE, Anthony and SMITH, Roger (1974) *Birmingham
1939–1970.* London: Oxford University Press.
The third volume of the official history of the city. Strong
emphasis on physical planning, stressing the difficulties caused
by rigid boundaries and central government restrictions.

Boston

5.38 MERINO, James Anthony (1968) A great city and its suburbs:
attempts to integrate metropolitan Boston, 1865–1920.
Unpublished Ph.D. thesis, University of Texas.
Principally a study of administrative and political
organization, this nevertheless covers the Metropolitan Sewerage

Commission (1889), the Parks Commission (1893), and the Water Board (1895), important though uncoordinated steps forward in the planning of the Boston region.

5.39 MERINO, James Anthony (1972) Cooperative schemes for Greater Boston, 1890–1920. *New England Quarterly*, **45**, pp. 196–226.
A distillation of his thesis—see 5.38.

Brasilia

5.40 *Brasilia: história, urbanismo, arquitetura, construção* (1960). São Paulo: Acropole.
A study of the planning and building of Brasilia.

5.41 EPSTEIN, David G. (1973) *Brasilia, Plan and Reality: A Study of Planned and Spontaneous Urban Development*. Berkeley: University of California Press.
A study of the planning and social problems generated by squatter settlements.

5.42 EVENSON, Norma (1973) *Two Brazilian Capitals: Architecture and Urbanism in Rio de Janeiro and Brasilia*. New Haven: Yale University Press.
An artistic appreciation of architecture and urban design in the two Brazilian cities, with some information of historical interest.

5.43 EVENSON, Norma (1975) Brasilia: 'yesterday's city of tomorrow', in Eldredge, H. Wentworth (ed.), *World Capitals: Toward Guided Urbanization*. Garden City, New York: Anchor Press/Doubleday, pp. 470–506.
A history and critique of the planning and architecture of Brasilia.

5.44 STAEUBLI, Willy (1966) *Brasilia*. London: Leonard Hill.
A general study of Brasilia with architectural emphasis. First published in German under the same title by Koch, Stuttgart, in 1965.

Budapest

5.45 PREISICH, Gábor (1960–4) *Budapest váosépűtésének története* (2 vols.). Budapest: Müszaki Könyvkiadó.
A general history of planning and architecture in Budapest.

Buenos Aires

5.46 *Introducción al planeamiento: su relación con el plan regulador de la ciudad de Buenos Aires (1968).* Buenos Aires: Organización del Plan Regulador.
Some relevance to the history of planning in Buenos Aires.

Calgary

5.47 CALGARY CITY PLANNING DEPARTMENT (1978) *The Historical Development of the Downtown and Inner City.* Calgary: City Council.
Covers municipal planning and its effect on building development.

5.48 FORAN, Max (1979) Land development patterns in Calgary, 1884–1945, in Artibise, A. F. J. and Stelter, G. A. (eds.), *The Usable Urban Past: Planning and Politics in the Modern Canadian City.* Toronto: Macmillan Company of Canada, pp. 293–315.
Analyses the pattern of physical development in Calgary and assesses the influence of city policies on it. Concludes that municipal planning policies and other related interventions, though not insignificant, largely conformed to the fundamental economic and social growth tendencies of the city.

Cambridge

5.49 REEVE, Frank Albert (1976) *The Cambridge That Never Was.* Cambridge: Oleander Press.
A collection of abortive planning proposals for Cambridge (England).

Canberra

5.50 HOLFORD, William Graham (1966) *A Review on the Growth of Canberra, 1958–1965 and 1965–1972.* Canberra: National Capital Development Commission.

Published as no. 338 of the Records of the Proceedings and the Printed Papers of the Australian Parliament.

Caracas

5.51 BERGAMIN, Rafael (1959) *20 años en Caracas, 1938–1958.* Madrid: publisher not stated.

On the recent planning and development of the city.

5.52 VIOLICH, Francis (1975) Caracas: focus on the new Venezuela, in Eldredge, H. Wentworth (ed.), *World Capitals: Toward Guided Urbanization.* Garden City, New York: Anchor Press/Doubleday, pp. 246–92.

Mainly a survey of current planning, but with some historical material.

Catania

5.53 PETINO, Antonio (ed.) (1976) *Catania contemporanea: cento anni di vita economica.* Catania: Istituto di storia economica dell'universita.

Includes a section (pp. 103–98) by Salvatore Boscarino on the physical development of Catania, with a discussion of modern planning policies (pp. 144–82).

Chandigarh

5.54 EVENSON, Norma (1966) *Chandigarh.* Berkeley: University of California Press.

An explanation and critique of Le Corbusier's planning and design at Chandigarh, and the execution of his ideas by the city's planning authorities. Much emphasis on architecture, but planning is fully discussed; and there is plenty of historical perspective.

5.55 EVENSON, Norma (1975) Chandigarh: monumental sculpture, in Eldredge, H. Wentworth (ed.), *World Capitals: Toward Guided Urbanization*. Garden City, New York: Anchor Press/Doubleday, pp. 391–429.

A partly historical treatment, amounting to a convenient precis of her book.

5.56 *Le Corbusier: Chandigarh, neue Hauptstadt des Punjab, Indien* (1969). Nuremburg: Städtebauinstitut.

Exhibition catalogue.

5.57 SARIN, Madhu (1975) *Planning and the Urban Poor: the Chandigarh Experience 1951–1975*. London: Development Planning Unit, School of Environmental Studies, University College.

A lengthy report on Chandigarh's inevitable tendency to attract poor workers who cannot be accommodated at the standards prescribed by Le Corbusier, and who therefore live in unofficial shanty-towns or in the streets. Much light is thrown on the design process which produced Chandigarh, and Le Corbusier's failure to comprehend the realities of Indian life.

5.58 SARIN, Madhu (1977) Chandigarh as a place to live in, in Walden, Russell (ed.), *The Open Hand: Essays on Le Corbusier*. Cambridge, Mass./London: MIT Press, pp. 374–411.

Analyses the present state of Chandigarh, and argues that both Le Corbusier's ideas, and the ways in which others have applied them, are inappropriate to Indian needs. Some historical perspective.

5.59 VON Moos, Stanislaus (1977) The politics of the Open Hand: notes on Le Corbusier and Nehru at Chandigarh, in Walden, Russell (ed.), *The Open Hand: Essays on Le Corbusier*. Cambridge, Mass./London: MIT Press, pp. 412–57.

Mainly a critique of the political and social foundations of Chandigarh's design, but throwing some light on the development and evolution of the plan and architecture. A virtually identical text appears as 'La politica de la Mano

Abierta: notas sobre Le Corbusier y Nehru en Chandigarh', in Sust, Xavier (ed.), *La arquitectura como símbolo de poder*. Barcelona: Tusquets, 1975, pp. 115–70.

Chicago

5.60 CONDIT, Carl W. (1973) *Chicago 1910–29: Building, Planning and Urban Technology*. Chicago: Chicago University Press.
A full study of the building history of Chicago, with much reference to planning.

5.61 CONDIT, Carl W. (1974) *Chicago 1930–70: Building, Planning and Urban Technology*. Chicago: Chicago University Press.
The sequel to the previous item.

5.62 McCARTHY, M. P. (1970) Chicago businessmen and the Burnham plan. *Journal of the Illinois State Historical Society*, **63**, pp. 228–56.
On the important role of business interests in the commissioning and subsequent partial execution of the Burnham plan of 1909.

Cleveland

5.63 HINES, T. S. (1973) The paradox of 'progressive' architecture: urban planning and public building in Tom Johnson's Cleveland. *American Quarterly*, **25**, pp. 426–48.
Discusses the significance of the lead which Cleveland took in the City Beautiful movement under Mayor Johnson.

Cologne

5.64 HEMDAHL, Reuel G. (1971) *Cologne and Stockholm: Urban Planning and Land-Use Controls*. Metuchen, N. J.: Scarecrow Press.
Some historical perspective.

Copenhagen

5.65 AYMONINO, Carlo (1960) Copenhagen: sviluppo storico e piano regolatore. *Urbanistica*, pp. 10–36.
A survey of the planning history of Copenhagen.

5.66 RASMUSSEN, Steen Eiler (1969) *København: Et bysamfunds saerpraeg og udvikling gennem tiderne*. Copenhagen: G.E.C. Gads Forlag.
A full study of the physical development of the town, including the planning policies of recent decades and their effects.

Coventry

5.67 GREGORY, Terence (1974) Coventry, in Holliday, John (ed.), *City Centre Redevelopment: A Study of British City Centre Planning and Case Studies of Five English City Centres*. London: Charles Knight, pp. 78–134.
A full survey of recent developments in the planning of central Coventry.

5.68 HODGKINSON, George (1970) *Sent to Coventry*. London: Robert Maxwell.
These memoirs of a Coventry councillor are of some relevance to the history of planning in the city since the war.

Dakar

5.69 SOMMER, John W. (1975) Dakar: post-colonial crisis, in Eldredge, H. Wentworth (ed.), *World Capitals: Toward Guided Urbanization*. Garden City, New York: Anchor Press/Doubleday, pp. 430–69.
Strongly historical treatment of the physical development and planning of Dakar.

Dallas

5.70 PRESNALL, P. C. (1972) Beginnings of city planning in Dallas,

Texas. Unpublished thesis, North Texas State University.
Concentrates on the early 1900s.

Dar Es Salaam

5.71 VORLAUFER, Karl (1970) *Koloniale und nachkoloniale Stadtplanung in Dar Es Salaam: Gesellschaftspolitische Zielvorstellungen und städtebauliche Ideen in ihrem Einfluss auf die Raumstruktur einer tropischen Grossstadt.* Frankfurt-am-Main: Selbstverlag des Seminars für Wirtschafts-geographie der Johann Wolfgang Goethe-Universität.
A discussion of the influence of colonial and post-colonial planning policies on the development and functions of Dar Es Salaam.

Detroit

5.72 Detroit plans its future (1953). *ASPO (American Society of Planning Officials) Newsletter*, 19 (10), pp. 73–84.
Includes a survey of city planning in Detroit since 1907.

Dortmund

5.73 *Die Ordnung von Grund und Boden in der Stadtgeschichte von Dortmund* (1962). Dortmund: Stadt Dortmund.
A general survey of the history of planning in Dortmund.

Easton

5.74 PFRETZSCHNER, Paul Alfred (1953) City planning and re-construction with special reference to the city of Easton, Pennsylvania. Unpublished Ph.D. thesis, University of Iowa.
Studies the history of planning in Easton between 1913 and 1953, concluding that it has failed to meet the city's real needs, owing partly to the fragmentation of planning functions among a number of authorities.

Edmonton

5.75 DALE, Edmund H. (1969) The role of successive town and city councils in the evolution of Edmonton, Alberta, 1892–1966. Unpublished Ph.D thesis, University of Alberta.
Includes discussion of municipal planning policies.

5.76 DALE, Edmund H. (1971) Decision-making at Edmonton, Alberta, 1913–1945; town planning without a plan. *Plan Canada*, 11 (2), pp. 134–47.
An account of planning policies in Edmonton in the period before a formal, master-plan strategy was adopted. The zoning schemes in force for much of this period caused many problems and produced a recognition that more thorough planning was needed.

5.77 WEAVER, John C. (1977) Edmonton's perilous course, 1904–1929. *Urban History Review*, No. 2, pp. 20–32.
A discussion of municipal reactions to generally depressed conditions after 1913, this throws much light on the city's land-purchase and development practices.

Essen

5.78 DICKHOFF, Erwin (1966) *Essen, 100 Jahre Stadtvermessung*. Essen: Amt für Wirtschafts- und Verkehrsförderung.
A planning and building history of one of the 'new towns' of the German industrial revolution.

Florence

5.79 PALLA, Marco (1977) Firenze nel periodo fascista: continuità e mutamenti nella compagine sociale, edilizia ed urbanistica. *Storia Urbana*, 1 (3), pp. 187–220.
Includes brief reference to the new regulating plan and central slum-clearance schemes in the 1930s.

5.80 SALVIOLI, L. (1953) Dal 1900 al 1950. *Urbanistica*, 12, pp. 29–42.

On planning developments in twentieth-century Florence, concentrating on the effects of the regulating plans.

Forlí

5.81 FREGNA, R. (1972) Forlí, città del Duce: dal 1° dopoguerra alla crisi del '29. *Parametro*, 14, pp. 26–47.

A history of planning in Forlí, Emilia Romagna, from 1918 to 1929, including discussion of the regulating plan of 1927.

Frankfurt

5.82 BANGERT, Wolfgang (1936) *Baupolitik und Stadtgestaltung in Frankfurt a.M.: ein Beitrag zur Entwicklungsgeschichte des deutschen Städtebaues in den letzten 100 Jahren.* Würzburg: Verlag Konrad Triltsch.

A rapid survey of planning and housing developments in Frankfurt between the early nineteenth century and the early 1930s. Was originally presented as a doctoral thesis at the Technische Hochschule, Berlin, in 1935.

5.83 DIEHL, Ruth (1974) *Stadtplanung in den Zwanziger Jahren.* Frankfurt: Frankfurter Stadt-Historisches Museum.

Not traced. Apparently an exhibition catalogue dealing with Frankfurt planning in the 1920s.

5.84 MULLIN, John R. (1975) German city planning in the 1920s: a North American perspective of the Frankfurt experience. Unpublished Ph.D. thesis, University of Waterloo.

A study of Frankfurt housing and planning in the 1920s, based mainly on the views of American observers.

5.85 MULLIN, John R. (1977) City planning in Frankfurt, Germany, 1925–1932: a study in practical utopianism. *Journal of Urban History*, 4 (1), pp. 3–28.

A full discussion of the housing and planning projects carried out under the aegis of Ernst May.

5.86 REBENTISCH, Dieter (1975) *Ludwig Landmann: Frankfurter*

Oberbürgermeister der Weimarer Republik (Frankfurter Historische Abhandlungen, Band 10). Wiesbaden: Franz Steiner Verlag.

Surveys the career of a distinguished mayor of Frankfurt, with much relevance to planning.

Genoa

5.87 DE MARPILLERO, G. (1966) Il piano di Piccapietra a Genova. *Casabella*, **308**, pp. 16–43.

Studies the origins and results of a 1953 plan for a central district of Genoa in the context of plans proposed for the city centre since 1825.

5.88 GABRIELLI, Bruno (1978) Il porto di Genova dalla donazione Galliera al progetto Gamba-Canepa, 1875–1919. *Storia Urbana*, **2** (4), pp. 141–84.

A narration of the development and fortunes of a number of schemes for the extension of the port of Genoa, with special emphasis on the interplay of state, municipal and private enterprise.

The Hague

5.89 BLIJSTRA, Reinder (1970) *Stedebouw 1900–1940 in 's-Gravenhage*. The Hague: City Council (?).

A brief survey of the development of planning in The Hague, 1900–40.

Hamburg

5.90 [ARCHITEKTEN- UND INGENIEUR-VEREIN, HAMBURG] (1953) *Hamburg und seine Bauten, 1929–53*. Hamburg: Hoffmann und Campe.

An architectural history of modern Hamburg, with some relevance to planning.

5.91 ASTENGO, G. (1962) Il piano della libera città anseatica di Amburgo. *Urbanistica*, **36**, pp. 72–108.

On the reconstruction and replanning of Hamburg since the last war.

Hanover

5.92 RIPPEL, J. K., WEYL, J. and HILLEBRECHT, R. (1968) Hannover. *Urbanistica*, **53**, pp. 36–94.
Includes a review of reconstruction and planning progress in post-1945 Hanover.

Harrisburg

5.93 WILSON, William H. (1975) 'More almost than the men': Mira Lloyd Dock and the beautification of Harrisburg. *Pennsylvania Magazine of History and Biography*, **99** (4), pp. 490–9.
Describes an episode in the City Beautiful movement.

Hartford

5.94 BELL, Gordon R. (1964) *Planning in Hartford 1907–1942*. Detroit: Walter H. Blucher.
Reproduction of a report of planning in Hartford, Connecticut, first printed in a limited edition c.1942.

Havana

5.95 GARNIER, Jean-Pierre (1973) *Une ville, une révolution: La Havane, de l'urbain au politique*. Paris: Anthropos.
A study of the urban policies pursued in Havana since Castro's revolution.

Indianapolis

5.96 SHADE, Philip A. (1970) *The Economics of City Planning: A Case Study of*

Indianapolis. Bloomington: Bureau of Business Research, Indiana University.

Some recent historical perspective.

Inverary

5.97 LINDSAY, I. G. and COSH, M. (1973) *Inverary and the Dukes of Argyll.* Edinburgh: Edinburgh University Press.

Discusses the influence of the Dukes of Argyll on the physical development of Inverary since 1745. The main emphasis is on the eighteenth and nineteenth centuries, but there is some discussion of planning in recent years.

Kansas City

5.98 WILSON, William H. (1964) *The City Beautiful Movement in Kansas City.* Columbia, Mo.: University of Missouri Press.

Based on a University of Missouri Ph.D. thesis of the same title (1962), this remains one of the best-known local studies of the City Beautiful movement. Much emphasis on park planning.

Leghorn

5.99 BORTOLLOTTI, Lando (1970) Livorno dal 1748 al 1958: profilo storio-urbanistico. Florence: L. S. Olschki.

A general survey of the building and planning of Leghorn, Tuscany.

Leicester

5.100 BROWN, Anthony Ernest (ed.) (1970) *The Growth of Leicester.* Leicester: Leicester University Press.

Composed of the texts of a series of radio talks on the history of the town, this is of some relevance to planning.

5.101 SMIGIELSKI, W. Conrad (1974) Leicester, in Holliday, J. (ed.), *City*

Centre Redevelopment. London: Charles Knight, pp. 135–74.
Outlines the recent history of the planning of the city centre of
Leicester.

Leiden

5.102 JOHNSON, Lisa J. (1978) *Post-war Planning in the Inner-Town of Leiden:
A Study of Changing Perception and Policies* (Working Paper no. 32).
Oxford: Department of Town Planning, Oxford Polytechnic.
A full narrative and analysis, with special reference to road
and urban renewal schemes.

Leningrad

5.103 BARANOV, Nikolai Varfolomeevich (1948) *Arkhitektura i stroitel'stvo
Leningrada*. Leningrad: Leningradskoy gazetno-phchrial'noe i
khnifoe izd-bo.
A full study of the architecture and planning of Leningrad,
with much historical perspective.

5.104 *Leningrad: planirovka i zastroyka, 1945–1957* (1958). Leningrad: Gos.
izd-vo lit-r'y po stroitel'stva i arkhitektury.
Surveys the planning and building history of Leningrad since
the Second World War.

5.105 SHAW, Denis J. B. (1978) Planning Leningrad. *Geographical Review*,
68, pp. 183–200.
A discussion of the planning of Leningrad in recent years,
with a brief survey of developments since the turn of the century.

Lisbon

5.106 AMARAL, Francisco Keil (1970) *Lisboa, uma cidade em transformação*.
Lisbon: Publicações Europa-América.
Of some historical relevance.

Liverpool

5.107 AMOS, Francis J. C. (1974) Liverpool, in Holliday, J. (ed.), *City Centre Redevelopment*. London: Charles Knight, pp. 175–206.
Surveys the history of the planning of the centre of Liverpool since the Second World War.

5.108 WHITE, B. D. (1951) *A History of the Corporation of Liverpool, 1835–1914*. Liverpool: Liverpool University Press.
This full municipal history gives some attention to Liverpool's leading role in the early development of British town planning.

London

5.109 BOR, Walter (1966) Städtebau in Grossbritannien am Beispiel London *and* Planungs- und Durchführungsverfahren in London, in [†Eggeling, Fritz, (ed.)], *Städtebau im Ausland*. Berlin: Zentralinstitut für Städtebau, Technische Universität Berlin, n.d. [1966], pp. 21–52.
Two linked articles on planning in London with much historical perspective.

5.110 CHALINE, Claude (1968) *Londres*. Paris: Armand Colin.
A general history of London by the distinguished French geographer. Modern planning is discussed on pp. 140–57.

5.111 CHALINE, Claude (1973) *La métropole londonienne: croissance et planification urbaine*. Paris: Armand Colin.
A detailed study of the recent development of a wide range of planning policies in London by a well-informed and sympathetic French observer.

5.112 GIBBON, Sir Gwilym and BELL, Reginald W. (1939) *History of the London County Council, 1889–1939*. London: Macmillan.
Includes an account of the activities of the Metropolitan Board of Works (pp. 27–61). Chapter on housing (pp. 363–402) covers L.C.C. slum clearance and housing estate planning. See also pp. 441–68 (street improvements), pp. 501–18 (parks), and

pp. 519–50 (control of land development, including town planning).

5.113 HALL, Peter (1966) London, in Hall, P. (ed.), *The World Cities*. London: Weidenfeld and Nicolson, pp. 30–58.

Discusses the planning problems and policies of the London area, with much historical perspective. Includes a comprehensive treatment of the post-1945 decentralization strategy.

5.114 JACKSON, W. Eric (1965) *Achievement: A Short History of the London County Council*. London: Longmans.

Concentrates on 1939–64 as a successor to Gibbon and Bell's *History of the London County Council, 1889–1939* (1939). Includes chapters on town planning (pp. 70–81), roads and traffic (pp. 82–92), housing (pp. 93–108), new and expanding towns (pp. 109–117), and parks and open spaces (pp. 118–26). Authoritative but uncritical 'official history' approach.

5.115 RASMUSSEN, Steen Eiler (1937) *London: The Unique City*. London: Jonathan Cape.

A personal but authoritative evocation of some of the distinctive elements in the physical growth of London, stressing the historical roots of parks, low densities, and good residential design. Includes some discussion of twentieth-century planning. It remains one of the best-known books ever written about London. Originally published in Danish in 1934 (see 5.116).

5.116 RASMUSSEN, Steen Eiler (1973) *London, den Vidtudbredte Storby: Det Nye London en Storbyregion*. Copenhagen: Gyldendal.

A new edition of the study first published in 1934 (see 5.115). It includes a whole new section on London planning since the 1930s, including regional planning and the new towns.

5.117 ROBSON, William Alexander (1939) *The Government and Misgovernment of London*. London: Allen and Unwin.

Though strongly polemical, this is an authoritative and still influential study of the weaknesses of London government. A second edition (1948) brings the story into the postwar years. Treatment of planning is largely negative, in the sense that

Robson argues that the institutions of London government, and particularly the L.C.C., have never controlled a sufficient area to be able to plan London effectively. However, the discussion of the series of expedients which had to meet the pressing needs of the world's largest city is pure planning history, and the book remains one of the finest studies ever written of the physical aspects of city government.

5.118 SHEPHERD, John W. (1975) London: metropolitan evolution and planning response, in Eldredge, H. Wentworth (ed.), *World Capitals: Toward Guided Urbanization*. Garden City, New York: Anchor Press/Doubleday, pp. 90–136.

A full survey of efforts to control and direct the development of London since the sixteenth century, but with the main emphasis on the nineteenth and twentieth centuries.

5.119 SUTCLIFFE, Anthony (1974) Deux capitales sous le poids de l'histoire. *L'Architecture d'Aujourd'hui*, **176**, pp. 2–7.

A brief comparison of the histories of London and Paris, stressing the constraints imposed by the past on present planning policies.

Manchester

5.120 REDFORD, A. and RUSSELL, I. S. (1939–40) *The History of Local Government in Manchester* (3 vols.). London: Longmans.

The full, official history of Manchester Corporation and its predecessors. Includes discussion of twentieth-century town planning and its antecedents. Written to celebrate the centenary of the Corporation.

5.121 SIMON, Lady S. D. (1938) *A Century of City Government: Manchester 1838–1938*. London: Allen and Unwin.

Shorter than the previous item, this study of municipal government, also written to celebrate the Corporation's centenary, includes discussion of twentieth-century planning by a noted participant in slum reform.

5.122 SIMON, E. D. and INMAN, J. (1935) *The Rebuilding of Manchester.* London: Longmans.

A study of slum improvement and clearance by two active participants in interwar housing reform. The history of town planning in Manchester up to 1935 is fully discussed, as is nineteenth-century slum clearance and environmental improvement. Town planning is portrayed as growing incrementally out of public-health and environmental controls.

Milan

.123 DE FINETTI, Giuseppe (1969) *Milano: costruzione di una città.* Milan: ETAS Kompass.

Collection of unpublished and published studies by De Finetti on the history and planning of Milan (and edited by Giovanni Cislaghi and others).

.124 DODI, L. (1956) L'urbanistica milanese dal 1860 al 1945. *Urbanistica,* **18–19,** pp. 24–38.

Outlines the development of Milan since the Unification, with special reference to city-centre improvements and the regulating plans of 1884, 1910–12, and 1934.

.125 EDALEO, A. (1956) L'attuazione del nuovo piano regolatore generale dopo la sua approvazione. *Urbanistica,* **18–19,** pp. 56–74.

On the problems created by the introduction of a new regulating plan for Milan in the early 1950s.

.126 EDALEO, A. (1956) Formazione e attuazione del nuovo piano regolatore generale. *Urbanistica,* **18–19,** pp. 39–55.

Traces the preparation of a new regulating plan for Milan between 1946 and its final approval in 1953.

.127 EDALEO, A. (1956) La realizzazione del P.R.G. dal 1953 al 1956. *Urbanistica,* **18–19,** pp. 77–148.

Discusses in detail some of the planning schemes prepared for Milan in the context of the general regulating plan approved in 1953.

5.128 FRANCHI, Dario and CHIUMEO, Rosa (1972) *Urbanistica a Milano in regime fascista*. Florence: La Nuova Italia.
A full study of planning in Milan between the 1920s and the early 1940s.

5.129 MACCHI CASSIA, C. (1967) Valore e significato dei lavori per il Pim nell' urbanistica italiana del dopoguerra. *Urbanistica*, 50–1, pp. 54–64.
Assesses the contribution of Milan's post-1945 planning experience to the general progress of planning in Italy.

5.130 REGGIORI, Ferdinando (1947) *Milano 1800–1943: itinerario urbanistico edilizio*. Milan: Edizioni del Milione.
A study of the building and planning development of Milan.

5.131 ROMANO, M. (1967) L'esperienza del piano intercomunale milanese. *Urbanistica*, 50–1, pp. 16–44.
Throws some light on planning in Milan between the later nineteenth century and the 1960s.

Montreal

5.132 MARSAN, Jean-Claude (1974) *Montréal en évolution: historique du développement de l'architecture et de l'environnement montréalais*. Montreal: Fides.
A history of the building and planning of Montreal.

Moscow

5.133 FROLIC, B. Michael (1975) Moscow: the socialist alternative, in Eldredge, H. Wentworth (ed.), *World Capitals: Toward Guided Urbanization*. Garden City, New York: Anchor Press/Doubleday, pp. 295–339.
Includes a lengthy and valuable discussion of the history of planning in Moscow, mainly since 1917.

5.134 HALL, Peter (1966) Moscow, in Hall, P. (ed.), *The World Cities*. London: Weidenfeld and Nicolson, pp. 158–81.

A discussion of planning problems and policies in the Moscow area, with much historical perspective.

5.135 *Moskva: planirovka i zastroyka goroda, 1945–1957* (1958) Moscow: Gos. izd-vo lit-r'y po stroitel'stva, arkhitektury i stroit. materialam.
A study of developments in the building and layout of Moscow between the end of the Second World War and 1957.

5.136 TAFURI, Manfredo (1974) Le prime ipotesi di pianificazione urbanistica nella Russia sovietica: Mosca 1918–1924. *Rassegna sovietica*, 1, pp. 80–93.
Discusses the impact of the Revolution on planning in Moscow, 1918–24.

Naples

5.137 GUIDI, Laura (1978) Napoli fra le due guerre: politica fascista nel settore delle trasformazioni edilizie ed urbanistiche. *Storia Urbana*, 2 (6), pp. 241–68.
Discusses housing conditions and building in Naples between the wars, with some reference to planning policy.

5.138 MARMO, Marcella (1977) Il piano di 'risanamento e ampliamento' dal 1885 a Napoli. *Storia Urbana*, 1 (2), pp. 145–54.
A brief discussion of some of the major influences on the formation of town-planning policy in Naples in the late nineteenth century.

New York

5.139 CARO, Robert A. (1974) *The Power Broker: Robert Moses and the Fall of New York*. New York: Alfred A. Knopf.
Includes discussion of Moses's influence on a variety of planning episodes.

5.140 COMMITTEE ON THE CITY PLAN (1914) *Development and Present Status of City Planning in New York City: Being the Report of the Committee on the City Plan, December 31, 1914, Together with Papers Presented at a Meeting of the Advisory Commission on City Plan, December 17, 1914.* New York: City of New York, Board of Estimate and Apportionment, Committee on the City Plan.

Includes studies (pp. 13–76) of a number of aspects of the development of public facilities and environmental control in New York.

5.141   FITCH, Robert (1977) Planning New York, in Alcaly, Roger and Mermelstein, David (eds.), *The Fiscal Crisis of American Cities.* New York: Random House, pp. 246–84.

A discussion of the history of planning in New York, concentrating on the regional planning of the 1920s and 1930s.

5.142   FORD, James (1936) *Slums and Housing, With Special Reference to New York City: History, Conditions, Policy.* Cambridge, Mass.: Harvard University Press.

Includes (pp. 17–254) a history of housing and environmental regulation in New York from the seventeenth century to the 1930s. Some reference is made to the development of zoning and other planning policies which developed out of building codes.

5.143   HALL, Peter (1966) New York, in Hall, P. (ed.), *The World Cities.* London: Weidenfeld and Nicolson, pp. 158–81.

Discusses planning problems and policies in the New York area, with much historical perspective.

5.144   KANTOR, Harvey A. (1971) Modern urban planning in New York City: origins and evolution, 1890–1933. Unpublished Ph.D. thesis, New York University.

A full study of the development of planning in New York from the civic-art stage of the 1890s to the regional planning of the 1920s.

5.145   KANTOR, Harvey A. (1973) The City Beautiful in New York. *New York Historical Society Quarterly,* **57**, pp. 149–71.

A narrative of efforts to secure an improvement programme worthy of New York between the late 1890s and the virtual pigeonholing of the New York City Improvement Plan of 1907.

5.146   KAPLAN, Barry J. (1979) Andrew H. Green and the creation of a planning rationale: the formation of Greater New York City, 1865–1890. *Urbanism Past and Present*, **8**, pp. 32–41.

Argues that Green's efforts from a number of official positions to secure the creation of an enlarged New York were largely the product of his awareness of the need to plan public facilities on a large scale, in advance of building development.

Newcastle-upon-Tyne

5.147 GALLEY, Kenneth A. (1974) Newcastle-upon-Tyne, in Holliday, J. (ed.), *City Centre Redevelopment*. London: Charles Knight, pp. 207–33.

Outlines the recent history of the planning of the city centre.

Nuremburg

5.148 WURMB, Dietrich von (1969) Die städtebauliche Entwicklung von Nürnberg von 1806–1944. Unpublished Diss. Ing., Technische Hochschule Munich.

A study of the building and planning development of Nuremburg.

Odessa

5.149 SKINNER, Frederick W. (1976) Trends in planning policies: the building of Odessa, 1794–1917, in Hamm, Michael F. (ed.), *The City in Russian History*. Lexington: Kentucky University Press, pp. 139–59.

A study of physical development and urban policies in Odessa during the nineteenth century.

Oslo

5.150 [BYPLANKONTORET, OSLO] (1960) *Oslo, planlegging og utvikling: oversikt over den geografiske og historiske bakgrunn, utviklingen av befolkning og*

naeringsliv m.m. og planlegging og utbygging etter krigen. Oslo: Oslo kommune.
Includes an account of post-1945 planning policies in Oslo.

Ottawa

5.151   EGGLESTON, Wilfrid (1961) *The Queen's Choice: A Story of Canada's Capital.* Ottawa: Queen's Printer.
Emphasizes the planning role of the National Capital Commission and its predecessors in the development of Ottawa since the mid-nineteenth century.

Padua

5.152   SCIMEMI, G. (1957) Padova città medievale. *Urbanistica,* **21,** pp. 32–42.
On planning developments in Padua since the beginning of the twentieth century, up to and including the new regulating plan approved in 1954.

Palermo

5.153   PIRRONE, G. (1950) Palermo, la sua storia e i suoi problemi. *Urbanistica,* **6,** pp. 34–46.
Outlines the development of the city since its origins, including the effects of modern planning.

Paris

5.154   BASTIÉ, Jean (1975) Paris: baroque elegance and agglomeration, in Eldredge, H. Wentworth (ed.), *World Capitals: Toward Guided Urbanization.* Garden City, New York: Anchor Press/Doubleday, pp. 55–89.
A discussion of the geography and planning of the Paris region, including a brief summary of the development of planning policy since the beginning of the twentieth century.

5.155 CORNU, Marcel (1972) *La conquête de Paris.* Paris: Mercure de France.

A polemic, but including a historical appreciation of aspects of Parisian planning policies since the mid-nineteenth century.

5.156 EVENSON, Norma (1979) *Paris: A Century of Change, 1878–1978.* New Haven/London: Yale University Press.

An authoritative survey of key aspects of the planning and architectural history of Paris—street planning, public transport, building regulations and the built form, housing, urban renewal, and the planning of the Paris region.

5.157 HALL, Peter (1966) Paris, in Hall, P. (ed.), *The World Cities.* London: Weidenfeld and Nicolson, pp. 59–94.

Discusses planning problems and policies in the Paris area, in the context of the city's development since the nineteenth century.

5.158 LAVEDAN, Pierre (1975) *Histoire de l'urbanisme à Paris.* Paris: Hachette.

A complete and authoritative study of the conscious shaping of Paris from Ancient times until the present day. Discussion of the nineteenth and twentieth centuries occupies pp. 327–557. Fully illustrated.

5.159 MORIZET, André (1932) *Du Vieux Paris au Paris moderne: Haussmann et ses successeurs.* Paris: Hachette.

A full discussion of the physical transformation of Paris achieved rapidly under Haussmann, and more slowly in later years.

5.160 MOSS, G. (1974) The taming of Paris. *Built Environment*, 3, pp. 507–11.

A brief outline of the history of planning in Paris.

5.161 SPECKTER, H. (1964) *Paris: Städtebau von der Renaissance bis zur Neuzeit.* Munich: Callwey.

Survey of urban design and planning in Paris from the Middle Ages to the present.

5.162 SUTCLIFFE, Anthony (1970) *The Autumn of Central Paris: The Defeat of Town Planning 1850–1970.* London: Edward Arnold.

Analyses the impact of planning policies on the physical evolution of the first four *arrondissements* of Paris since Haussmann.

Perm

5.163 STEPANOV, M. N. (1962) Development of the satellite places of Perm. *Soviet Geography: Review and Translation,* 3 (3), pp. 65–8.

A case study of planned decentralization around the city of Perm (Molotov).

Perugia

5.164 COPPA, M. (1960) Rendiconto sulla formazione del piano. *Urbanistica,* 30, pp. 65–75.

Survey of planning in Perugia since the development plan of 1933.

Perth

5.165 WEBB, Martyn J. (1979) Urban expansion, town improvement and the beginning of town planning in metropolitan Perth, in Gentilli, J. (ed.), *Western Landscapes.* Perth: University of Western Australia, pp. 359–82.

An account of the spectacular progress in urban improvement and, ultimately, urban planning achieved in Perth, Western Australia, between 1899 and 1914. Lays much stress on the international diffusion of planning ideas, and the leading role played by W. E. Bold, Perth's Town Clerk.

Philadelphia

5.166 WARNER, Sam Bass, Jr. (1968) *The Private City: Philadelphia in Three Periods of its Growth.* Philadelphia: University of Pennsylvania Press.

There is a discussion of twentieth-century planning on pp. 205–14, with Warner arguing that the strength of the

American 'privatist' tradition devalued the city's planning effort.

Pittsburgh

5.167 LUBOVE, Roy (1969) *Twentieth-Century Pittsburgh: Government, Business, and Environmental Change.* New York: John Wiley.
Includes discussion of urban planning.

Portmeirion

5.168 WILLIAMS-ELLIS, Clough (1963) *Portmeirion: The Place and Its Meaning.* London: Faber.
An autobiographical account by its creator of the foundation, growth, and present state of the unique pastiche community in Wales.

Pretoria

5.169 *Pretoria: rante en spruite: 'n inleidende verslag oor beheer en ontwikkeling* (1967). Pretoria: Afdeling Stadsbeplanning en Argitektuur.
A brief survey of the planning and development of Pretoria with some historical perspective.

Rome

.170 BENEVOLO, Leonardo (1958) Osservazioni sui lavori per il piano regolatore di Roma. *Casabella,* **219**, pp. 4–15.
Outlines the preparation of a new regulating plan for Rome since 1953, with some reference to the application of the previous plan, approved in 1931.

.171 BENEVOLO, Leonardo, *et al.* (1959) L'ultima lezione: un passo avanti e due salti indietro. *Urbanistica,* **28**, pp. 91–196.
A group of articles dealing with various aspects of the planning of Rome since 1945.

5.172 CARACCIOLO, Alberto (1956) *Roma capitale dal Risorgimento alla crisi dello Stato liberale*. Rome: Edizioni Rinascita.
A history of Rome from the mid-nineteenth to early twentieth centuries, with main emphasis on physical development, including planning.

5.173 COSTA, Frank J. (1977) The evolution of planning styles and planned change: the example of Rome. *Journal of Urban History*, 3 (3), pp. 263–94.
An outline of the planning history of Rome from the days of the Republic to the 1960s, arguing that power relationships have always been mirrored in the urban form.

5.174 FRIED, Robert C. (1973) *Planning the Eternal City: Roman Politics and Planning Since World War II*. New Haven and London: Yale University Press.
A full study of the political context of Roman planning since 1945, emphasizing the obstacles to effective public action.

5.175 INSOLERA, Italo (1959) L'istituto del Regolamento edilizio nell'ultimo secolo di urbanistica romana. *Urbanistica*, 28, pp. 197–208.
A survey of Roman building regulations and their impact since 1874.

5.176 INSOLERA, Italo (1959) I piani regolatori dal 1880 alla seconda guerra mondiale; Gli ultimi sventramenti; Le borgate; and Il nuovo volto di Roma. *Urbanistica*, 28, pp. 6–90.
A collection of articles on the planning history of Rome since 1880.

5.177 INSOLERA, Italo (1959) Storia del primo Piano Regolatore di Roma, 1870–1874. *Urbanistica*, 27, pp. 74–94.
A full analysis of the detail and context of the first regulating plan for Rome.

5.178 INSOLERA, Italo (1962) *Roma moderna: un' secolo di storia urbanistica*. Rome: Einaudi.
The best-known building and planning history of post-unification Rome. A second edition appeared in 1971.

5.179 KOSTOF, Spiro (1973) *The Third Rome, 1870–1950: Traffic and Glory.*
Berkeley: University Art Museum.
Exhibition catalogue.

5.180 KOSTOF, Spiro (1976) The drafting of a master plan for *Roma capitale:* an exordium. *Journal of the Society of Architectural Historians,* **35** (1), pp. 4–21.
On the preparation and results of the 1883 city plan.

5.181 MELOGRANI, C. (1971) La battaglia di idee per il piano di Roma. *Città e Società,* **5,** pp. 23–33.
Analyses the Roman planning debate between the end of the Second World War and the regulating plan of 1962.

5.182 PIACENTINI, Marcello and GUIDI, Francesco (1952) *Le vicende edilizie di Roma dal 1870 ad oggi.* Rome: Fratelli Palombi.
A study of building and planning in modern Rome.

5.183 Roma (1948). *Metron,* **23,** pp. 2–36.
Studies the development of Rome since the mid-nineteenth century with particular reference to the effect of the regulating plans on the evolution of the city's economic and social structure.

Rotterdam

5.184 BLIJSTRA, Reinder (1965) *Rotterdam, stad in beweging.* Amsterdam: De Arbeiderspers.
A full study of the planning and development of Rotterdam, with much historical content.

St. Louis

5.185 JUDD, Dennis R. and HENDELSON, Robert E. (1973) *The Politics of Urban Planning: The East St. Louis Experience.* Urbana: Illinois University Press.
A number of case studies, providing some very recent historical perspective on developments in St. Louis since the 1960s.

Saskatoon

5.186 RAVIS, Don (1973) *Advanced Land Acquisition by Local Government: The Saskatoon Experience.* Ottawa: Community Planning Association of Canada.

A detailed account of Saskatoon's ambitious land-purchase policy, confirmed in 1953, and unique in Canada. Originally published in 1972 by the City of Saskatoon.

Sheffield

5.187 HAWSON, Herbert Keeble (1968) *Sheffield: The Growth of a City, 1893–1926.* Sheffield: J. W. Northend Ltd.

A detailed study of municipal administration, including planning.

5.188 STAINTON, J. H. (1924) *The Making of Sheffield, 1865–1914.* Sheffield: Weston.

Includes a brief section (pp. 220–3) on planning.

Sienna

5.189 PICCINATO, Luigi (1958) Siena: città e piano. *Urbanistica,* **23,** pp. 7–16.

A brief outline of the building development of the city.

Siracusa

5.190 CABIANCA, V., LACAVA, A. and ROSCIOLI, S. V. (1956) Siracusa. *Urbanistica,* **20,** pp. 96–115.

A profile of the development of the town, including the effects of modern planning.

Stockholm

5.191 FERRARI, M. (1950) Corrispondenza da Stoccolma. *Urbanistica,* **5,** pp. 16–37.

Outlines the development of the city with particular reference to the influence of town planning.

5.192 GEJVALL, Birgit (1954) *1800-talets Stockholmsbostad: en studie över den borgerliga bostadens planlösning i hyreshusen.* Stockholm: Almqvist and Wiksell.

A study of middle-class housing in nineteenth-century Stockholm, with some reference to planning.

5.193 LUNDÉN, Thomas (1979) Stockholm—a hundred years of suburban growth: agents, flows and restrictions, in Hammarström, Ingrid and Hall, Thomas (eds.), *Growth and Transformation of the Modern City.* Stockholm: Swedish Council for Building Research, pp. 127–38.

Makes some reference to planning as a rationalizing element in twentieth-century suburban growth in the Stockholm area.

5.196 MARKELIUS, S. (1963) Il nuovo centro di Stoccolma. *Casabella,* 275, pp. 3–25.

A discussion of plans for the redevelopment of central Stockholm, including a review of the planning of the area since the seventeenth century.

5.195 SELLING, Gösta (1970) *Esplanadsystemet och Albert Lindhagen: Stadsplanering i Stockholm åren 1857–1887.* Stockholm: Stockholm City Council.

A full account of the reconstruction and planning strategy pursued in Stockholm between the late 1850s and late 1880s, under the principal inspiration of Lindhagen (1823–87), Stockholm city councillor and member of parliament. Numerous illustrations and plans. English summary.

5.196 SIDENBLADH, Göran (1966) Die städtebauliche Entwicklung und Planung von Stockholm, in [†Eggeling, Fritz (ed.)], *Städtebau im Ausland.* Berlin: Zentralinstitut für Städtebau, Technische Universität Berlin, n.d. [1966], pp. 95–123.

A survey of the development of planning in Stockholm since the Second World War.

5.197 SIDENBLADH, Göran (1967) Stockholm: a planned city, in *Cities*

(Pelican A892). Harmondsworth: Penguin, pp. 86–98.

A brief but informative outline history of the planning of Stockholm since the seventeenth century. Reprinted in Davis, Kingsley (ed.), *Cities: Their Origin, Growth and Human Impact.* San Francisco: Freeman, 1973, pp. 187–94.

5.198 SIDENBLADH, Göran (1975) Stockholm: three hundred years of planning, in Eldredge, H. Wentworth (ed.), *World Capitals: Toward Guided Urbanization.* Garden City, New York: Anchor Press/ Doubleday, pp. 25–53.

A very full survey of planning in Stockholm since the seventeenth century, including extensive consideration of post-1945 regional planning and central redevelopment.

5.199 *Stockholm: Regional and City Planning* (1964). Stockholm: Planning Commission of the City of Stockholm.

A collection of seven articles on planning problems and policies in Stockholm, with some historical perspective.

5.200 SUNDSTRÖM, T. (1972) Environmental policies of the City of Stockholm. *Studies in Comparative Local Government*, **6**, pp. 26–32.

Some historical perspective.

Strasbourg

5.201 RIMBERT, Sylvie (1967) *La banlieue résidentielle du sud de Strasbourg: genèse d'un paysage suburbain.* Paris: Les Belles Lettres.

Includes discussion of urban planning policies and their effect on private residential development in the Strasbourg suburbs since the late nineteenth century.

Swindon

5.202 HARLOE, Michael (1975) *Swindon: A Town in Transition: A Study in Urban Development and Overspill Policy.* London: Heinemann (for Centre for Environmental Studies).

Strong historical emphasis, containing a lengthy chronological account of the growth of Swindon, Wiltshire, and planning policies since the nineteenth century, when the town was founded as a deliberately laid-out railway community.

Tokyo

5.203 HALL, Peter (1966) Tokyo, in Hall, P. (ed.), *The World Cities*. London: Weidenfeld and Nicolson, pp. 217–33.

Discusses planning problems and policies in the Tokyo area, with some historical perspective.

5.204 HONJO, Masahiko (1975) Tokyo: giant metropolis of the Orient, in Eldredge, H. Wentworth (ed.), *World Capitals: Toward Guided Urbanization*. Garden City, New York: Anchor Press/Doubleday, pp. 340–87.

Not primarily a historical study but throws some light on the development of planning in Tokyo in the twentieth century.

Toronto

5.205 DAKIN, A. John (1974) *Toronto Planning: A Planning Review of the Legal and Jurisdictional Contexts from 1912 to 1970* (Papers on Planning and Design, no. 3). Toronto: Department of Urban and Regional Planning, University of Toronto.

Surveys the development of modern planning powers in Toronto.

5.206 DAKIN, A. John (1975) Toronto: a federated Metro, in Eldredge, H. Wentworth (ed.), *World Capitals: Toward Guided Urbanization*. Garden City, New York: Anchor Press/Doubleday, pp. 207–45.

Much discussion of the historical development of planning in Toronto since the early twentieth century.

5.207 DAKIN, A. John (1978) *Historical Instrument for Considering Toronto Planning* (Papers on Planning and Design, no. 16). Toronto: Department of Urban and Regional Planning, University of Toronto.

A set of notes and remarks intended to throw light on the planning history of Toronto.

5.208 DAKIN, A. John and MANSON-SMITH, P. M. (1974) *Toronto Urban Planning: A Selected Bibliography 1788–1970*. Monticello, Ill.: Council of Planning Librarians.

A list of primary and secondary materials relevant to the history of planning in Toronto.

5.209 KNAPPE, C. F. (1974) The development of planning in Toronto 1893–1922: a survey. Unpublished Master's thesis, University of Toronto.

No information.

5.210 MOORE, Peter W. (1979) Zoning and planning: the Toronto experience, 1904–1970, in Artibise, A. F. J. and Stelter, G. A. (eds.), *The Usable Urban Past: Planning and Politics in the Modern Canadian City*. Toronto: Macmillan Company of Canada, pp. 316–41.

Investigates the relationship between planning and zoning in Toronto, arguing that they developed from different sets of values, the one collectivist and the other purely self-interested. However, since the 1940s they have come to be more fully integrated.

5.211 SMALLWOOD, F. (1963) *Metro Toronto: A Decade Later*. Toronto: Bureau of Municipal Research.

Reviews the first ten years of metropolitan government in the Toronto area, including planning.

5.212 WEAVER, John C. (1979) The modern city realized: Toronto civic affairs, 1880–1915, in Artibise, A. F. J. and Stelter, G. A. (eds.), *The Usable Urban Past: Planning and Politics in the Modern Canadian City*. Toronto: Macmillan Company of Canada, pp. 39–72.

Makes brief reference to progress towards city planning in the early 1900s as one aspect of a general movement of civic reform.

Turin

5.213 CASTRONOVO, Valerio (1977) Lo sviluppo urbano di Torino nell'età del decollo industriale. *Storia Urbana*, 1 (2), pp. 3–44.

Outlines the development of Turin 1800–1914, with much

consideration of town-planning policies and their effects from the later nineteenth century.

5.214 GABRIELLI, B. (1967) Formazione e crisi del Piano intercomunale torinese. *Urbanistica*, 50/51, pp. 66–98.
Discusses the huge growth of Turin in the 1950s in relation to the development plan of 1951.

Ujung Pandang

5.215 MCTAGGART, W. Donald (1976) Urban policies in an Indonesian city: the case of Ujung Pandang, South Sulawesi. *Town Planning Review*, 47 (1), pp. 56–81.
Some historical perspective.

Urbino

5.216 DE CARLO, Giancarlo (1966) *Urbino: la storia di una città e il piano della sua evoluzione urbanistica.* Padua: Marsilio.
A building and planning history.

Västerås

5.217 DRAKENBERG, Sven (1962) *Västerås stads byggnadshistoria: från 1800-talets mitt.* Västerås: Västerås stad.
This is volume V(2) in a series of monographs on the history of Västerås published by the municipality and entitled *Västerås genom tiderna.* It deals with the building development of the town from the mid-nineteenth century, including planning policies.

Valencia

5.218 HEALEY, Patsy (1975) Urban planning in a Venezuelan city: five plans for Valencia. *Town Planning Review*, 46 (1), pp. 63–82.
Analyses a series of development plans proposed since 1953.

Vancouver

5.219 BOTTOMLEY, John (1977) Ideology, planning and the landscape: the business community, urban reform and the establishment of town planning in Vancouver, British Columbia, 1900–1940. Unpublished Ph.D. thesis, University of British Columbia.

An analysis of the relationship between Vancouver planning, 1900–40, the municipal reform movement, and the local business community. Aims to show that the physical form of cities reflects the attitudes of dominant social groups.

Venice

5.220 CHIRIVI, R. (1968) Eventi urbanistici dal 1846 al 1962. *Urbanistica*, 52, pp. 84–113.

A history of planning and improvement work in Venice since the mid-nineteenth century.

5.221 DOLCETTA, B. (1972) Venezia dal 1959 ad oggi. *Urbanistica*, 59/60, pp. 5–48.

A full study of planning policies and their social and economic contexts in Venice from 1959 to 1972.

5.222 ROMANELLI, Giandomenico (1977) *Venezia Ottocento: materiali per una storia architettonica e urbanistica della città nel secolo XIX*. Rome: Officina Edizioni.

A full study of the evolution of the built form of Venice during the nineteenth century, with main emphasis on architecture and civic design. Principally takes the form of an analysis of various official projects of embellishment and improvement, which culminate in 1886–91 in a city-wide regulating and reconstruction plan. Profuse illustrations.

Verona

5.223 MARCONI, P. (1957) Verona, lo sviluppo storico e il piano regolatore generale della città. *Urbanistica*, 22, pp. 45–74.

Outlines the whole of the city's building development, including modern town planning.

Victoria

5.224 LEE, C. L. (1969) The effect of planning controls on the morphology of the city of Victoria, British Columbia. Unpublished M.A. thesis, University of Victoria.
No information other than title.

Vienna

5.225 ABERCROMBIE, Patrick (1910–11) Vienna. *Town Planning Review*, 1, pp. 220–34, 279–93.
Surveys the growth and planning of Vienna, with much emphasis on recent policies.

5.226 BOBEK, Hans and LICHTENBERGER, Elisabeth (1966) *Wien: bauliche Gestalt und Entwicklung seit der Mitte des 19. Jahrhunderts*. Graz/Cologne: Böhlau.
A building and planning history of Vienna since the middle of the nineteenth century.

5.227 POSCH, Wilfried (1976) Lebensraum Wien: die Beziehungen zwischen Politik und Stadtplanung 1918–1954. Unpublished dissertation, University of Graz.
Discusses political limitations on the planned expansion of Vienna in the twentieth century.

5.228 TAFURI, Manfredo (1971) Austromarxismo e città: das Rote Wien. *Contropiano*, 2, pp. 259–312.
A review of the planning policies pursued by the Social Democratic municipality in Vienna between 1920 and 1933.

Warsaw

5.229 DZIEWULSKI, S. (1961) Versavia 1945–1965. *Urbanistica*, 34, pp. 18–27.

On the postwar reconstruction of Warsaw and the development of new planning policies.

Washington

5.230 BOZARTH, Donald F. (1975) Washington, D.C.: symbol and city. Tomorrow: community development planning, in Eldredge, H. Wentworth (ed.), *World Capitals: Toward Guided Urbanization*. Garden City, New York: Anchor Press/Doubleday, pp. 161–206.

Amounts to a full history of planning in Washington since the 1950s.

5.231 FEISS, Carl (1975) Washington, D.C.: symbol and city. Today: a critique of the physical plan in its socio-geographic setting, in Eldredge, H. Wentworth (ed.), *World Capitals: Toward Guided Urbanization*. Garden City, New York: Anchor Press/Doubleday, pp. 139–60.

Despite its title, this article contains a modicum of historical discussion of the L'Enfant plan and its influence on the growth of the city.

5.232 *The Grand Design: An Exhibition Tracing the Evolution of the L'Enfant Plan and Subsequent Plans for the Development of Pennsylvania Avenue and the Mall Area* ... (1967). Washington: Library of Congress.

An exhibition catalogue, composed mainly of maps and plans.

5.233 JUSTEMENT, Louis (1946) *New Cities for Old: City Building in Terms of Space, Time and Money*. New York/London: McGraw-Hill.

Contains (pp. 95–144) a full account of the history of planning in Washington from L'Enfant to the present, mainly using captioned illustrations.

5.234 REPS, John W. (1967) *Monumental Washington: The Planning and Development of the Capital Center*. Princeton: Princeton University Press.

An architectural and planning history of the major public areas of Washington.

Whitehorse

5.235 KOROSCIL, Paul M. (1978) Planning and development in Whitehorse, Yukon Territory. *Plan Canada*, **18** (1), pp. 30–45.
Reviews the entire history of planning in Whitehorse since its Gold Rush origins in the 1890s.

Winnipeg

5.236 ARTIBISE, Alan F. J. (1975) Winnipeg and the city planning movement, 1910–1915, in Bercuson, D. J. (ed.), *Western Perspectives I*. Toronto: Holt, Rinehart and Winston, pp. 1–10.
On Winnipeg's role in the early years of Canadian planning.

5.237 ARTIBISE, Alan F. J. (1975) *Winnipeg: A Social History of Urban Growth, 1874–1914*. Montreal: McGill-Queen's University Press.
Includes discussion of pre-1914 planning in the town.

For town and city references in the 'Additional entries' section, see: Atlanta, 9.105; Berlin, 9.50, 9.62; Canberra, 9.70; Chicago, 9.141; Paris, 9.6, 9.40; Rome, 9.34; Tokyo, 9.26; Toronto, 9.56, 9.97; Vienna, 9.124; Washington, 9.57.

6.

Individual planners

This lengthy section demonstrates the great attraction of the biographical approach to planning historians. It also reflects the immaturity of planning historiography, given that biography is a declining genre elsewhere in the historical sciences, and even in political history. Historians no longer attach the same importance to the role of the individual as they did fifty or a hundred years ago; instead, much broader processes seem to them to be shaping the world.

Why then are planning historians so interested in the individual? There are some purely practical reasons. For instance, the work of one man makes a manageable thesis topic, from which articles or a book often follow. Even in the absence of private papers, leading planners have usually published enough, or stimulated enough published comment, to provide an adequate source-base for the researcher. It also has to be recognized that planning, until very recent decades, was indeed greatly advanced by the work of a few creative or influential people. Most of the studies here are of planning pioneers, and few of those who have participated in planning since its institutionalization as a bureaucratic activity have qualified for personal treatment. In fact, planning biography may already be on a downward path as the leading pioneers are mopped up by authoritative studies, leaving only minor figures from the early years, and the more anonymous contemporary planners, to be studied.

However, behind these objective considerations there lies a further potent, irrational, stimulus to biography. This is the planner's tendency to view himself as a lone hero figure, able to grasp realities which escape lesser mortals, but frequently thwarted by incompetence and inertia elsewhere. No doubt the routinization of planning will ultimately destroy this mentality, but it remains quite strong especially among people just leaving the planning schools. As some of the more able of these move almost immediately into planning teaching, they are liable to retain this Nietzschean vision and impose it on the history of planning. Patrick Geddes and Le Corbusier have benefited most from this attention, but Cerdà and Sitte run them close. Interestingly, there is in many cases an inverse relationship between the amount of planning work undertaken and the degree of historical attention secured. It was largely because Geddes and Le Corbusier were allowed to do so little planning that they wrote and lectured so profusely, inadvertently allowing generations of researchers to pore through their works, seeking their 'true' message. Meanwhile, we lack adequate studies of Joseph Stübben, Patrick Abercrombie, and many more full-time, working planners (though some of these gaps will soon be filled by research already in progress).

Even when the biographical canon is rounded out, however, we shall have to remain alive to the dangers of the genre. Biographers are, as a rule, sympathetic to their subjects. Most of the studies listed below are uncritical, and many are positively eulogistic. As a result, biography peoples the past with larger-than-life figures and over-rated ideas. Historical reality does not have room for them all, and, as planning historiography develops, some of these figures are likely to be cut down to a more human scale.

(For cross-references, and names not included in this section, see the index of names, p. 265.)

Adams

6.1 HULCHANSKI, John David (1978) *Thomas Adams: A Biographical and Bibliographic Guide* (Papers on Planning and Design, no. 15). Toronto: Department of Urban and Regional Planning, University of Toronto.

A brief outline of Adams's career, followed by a full list of his writings.

Bartholomew

6.2 JOHNSTON, Norman J. (1964) Harland Bartholomew: his comprehensive plans and science of planning. Unpublished Ph.D. thesis, University of Pennsylvania.

A full study of the work of the early American planner.

Bassett

6.3 BASSETT, Edward Murray (1939) *Autobiography of Edward M. Bassett.* New York: The Harbor Press.

Covers the active career of the pioneer New York planner (1863–1948), key architect of the zoning policy and the regional plan.

Bettman

6.4 VITZ, M. H. (1964) The contribution of Alfred Bettman to city and regional planning. Unpublished Master of City Planning thesis, Ohio State University.

An assessment of the career of the early American planner.

Blumenfeld

6.5 PRESSMAN, Norman E. P. (1976) Hans Blumenfeld: humanist and urban planner. *Plan Canada*, 16, pp. 25–35.

A brief appreciation of Blumenfeld's contribution to planning in North America.

Buckingham

6.6 ABERCROMBIE, Patrick (1921) Ideal cities, no. 2: Victoria. *Town Planning Review*, 9 (1), pp. 15–20.

A brief analysis of James Silk Buckingham's ideal scheme.

6.7 TURNER, R. E. (1934) *J. S. Buckingham, 1786–1855: A Social Biography.* London: Williams and Norgate.
Makes brief reference to Buckingham's interest in urban reform and his ideal town of Victoria.

Burnham

6.8 HINES, Thomas Speight (1972) The imperial facade: Daniel H. Burnham and American architectural planning in the Philippines. *Pacific Historical Review*, 41, pp. 33–53.
Analysis of Burnham's government-commissioned plans for Manila and other places in the Philippines.

6.9 HINES, Thomas Speight (1974) *Burnham of Chicago: Architect and Planner.* New York: Oxford University Press.
A full, authoritative, and critical biography, replacing Moore's hagiographical piece (see below). This study was preceded by the author's University of Wisconsin Ph.D. thesis, Daniel Hudson Burnham: a study in cultural leadership, 1971.

6.10 MOORE, Charles (1921) *Daniel H. Bu.nham: Architect: Planner of Cities* (2 vols.). Boston/New York: Houghton Mifflin.
Mainly hagiographical, and now superseded by Hines's 1974 biography.

Cerdà

6.11 CID, Salvador Tarragó (1977) Genesis y estructura de la obra de Cerdà. *Construcción de la Ciudad*, 6–7, pp. 19–37.
Briefly summarizes the development of Cerdà's ideas, lists his projects and published works, and prints two unpublished fragments.

6.12 CID, Salvador Tarragó (1977) La ultima obra de Cerdà: comarcalización de la provincia de Barcelona. *Construcción de la Ciudad*, 6–7, pp. 56–61.

A brief discussion of Cerdà's proposals for a regional plan (principally communications) for the province of Barcelona.

6.13 CORT, Cesar *et al.* (1959) *Ildefonso Cerdà, el Hombre y su Obra.* Barcelona: Ayuntamiento.

An early attempt to rehabilitate the reputation of Cerdà, published to celebrate the centenary of the approval of his Barcelona extension plan.

6.14 CREÍXELL, Santiago Padrés and PARÉS, Santiago Vela (1977) El modelo teorico del plan Cerdà. *Construcción de la Ciudad,* **6–7,** pp. 46–55.

A discussion of the origins and development of Cerdà's theories of urban structure, and their application in his Barcelona plan.

6.15 ESTAPÉ, Fabian (1971) *Vida y Obra de Ildefonso Cerdà.* Barcelona: Instituto de Estudios Fiscales.

Volume 3 of a re-edition of Cerdà's *Teoría general de la urbanización.* An authoritative professional biography.

6.16 Materiàles para una biografia (1977). *Construcción de la Ciudad,* **6–7,** pp. 10–18.

Reproduces a number of documents relating to the career of Cerdà.

6.17 MILLER, Bernard (1978) Ildefonso Cerdà: an introduction. *Architectural Association Quarterly,* **9** (1), pp. 12–22.

An account of Cerdà's career and an analysis of his Barcelona plan, based on an exhibition.

6.18 ORTÍZ, Augusto (1977) Perspectiva y prospectiva desde Cerdà: una linea de tendencia. *Construcción de la Ciudad,* **6–7,** pp. 62–70.

Discusses the parallels between Cerdà's ideas and those of later planners (Soria y Mata, Garnier, Le Corbusier, Miliutin, Sert, Hilberseimer).

6.19 SORIA Y PUIG, Arturo (1977) Los pasos previos a la fundación de una ciencia urbanizadora. *Construcción de la Ciudad,* **6–7,** pp. 38–45.

Discusses the intellectual background to Cerdà's theories.

Copeland

6.20 WEISS, Ellen (1975) Robert Morris Copeland's plans for Oak Bluffs. *Journal of the Society of Architectural Historians*, **34**, pp.60–6.
Discusses an early example of upper-class residential planning in mid-nineteenth century America.

Eggeling

6.21 FRICK, Dieter and WITTWER, Georg (eds.) (1972) *Fritz Eggeling: Theorie und Praxis im Städtebau: sein Werk als Stadtplaner, Architekt und Lehrer*. Stuttgart/Berne: Karl Krämer Verlag.
A collection of documents, preceded by an introduction, relating to the work of the modern German planner (died 1966).

Fassbender

6.22 WURZER, Rudolf (1974) Eugen Fassbender. *Stadtbauwelt*, **44**, p. 299.
Brief appreciation of his qualities as one of Austria's leading planners c. 1890–1914.

Fischer

6.23 PFISTER, Rudolf (1968) *Theodor Fischer: Leben und Wirken eines deutschen Baumeisters*. Munich: Verlag Callwey.
Covers his work in model settlement design in Germany before and after the First World War.

Garnier

6.24 PAWLOWSKI, Christophe (1967) *Tony Garnier et les débuts de l'urbanisme fonctionnel en France*. Paris: Centre de Recherche d'Urbanisme.
An outline of Garnier's career and an appreciation of his major contribution to French planning.

6.25 VERONESI, Giulia (1948) *Tony Garnier*. Milan: il Balcone.
A critical appreciation of his contribution to twentieth-century architecture and planning.

6.26 WIEBENSON, Dora (1958) Tony Garnier's *Cité Industrielle*: its relation to its nineteenth and early twentieth century background. Unpublished Master's thesis, New York University (Institute of Fine Arts).
The predecessor of 6.28.

6.27 WIEBENSON, Dora (1960) Utopian aspects of Tony Garnier's *Cité Industrielle. Journal of the Society of Architectural Historians*, **19** (1), pp. 16–24.
A discussion of the idealist features of Garnier's model planning project.

6.28 WIEBENSON, Dora (1970) *Tony Garnier: The Cité Industrielle*. London: Studio Vista.
An outline of Garnier's career and a critique of his major model planning projects. Copiously illustrated.

Geddes

6.29 BOARDMAN, Philip (1944) *Patrick Geddes: Maker of the Future*. Chapel Hill: University of North Carolina Press.
A full survey of the life and ideas of Geddes, somewhat adulatory in tone.

6.30 BOARDMAN, Philip (1978) *The Worlds of Patrick Geddes: Biologist, Town Planner, Re-educator, Peace-warrior*. London: Routledge and Kegan Paul.
A second attempt by Boardman to capture the essence of Geddes's message, retaining the features of his earlier work.

6.31 DEFRIES, Amelia Dorothy (1927) *The Interpreter: Geddes, the Man and his Gospel*. London: Routledge and Kegan Paul.
Basically a promotional piece, but with some historical relevance.

6.32 GOIST, Park Dixon (1974) Patrick Geddes and the city. *Journal of the American Institute of Planners*, **40**, pp. 31–7.
      A brief appreciation of Geddes's contribution to town planning.

6.33 KITCHEN, Paddy (1975) *A Most Unsettling Person: An Introduction to the Ideas and Life of Patrick Geddes*. London: Gollancz.
      A recent effort to encapsulate Geddes's contribution to a number of branches of theory, including town planning.

6.34 KITCHEN, Paddy (1975) Patrick Geddes: nurterer of life. *Built Environment*, **1** (1), pp. 61–5.
      Resumes some of the main points of her book (see previous item).

6.35 LESSER, Wendy (1974) Patrick Geddes: the practical visionary. *Town Planning Review*, **45** (3), pp. 311–27.
      Attempts to define the true essence of Geddes's contribution to planning, and suggests why his ideas have had so little real impact.

6.36 McGEGAN, E., GEDDES, Arthur and MEARS, F. C. (1940) The life and work of Sir Patrick Geddes. *Journal of the Town Planning Institute*, **26**, pp. 189–95.
      A brief assessment of his contribution to town planning.

6.37 MAIRET, Philip (1957) *A Pioneer of Sociology: Life and Letters of Patrick Geddes*. London: Lund Humphries.
      A full biography, using correspondence not seen by Boardman in his 1944 biography. Includes discussion of his work in town planning.

6.38 MELLER, Helen E. (1973) Patrick Geddes: an analysis of his theory of civics, 1880–1904. *Victorian Studies*, **16**, pp. 291–316.
      An exposition and critical appraisal of Geddes's civics, the basis of his approach to urban planning.

6.39 MUMFORD, Lewis (1950) Mumford on Geddes. *Architectural Review*, **108** (644), pp. 81–7.
      A brief appraisal of the importance of Geddes by one of his best-known admirers.

6.40 NICOLINI, Laura (1979) *La vita e le opere di Patrick Geddes*: un recente studio di P. Boardman. *Storia Urbana*, 3 (7), pp. 217–22.
A review article, summarizing Geddes's career and welcoming Boardman's *The Worlds of Patrick Geddes*.

6.41 PEPLER, George L. (1955) Geddes' contribution to town planning. *Town Planning Review*, 26 (1), pp. 19–24.
An assessment of Geddes's importance by a distinguished British planning pioneer.

6.42 STALLEY, Marshall (1972) *Patrick Geddes: Spokesman for Man and the Environment: A Selection*. New Brunswick, N.J.: Rutgers University Press.
A selection from the writings of Geddes with an introduction by Stalley.

6.43 TYRWHITT, Jacqueline (ed.) (1947) *Patrick Geddes in India*. London: Lund Humphries.
A full study of Geddes's valuable town-planning work in India in the 1920s.

Griffin

6.44 BIRRELL, James (1964) *Walter Burley Griffin*. St. Lucia: University of Queensland Press.
A study of the distinguished American planner, creator of Canberra.

6.45 JOHNSON, D. L. (1973) Walter Burley Griffin: an expatriate planner at Canberra. *Journal of the American Institute of Planners*, 39, pp. 326–36.
A survey of Griffin's work in planning the Australian capital.

Hegemann

6.46 CALABI, Donatella (1976) Werner Hegemann, o dell'ambiguità borghese dell'urbanistica. *Casabella*, 428, pp. 54–60.

A critique of Hegemann's career as both planner and publicist.

6.47 CALABI, Donatella and FOLIN, Marino (eds.) (1975) *Werner Hegemann, Catalogo delle Esposizioni Internazionali di Urbanistica di Berlino e Düsseldorf, 1910–12.* Milan: il Saggiatore.

Extracts from the writings of Hegemann on the Berlin planning exhibition, of which he was the main organizer, and the subsequent Düsseldorf exhibition, with an introduction by the editors.

Hénard

6.48 BARDET, Gaston (1939) Un précurseur: Eugène Hénard. *L'Architecture d'Aujourd'hui*, **10**, p. 18.

One of the earliest historical appreciations of Hénard's important contribution to the development of planning in France.

6.49 CALABI, Donatella and FOLIN, Marino (eds.) (1972) *Alle origini dell'urbanistica: la costruzione della metropoli.* Padua: Marsilio.

Mainly consists of selections from the writings of Eugène Hénard.

6.50 ROTIVAL, Maurice E. H. (1960) Hommage à Eugène Hénard: urbaniste de Paris, 1900–1909. *L'Architecture d'Aujourd'hui*, **88**, pp. 3–5.

A brief appreciation of Hénard's proposals for new public works in Paris in the early 1900s.

6.51 WOLF, P. M. (1967) The first modern urbanist. *Architectural Forum*, **127**, pp. 50–5.

Summarizes his book (see next item).

6.52 WOLF, P. M. (1968) *Eugène Hénard and the Beginning of Urbanism in Paris, 1900–1914.* Paris: Centre de Recherche d'Urbanisme.

An authoritative analysis of Hénard's contribution to the emergence of modern planning in France, somewhat exaggerating his importance. Fully illustrated.

Hilberseimer

6.53 HILBERSEIMER, L. (1963) *Entfaltung einer Planungsidee*. Berlin: Ullstein.
Hilberseimer traces the development of his own ideas on town planning.

Horsfall

6.54 REYNOLDS, Josephine P. (1952) Thomas Coglan Horsfall and the town planning movement in England. *Town Planning Review*, 23, pp. 52–60.
A summary of her thesis (see next item).

6.55 REYNOLDS, Josephine P. (1953) Thomas Coglan Horsfall, 1841–1932: a pioneer of the town planning movement in England. Unpublished M.A. thesis, University of Liverpool.
The first full historical study of Horsfall, still much quoted. Established Horsfall as a major influence on the development of the town-planning idea in Britain.

Howard

6.56 BUDER, Stanley (1969) Ebenezer Howard: the genesis of a town planning movement. *Journal of the American Institute of Planners*, 35 (6), pp. 390–8.
A brief appreciation of Howard's work and ideas.

6.57 EDEN, W. A. (1943–47) Studies in urban theory, II: Ebenezer Howard and the garden city movement. *Town Planning Review*, 19 (3–4), pp. 123–43.
On the origins of Howard's idea, and his development of it.

6.58 FISHMAN, Robert (1974) Ideal cities: the social thought of Ebenezer Howard, Frank Lloyd Wright and Le Corbusier. Unpublished Ph.D. thesis, Harvard University.

This was published, with little alteration, three years later (see following item).

6.59 FISHMAN, Robert (1977) *Urban Utopias of the Twentieth Century: Ebenezer Howard, Frank Lloyd Wright and Le Corbusier*. New York: Basic Books.

A thorough study of all three as 'utopian' urban and social planners, stressing similarities of motivation and contrasts in their proposals, which the author sees as spanning the entire range of solutions open to those who would replan the urban environment, from extreme centralization to extreme decentralization.

6.60 HARMSWORTH, Cecil B. (1936) *Some Reflections on Sir Ebenezer Howard and His Movement*. London: Garden Cities and Town Planning Association.

A promotional piece, with some historical relevance.

6.61 MACFADYEN, Dugald (1933) *Sir Ebenezer Howard and the Town Planning Movement*. Manchester: Manchester University Press.

A hagiographical, but comprehensive, study. Reprinted by Manchester University Press in 1970.

6.62 MOSS-ECCARDT, John (1973) *Ebenezer Howard: An Illustrated Life of Sir Ebenezer Howard, 1850–1928*. Aylesbury: Shire Publications.

A brief biography by the curator of the Letchworth Museum.

6.63 OSBORN, Frederic James (1950) Sir Ebenezer Howard: the evolution of his ideas. *Town Planning Review*, **31**, pp. 221–35.

A brief exposition by one of Howard's most distinguished followers.

6.64 OSBORN, Frederic James (1971) The history of Howard's 'Social Cities'. *Town and Country Planning*, **39** (12), pp. 539–45.

Studies the changes which Howard made to the 'social cities' chapter in the 1902 edition.

6.65 OSTROWSKI, Waclaw (1966) Sir Ebenezer Howard in Poland. *Town and Country Planning*, **34** (11), pp. 511–13.

On Howard's stay in Cracow in 1921, and the influence of his ideas on the planning of the town.

Howe

5.66 HUFF, Robert Arthur (1967) Frederic C. Howe, Progressive. Unpublished Ph.D. thesis, University of Rochester.
A detailed study of Howe's public career from his early years in Cleveland until his resignation from Federal service in 1919. Suggests that the enthusiasm for urban life which involved him so closely in planning before the war was dispelled thereafter.

5.67 LUBOVE, Roy (1977) Frederic C. Howe and the quest for community in America. *The Historian*, 39 (2), pp. 270–91.
An outline and critique of Howe's various reform proposals, including his role in the city-planning movement.

Josimović

6.68 MAKSIMOVIĆ, Branko (1969) *Emilijan Josimović, prvi srpski urbanist.* Belgrade: Institut za arhitektura i urbanizam Srbije.
A study of the career of the Serbian urban reformer (1823–97).

Kahn

6.69 SCULLY, Vincent Joseph (1962) *Louis I. Kahn.* London: Prentice-Hall.
A presentation and critique of the work of the American architect-planner, best noted for his planning work in Philadelphia between 1952 and 1961.

Korn

6.70 FRY, Maxwell (1967) Arthur Korn and the English MARS group, in Sharp, Dennis (ed.), *Planning and Architecture.* London: Barrie and Rockliff, pp. 127–8.

A brief note on Korn's contributions to the wartime London plans of the MARS group.

6.71 JOHNSON-MARSHALL, Percy (1967) Arthur Korn: planner, in Sharp, Dennis (ed.), *Planning and Architecture*. London: Barrie and Rockliff, pp. 129–30.
A brief appreciation.

Le Corbusier

6.72 ANTHONY, Harry Antoniades (1966) Le Corbusier: his ideas for cities. *Journal of the American Institute of Planners*, **32** (5), pp. 279–88.
Summarizes Le Corbusier's approach to urban design and planning.

6.73 BOESIGER, Willy (ed.) (1972) *Le Corbusier*. London: Thames and Hudson.
A fully-illustrated selection from the *Oeuvre Complète*, covering Le Corbusier's entire output, including his urban planning schemes and theories.

6.74 EVENSON, Norma (1970) *Le Corbusier: The Machine and the Grand Design*. London: Studio Vista.
An extensively illustrated exposition of Le Corbusier's urban planning ideas.

6.75 FISHMAN, Robert (1977) From the Radiant City to Vichy: Le Corbusier's plans and politics, 1928–1942, in Walden, Russell (ed.) *The Open Hand: Essays on Le Corbusier*. Cambridge, Mass./ London: MIT Press, pp. 244–83.
Analyses the relationship between Le Corbusier's changing political views, his approach to city planning, and his efforts to influence authority during his crucial middle years.

6.76 FRAMPTON, Kenneth (1969) The city of dialectic. *Architectural Design*, **39** (10), pp. 541–6.
An interpretation of Le Corbusier's *Ville Radieuse*. Suggests that the rigid separation of functions envisaged by Le Corbusier allowed the city to function in a dialectical manner. This is

highly questionable, but Frampton has some interesting things to say about Le Corbusier's links with the syndicalist movement in the 1920s and 1930s.

6.77 FRY, Maxwell (1977) Le Corbusier at Chandigarh, in Walden, Russell (ed.), *The Open Hand: Essays on Le Corbusier*. Cambridge, Mass./London: MIT Press, pp. 350–63.

Illuminating reminiscences by a distinguished associate of Le Corbusier's appointment as chief planner of Chandigarh and the subsequent elaboration of the master plan and the capitol complex.

6.78 SUTCLIFFE, Anthony (1977) A vision of utopia: optimistic foundations of Le Corbusier's *doctrine d'urbanisme*, in Walden, Russell (ed.), *The Open Hand: Essays on Le Corbusier*. Cambridge, Mass./London: MIT Press, pp. 217–43.

Outlines his approach to town planning and argues that its weaknesses were largely the product of an over-optimistic view of humanity and an uncritical acceptance of technical change.

6.79 VON MOOS, Stanislaus (1971) *Le Corbusier: l'architecte et son mythe.* Paris: Horizons de France.

A detailed analysis of Le Corbusier's development as an architect and planner, firmly based on documentary sources. One of the best recent studies of Le Corbusier, with full attention paid to urban and regional planning.

Lichtwark

6.80 FISCHER, Alice (1961) An analysis of the writings of Alfred Lichtwark as they apply to the city and civic improvement. Unpublished Master's essay, Columbia University.

No information.

Lutyens

6.81 BUTLER, A. S. G. (1950) *The Architecture of Sir Edwin Lutyens* (3 vols.). London: Country Life.

Lutyens's plans for New Delhi, and other schemes of urban design, are discussed in volume 2.

6.82 HUSSEY, Christopher E. C. (1950) *The Life of Sir Edwin Lutyens.* London: Country Life.
Includes discussion of his work at New Delhi.

6.83 LUTYENS, Robert (1970) *Notes on Sir Edwin Lutyens.* Newcastle: Oriel for Art Workers Guild.
The text of a brief lecture of some relevance to Lutyens's work as a planner.

McAneny

6.84 MCANENY, George (1949) *Reminiscences.* New York: Columbia University Oral History Project.
Includes McAneny's recollections of his role in the formulation of zoning and other planning policies for New York between the early 1900s and the First World War, together with his subsequent interest in the promotion of city planning.

Marsh

6.85 KANTOR, Harvey A. (1974) Benjamin C. Marsh and the fight over population congestion. *Journal of the American Institute of Planners,* **40** (6), pp. 422–9.
A full discussion of Marsh's career as a housing and planning reformer in New York between 1907 and the First World War. Claims that Marsh's land-reform intransigence was partly responsible for splitting the American planning movement in 1910.

6.86 MARSH, Benjamin Clarke (1953) *Lobbyist for the People: A Record of Fifty Years.* Washington: Public Affairs Press.
The autobiography of the versatile American reformer, who was one of the leaders of the American planning and land-reform movements before the First World War.

Mawson

6.87 MAWSON, Thomas H. (1927) *The Life and Work of an English Landscape Architect.* New York: Charles Scribner's Sons.

An autobiography of considerable interest for the early history of modern planning, from the early 1900s to the 1920s.

May

6.88 BUEKSCHMITT, J. (1963) *Ernst May.* Stuttgart: Koch.

The authoritative biography of the noted German planner and housing expert, active in Frankfurt until his transfer to the Soviet Union in the early 1930s.

Miliutin

6.89 MILIUTIN, N. A. (1974) *Sotsgorod: The Problem of Building Socialist Cities.* Cambridge, Mass.: MIT Press.

This translation by Arthur Sprague of Miliutin's major work includes a long essay on Miliutin by the translator.

Nolen

6.90 HANCOCK, John Loretz (1960) John Nolen: the background of a pioneer planner. *Journal of the American Institute of Planners,* **26** (4), pp. 302–12.

Review Nolen's background, education, and early career in planning until about 1909.

6.91 HANCOCK, John Loretz (1964) John Nolen and the American city planning movement, a history of culture change and community response, 1900–1940. Unpublished Ph.D. thesis, University of Pennsylvania.

Rather broader than its title suggests, this study attempts to trace, through Nolen's rise to the leadership of the American planning profession, the origins and dynamic of the growth of planning in the United States.

6.92 HANCOCK, John Loretz (1976) *John Nolen: A Bibliographic Record of Achievement.* Cornell University, Urban and Regional Studies Research Report.
A guide to Nolen's published work.

Olmsted

6.93 BARLOW, Elizabeth and ALEX, William (1972) *Frederick Law Olmsted's New York.* New York/London: Praeger.
Sets Olmsted's plans for Central Park in the context of mid-nineteenth-century New York.

6.94 BENDER, Thomas (1975) *Toward an Urban Vision: Ideas and Institutions in Nineteenth-Century America.* Lexington: University Press of Kentucky.
Includes a detailed analysis of the ideology of Frederick Law Olmsted (pp. 159–87) as part of a broader study of the response of American intellectuals to nineteenth-century urbanization.

6.95 BEVERIDGE, Charles Eliot (1966) Frederick Law Olmsted: the formative years, 1822–1865. Unpublished Ph.D. thesis, University of Wisconsin.
A narrative of Olmsted's early wonderings, wanderings and writings. Includes Central Park but ends rather abruptly in 1865, as Olmsted resumes his landscape-architecture partnership with Calvert Vaux.

6.96 BLODGETT, Geoffrey (1976) Frederick Law Olmsted: landscape architecture as conservative reform. *Journal of American History*, **62** (4), pp. 869–89.
Investigates the social objectives of Olmsted's park and residential planning.

6.97 FABOS, J. G., MILDE, G. T. and WEINMAYR, V. M. (1968) *Frederick Law Olmsted, Sr.: Founder of Landscape Architecture in America.* Amherst: University of Massachusetts Press.
An authoritative biography and review of Olmsted's work.

6.98 FEIN, Albert (ed.) (1968) *Landscape into Cityscape: Frederick Olmsted's*

Plans for a Greater New York City. Ithaca: Cornell University Press.
A collection of documents, with an introduction by Fein.

6.99 FEIN, Albert (1972) *Frederick Law Olmsted and the American
Environmental Tradition*. New York: Braziller.
   A richly illustrated, succinct commentary on all the main
aspects of Olmsted's creative activity, stressing his commitment
to a unified, organic, enlightened society. This study was
preceded by a Columbia University Ph.D. thesis, Frederick Law
Olmsted: his development as a theorist and designer of the
American city, 1969.

6.100 FISHER, Irving David (1976) Frederick Law Olmsted and the
philosophic background to the city planning movement in the
United States. Unpublished Ph.D. thesis, Columbia University.
   Sets Olmsted's career in the context of the park movement
and the broader progression towards an ideology of urban
planning in nineteenth-century America.

6.101 MCLAUGHLIN, Charles Capen (1960) Selected letters of Frederick
Law Olmsted. Unpublished Ph.D. thesis, Harvard University.
   No information.

6.102 OLMSTED, Frederick Law Jr. and KIMBALL, Theodora (1922–28)
Forty Years of Landscape Architecture (2 vols.). New York: Putnam.
   Mostly a collection of documents. Volume 1 covers the early
years of Olmsted's career, and Volume 2 is devoted to Central
Park.

6.103 PHILIPP-NEHRING, Dorothee (1973) Stadtväter: Frederick Law
Olmsted (1822–1903): zur Entstehung des Central Parks in New
York City. *Stadtbauwelt*, **37**, p. 68.
   A brief tribute to Olmsted's achievement as creator of Central
Park.

6.104 ROPER, Laura Wood (1973) *F.L.O.: A Biography of Frederick Law
Olmsted*. Baltimore/London: Johns Hopkins University Press.
   A thorough, comprehensive biography, now the main
authority on Olmsted.

6.105 SIMUTIS, Leonard J. (1971) Frederick Law Olmsted's later years: landscape architecture and the spirit of place. Unpublished Ph.D. thesis, University of Minnesota.
Includes detailed study of a number of park and other landscape schemes.

6.106 SIMUTIS, Leonard J. (1972) Frederick Law Olmsted, Sr.: a reassessment. *Journal of the American Institute of Planners*, **38** (5), pp. 276–84.
A brief discussion of Olmsted's contribution to the growth of planning in the United States.

6.107 SUTTON, S. B. (ed.) (1971) *Civilizing American Cities: A Selection of Frederick Law Olmsted's Writings on City Landscapes.* Cambridge, Mass.: MIT Press.
A collection of documents with an introduction by the editor.

Paxton

6.108 CHADWICK, George Fletcher (1961) *The Works of Sir Joseph Paxton, 1803–1865.* London: Architectural Press.
Includes Paxton's park and urban engineering schemes.

Prost

6.109 *L'oeuvre de Henri Prost, architecture et urbanisme* (1960). Paris: Académie d'Architecture.
A collection of studies by different authors on periods of Prost's career and aspects of his work.

6.110 SÉASSAL, Roger (1960) *Notice sur la vie et les travaux de Henri Prost, 1874–1959.* Paris: Institut de France.
A brief, commemorative study.

Richardson

6.111 MACNALTY, Arthur Salusbury (1950) *A Biography of Sir Benjamin Ward Richardson.* London: Harvey and Blythe.

A brief biography, with only passing references to Richardson's scheme for a model city of health, Hygeia.

Sant'Elia

6.112 APOLLONIO, Umbro (1958) *Antonio Sant'Elia: documenti, note storiche e critiche.* Milan: il Balcone.
A compilation of materials relevant to the work of the leading Italian Futurist, with some discussion of his views of cities.

6.113 BRION-GUERRY, Liliane (1973) Antonio Sant'Elia: message— l'architecture futuriste, in Brion-Guerry, L. (ed.), *L'année 1913*, vol. 3. Paris: Klincksieck, pp. 75–82.
A brief memorandum on Sant'Elia's architectural theories, with some bearing on urban design.

6.114 CARAMEL, Luciano and CONGATTI, Alberto (eds.) (1962) *Antonio Sant'Elia.* Como: Ente Villa Olmo.
Exhibition catalogue.

Schumacher

6.115 KALLMORGEN, Werner (1969) *Schumacher und Hamburg: eine fachliche Dokumentation zu seinem 100. Geburtstag.* Hamburg: Christians.
A study of the work of Fritz Schumacher in Hamburg.

6.116 OCHERT, Erich (1950) *Fritz Schumacher: sein Schaffen als Städtebauer und Landesplaner.* Tübingen: Ernst Wasmuth Verlag.
Biography of the town planner, active in Germany between the wars.

Sert

6.117 BASTLUND, Knud (1967) *José Luis Sert: Architecture, City Planning, Urban Design.* New York: Praeger.
A full review of Sert's career and achievement.

Sitte

6.118 ADSHEAD, S. D. (1930) Camillo Sitte and Le Corbusier. *Town Planning Review*, 14 (2), pp. 85–94.
Compares and contrasts the philosophies of the two great planning prophets.

6.119 BOYARSKY, Alvin Simon (1959) Camillo Sitte: city builder. Unpublished Master of Regional Planning thesis, Cornell University.
An early analysis of Sitte's approach to urban design, soon to be upstaged by the work of Collins.

6.120 COLLINS, George R. and COLLINS, Christiane C. (1965) *Camillo Sitte and the Birth of Modern City Planning*. London: Phaidon Press.
The first study of Sitte and his influence to make full use of the original German text of his book. By showing that Sitte admired Renaissance, rather than medieval, design, the book invalidated in one stroke over half a century of orthodoxy.

6.121 PEETS, Elbert (1927) Camillo Sitte. *Town Planning Review*, 12, pp. 249–59.
One of a series on great urban designers, this concentrates on Sitte's aesthetics. It was reprinted in Peets, *The Art of Designing Cities*. Cambridge, Mass.: MIT Press, 1968, pp. 143–50.

Soria y Mata

6.122 BOILEAU, I. (1959) La Ciudad Lineal: a critical study of the Linear Suburb of Madrid. *Town Planning Review*, 30, pp. 230–8.
Discusses Soria y Mata's original scheme and the extent to which the eventual development lived up to his hopes.

6.123 *La Ciudad Lineal: memoria presentada al XIII Congreso Internacional de la Habitacion y del Urbanismo por la Compania Madrileña de Urbanizacion* (1931). Madrid: Impr. Ciudad Lineal.
A history of the origins and development of the suburb.

6.124 COLLINS, George R. (1959) The Ciudad Lineal of Madrid. *Journal of*

the Society of Architectural Historians, **18**, pp. 38–53.
A study of Soria y Mata's linear theories and their implementation.

6.125 COLLINS, George R. and FLORES, Carlos (1968) *Arturo Soria y la Ciudad Lineal.* Madrid: Revista de Occidente.
A collection of documents with a biographical essay on Soria y Mata by Arturo Soria y Puig.

Tange

6.126 KULTERMANN, Udo (ed.) (1970) *Kenzo Tange 1946–1969: Architecture and Urban Design.* London: Pall Mall Press.
Selections from Tange's designs and writings.

Taut

6.127 JUNGHANNS, Kurt (1970) *Bruno Taut, 1880–1928.* Berlin (East): Henschelverlag.
A weighty, fully-illustrated study of Taut's architecture and urban planning.

Taylor

6.128 GILES, J. M. (ed.) (1959) *Fifty Years of Town Planning with Florence M. Taylor.* Sydney: Building Pub. Co.
A collection of writings of Florence M. Taylor, Australian planner.

Tugwell

6.129 MYRHA, D. (1974) Rexford Guy Tugwell: initiator of America's greenbelt new towns, 1935 to 1936. *Journal of the American Institute of Planners,* **40** (3), pp. 176–88.
A thorough review and analysis of the greenbelt town programme, stressing Tugwell's important initiating role.

6.130 STERNSHER, B. (1964) *Rexford Tugwell and the New Deal.* New Brunswick: Rutgers University Press.

An assessment of Tugwell's leading role in New Deal planning.

Unwin

6.131 CREESE, Walter L. (1967) *The Legacy of Raymond Unwin: A Human Pattern for Planning.* Cambridge, Mass.: MIT Press.

A selection of Unwin's writings, with an introductory essay by Creese on the ideas and assumptions of the pioneer British planner.

6.132 DAY, Michael G. (1973) Sir Raymond Unwin (1863–1940) and R. Barry Parker (1867–1947): a study and evaluation of their contribution to the development of site planning theory and practice (2 vols.). Unpublished M.A. thesis, University of Manchester.

After tracing the education and early career of the two men, Day analyses their work in the planning and design of New Earswick, Letchworth, Hampstead, Gretna and other munitions estates during the First World War, and Wythenshawe and other municipal estates between the two wars. These detailed studies are woven throughout into a general consideration of their development as designers and social reformers, and some consideration is given to their influence on the broader evolution of domestic design and town planning.

6.133 DAY, Michael and GARSTANG, Kate (1975) Socialist theories and Sir Raymond Unwin. *Town and Country Planning*, 43 (7–8), pp. 346–9.

Investigates Unwin's early years as a socialist in Manchester and suggests that a social-reform ideology continued to influence his planning work throughout his career.

6.134 HAWKES, Dean (1978) The architectural partnership of Barry Parker and Raymond Unwin, 1896–1914. *Architectural Review*, 163 (976), pp. 327–32.

A brief but interesting and well-illustrated discussion of

Parker's and Unwin's contribution to domestic design and urban layout.

6.135 PARKER, Barry (1940) Raymond Unwin: his life and work. *Journal of the Town Planning Institute*, **26** (5), pp. 159–62.
An extended obituary by Unwin's former partner.

Verhaeren

6.136 ABERCROMBIE, Patrick (1912) The many-tentacled town: the vision of Emile Verhaeren. *Town Planning Review*, **3**, p. 135.
A brief tribute to Verhaeren's poetic critique of the nineteenth-century city, which became a big stimulus to early planners in France and the Low Countries.

6.137 JONES, Percy Mansell (1926) *Emile Verhaeren: A Study in the Development of His Art and Ideas*. Cardiff: University of Wales.
Mainly a literary study.

6.138 ZWEIG, Stefan (1914) *Emile Verhaeren*. London: Constable.
An early appreciation of Verhaeren's vision, translated from the German edition (Leipzig, 1910).

Wagner

6.139 GERETSEGGER, Heinz and PEINTNER, Max (1970) *Otto Wagner, 1841–1918: The Expanding City: The Beginning of Modern Architecture*. London: Pall Mall Press.
A full survey of Wagner's career and achievement, concentrating on his architecture and engineering schemes, but including much information on his urban design work.

6.140 GRAF, Otto A. (1963) *Otto Wagner: das Werk des Wiener Architekten, 1841–1918*. Darmstadt: Hessisches Landesmuseum.
Exhibition catalogue.

6.141 PIRCHAN, Emil Karl (1956) *Otto Wagner: der grosse Baukünstler*. Vienna: Bergland.
A brief appreciation.

Wright, F. L.

6.142 GRABOW, Stephen (1977) Frank Lloyd Wright and the American city: the Broadacres debate. *Journal of the American Institute of Planners*, **43** (2), pp. 115–24.

Summarizes Wright's Broadacre model and analyses critical reaction to it between 1933 and the present day. Concludes that Wright's ideas, though idiosyncratic, were also prophetic.

Wright, H.

6.143 CHURCHILL, Henry (1960) Henry Wright: 1878–1936. *Journal of the American Institute of Planners*, **26** (4), pp. 293–301.

A brief survey by an acquaintance of the life and work of a leading American residential planner, particularly active in the 1920s and 1930s, and the designer of Greenbrook.

For individual planner references in the 'Additional entries' section, see: Geddes, 9.91; Griffin, 9.70; Le Corbusier, 9.51; Sitte, 9.29, 9.42.

7.
Nineteenth-century antecedents of urban and regional planning

The selection of titles for this section is based on the assumption that until the very end of the nineteenth century progress towards comprehensive urban planning was being made in several important, but discrete, areas. In these areas, the resolution of specific problems was leading those concerned to take a broad view of the relationship between their actions and the general development of towns. To prevent this section expanding out of all proportion to the rest of the bibliography, a number of rigorous exclusions have been made, with housing, public health, and private estate development notable among them. There was, after all, nothing new about housing and housing reform, and private estates in towns had been laid out to a plan since long before industrialization. Public health, for its part, is much too broad a topic and we have preferred to leave it on one side rather than make an artificial selection from the hundreds of titles available.

Urban reconstruction

The rapid urban growth of the nineteenth century generated, for the first time in the history of towns, a perceived need to tear down and reconstruct parts of the central areas of the largest cities. In previous centuries many towns had been rebuilt after fires, sometimes on a new plan, but organic growth had otherwise met all needs. In the nineteenth century, on the contrary, towns (except in North America) largely ceased to burn down, thanks to stronger building regulations and a better quality of construction. At the same time, however, their built forms partially failed to respond to economic and demographic change, particularly in their inner districts. The main problems were the inadequacy of the traditional street system, and the deterioration of large areas of poor housing to the point where private redevelopment was completely discouraged. Only public authority could resolve these difficulties.

The first major steps were taken in the 1850s, when Paris and London undertook concerted programmes of central-area improvements. Paris was much more ambitious than the British capital, and its efforts were emulated in the provinces much more than was the case in Britain. However, renewal in London and other British towns was greatly furthered by the use of area-clearance powers, available in some Scottish cities from the 1860s and in England from 1875. Complemented by municipal housing, virtually unknown abroad, these powers allowed Britain to take a world lead in slum replanning by the turn of the century. By this time, however, Italy too had risen to prominence in this area. Although the early town-planning movement was more interested in the suburbs than the city centres, the existence of a long-established programme of intervention in the central areas contributed to the comprehensiveness of the new urban strategies generated after about 1890.

See also 3.62, 3.82, 4.49, 5.112, 5.124, 5.159, 5.162, 5.195, 5.222, 5.229, 9.68, 9.120.

7.1 ALLAN, C. M. (1965) The genesis of British urban redevelopment with special reference to Glasgow. *Economic History Review*, 2nd series, **18**, pp. 598–613.

A study of the work of the Glasgow Improvement Trust in clearing slums and arranging for their reconstruction between the mid-1860s and the later nineteenth century.

7.2 BORSI, Franco (1970) *La capitale a Firenze e l'opera di G. Poggi*. Rome: Colombo Editore.

A full study of the street improvement and other modernization work undertaken in Florence during its brief period as capital of Italy in the mid-nineteenth century.

7.3 CHAPMAN, Brian (1953–54) Baron Haussmann and the planning of Paris. *Town Planning Review*, 24 (3), pp. 177–92.

An overview of Haussmann's contribution to the massive public-works programme undertaken in Paris in the 1850s and 1860s.

7.4 COX, R. C. W. (1973) The old centre of Croydon: Victorian decay and redevelopment, in Everitt, Alan (ed.), *Perspectives in English Urban History*. London: Macmillan, pp. 184–212.

Detailed account of a late-Victorian improvement scheme in the centre of a small but growing town.

7.5 CRESTI, Carlo and FREI, Silvano (1977) Le vicende del 'risanamento' di Mercato Vecchio a Firenze. *Storia Urbana*, 1 (2), pp. 99–126.

A detailed study of a large slum redevelopment scheme in Florence in the 1870s and 1880s.

7.6 DYOS, H. J. (1957) Urban transformation: a note on the objects of street improvements in Regency and Early Victorian London. *International Review of Social History*, 2, pp. 259–65.

A stimulating discussion of a number of factors which bore on nineteenth-century London street improvements.

7.7 EDWARDS, Percy J. (1898) *History of London Street Improvements, 1855–1897*. London: London County Council.

The main source of information on the street improvement work of the Metropolitan Board of Works and of the London County Council in its early years.

7.8 GAILLARD, Jeanne (1977) *Paris, la ville, 1852–1870*. Paris: Honoré Champion.

Throws much light on the strategy of reconstruction and development pursued by Haussmann, especially pp. 6–66. Thoughtful discussion of the relationship between public works and the various private forces shaping Paris.

7.9 GIRARD, Louis (1952) *La politique des travaux publics du Second Empire*. Paris: A. Colin.

An authoritative study of the public works policy of the

government of Napoleon III, including full consideration of the political and financial aspects of the improvement programmes pursued in Paris and other large cities.

7.10 HAUSSMANN, Georges (1890–93) *Mémoires* (3 vols.). Paris: Victor-Havard.

A full account of his career, with special emphasis on his Paris programme of public works. Though intended largely as a piece of self-justification, it is highly informative and a major source for the history of mid-nineteenth-century Paris. The disjointed and uneven treatment, concentrating on details, and blandly avoiding all criticism of individuals, fails however to convey the rough-and-tumble of the period, and the comprehensive view of the city and its problems which Haussmann undoubtedly possessed.

7.11 JONES, Gareth Stedman (1971) *Outcast London: A Study in the Relationship Between Classes in Victorian Society*. Oxford: Clarendon Press.

A study of poverty, housing and social protest in East London, c.1880–c.1900. Argues that many poor people were displaced by street improvement schemes, and sustains this view with a wide-ranging and thorough discussion of London improvements in the nineteenth century (pp. 159–284).

7.12 KAIN, Roger (1978) Urban planning and design in Second Empire France. *The Connoisseur*, December, pp. 236–46.

An outline of the urban reconstruction programme in Paris c.1850–70, with some reference to comparable work in the provinces.

7.13 LAMEYRE, Gérard (1968) *Haussmann: 'Préfet de Paris'*. Paris: Flammarion.

A popular study of Haussmann's work in Paris, but comprehensive and thoroughly researched.

7.14 LEONARD, Charlene Marie (1961) *Lyon Transformed: Public Works of the Second Empire, 1853–1864*. Berkeley: University of California Press.

A thorough study of the improvement work undertaken in France's second city.

7.15 MALET, Henri (1973) *Le Baron Haussmann et la rénovation de Paris.* Paris: Editions Municipales.
An attractively written narrative aimed at a general readership, but thoroughly researched.

7.16 MARMO, Marcella (1976) Speculazione edilizia e Credito Mobiliare a Napoli nella congiuntura degli anni Ottanta. *Quaderni Storici,* 11 (2), pp. 646–83.
Of relevance to slum clearance in Naples in the 1880s.

7.17 MERRUAU, Charles (1875) *Souvenirs de l'Hôtel de Ville de Paris, 1848–1852.* Paris: E. Plon.
Memoirs of one of Haussmann's early aides in Paris; source of valuable sidelights on the early stages of the reconstruction of Paris between the 1840s and the early 1850s.

7.18 MICHELUCCI, G. and MIGLIORINI, F. (1953) Storia dello sviluppo urbanistico. *Urbanistica,* 12, pp. 5–28.
Outlines the development of Florence from the sixteenth century until the end of the nineteenth, including the improvement schemes of the mid-nineteenth century.

7.19 PEETS, Elbert (1927) Haussmann and the rebuilding of Paris. *Town Planning Review,* 12, pp. 181–90.
Primarily an aesthetic appreciation. Reprinted in Peets, *On the Art of Designing Cities.* Cambridge, Mass.: MIT Press, 1968, pp. 133–42.

7.20 PINKNEY, David Henry (1955) Napoleon III's transformation of Paris: the origins and development of the idea. *Journal of Modern History,* 27, pp. 125–34.
A synthesis of his book (see 7.22).

7.21 PINKNEY, David Henry (1957) Money and politics in the rebuilding of Paris, 1860–70. *Journal of Economic History,* 17, pp. 45–60.
An investigation of some of the inventive financial methods

used by Haussmann to sustain the later years of his improvement programme.

7.22 PINKNEY, David Henry (1958) *Napoleon III and the Rebuilding of Paris*. Princeton: Princeton University Press.
The best general study in English of the Second Empire improvement programme.

7.23 RANIERI, Liane (1973) *Léopold II, urbaniste*. Brussels: Hayez.
A study of royal efforts to modernize and reconstruct Belgian towns, notably Brussels, in the second half of the nineteenth century.

7.24 RÉAU, Louis *et al.* (1954) *L'oeuvre du baron Haussmann*. Paris: Presses Universitaires de France.
A collection of essays on aspects of Haussmann's work in Paris. Informative and original.

7.25 RIVET, Félix (1955) *L'aménagement du quartier Grôlée, 1887–1908: une réalisation d'urbanisme à Lyon à la fin du XIX*^e*siècle*. Lyon: Revue de Géographie de Lyon.
On the somewhat prolonged reconstruction of one of Lyon's worst slum districts, typical of the reduced scale on which urban improvement was carried out in France between 1870 and 1914.

7.26 SAALMAN, Howard (1971) *Haussmann: Paris transformed*. New York: G. Braziller.
A well-illustrated but otherwise superficial, derivative study of the reconstruction of Paris under the Second Empire.

7.27 SCHUMACHER, Fritz (1920) *Wie das Kunstwerk Hamburg nach dem grossen Brande entstand: ein Beitrag zur Geschichte des Städtebaus*. Berlin: K. Curtius.
An account of the rebuilding of Hamburg after the fire of 1842, according to the plans of William Lindley, by the noted twentieth-century Hamburg planner.

7.28 SPADOLINI, G. (1966) Firenze capitale. *Nuova Antologia*, **498**, pp. 291–312.

Includes discussion of the improvement work undertaken in Florence to fit it for its short-lived role as capital of Italy.

7.29 STEFFEL, R. Vladimir (1976) The Boundary Street estate: an example of urban redevelopment by the London County Council, 1889–1914. *Town Planning Review*, 47 (2), pp. 161–73.
A study of the L.C.C.'s first large slum redevelopment scheme, regarded in the 1890s and early 1900s as the most ambitious public-housing venture in the world.

Extension planning

In Germany, Italy, Spain and Scandinavia, powers were inherited from pre-industrial times to plan street-systems for new, peripheral districts of towns. In Britain, on the contrary, no such powers had ever existed and none were taken in the late eighteenth and the nineteenth centuries. Instead, decisions on street planning were left largely to the landowners, who held their property in sufficiently large blocks to make this solution practicable. When on the Continent, however, many towns built up a strong expansionary pressure in the mid-nineteenth century, the extension plan was pressed into service to order building which would otherwise have been seriously disrupted by the small size of many peasant plots. In most of Europe this planning was so crude that no particular value was attached to it, but in Germany, when combined with a frenetic urbanization rate and large-scale land speculation, it led on to more ambitious public intervention. Ultimately, the idea of urban planning in Germany (*Städtebau*) arose directly from extension planning. Moreover, German influence on Britain, the United States and France in the early 1900s was founded largely on its lead in extension planning.
See also 3.82, 4.65, 4.140, 4.142, 4.313, 5.195, 9.18, 9.78, 9.81, 9.108, Barcelona, Cerdà, Berlin, Rome.

7.30 ABERCROMBIE, Patrick (1914) Berlin: its growth and present state. II, the nineteenth century. *Town Planning Review*, 4 (4), pp. 302–11.

Part of a series by Abercrombie on the growth of European cities, this discusses the Hobrecht and other extension plans of the nineteenth century.

7.31   ÅSTRÖM, Sven-Erik (1979) Town planning in Imperial Helsingfors 1810–1910, in Hammarström, Ingrid and Hall, Thomas (eds.), *Growth and Transformation of the Modern City*. Stockholm: Swedish Council for Building Research, pp. 59–67.

A brief discussion of the rationale and impact of nineteenth-century extension planning in Helsinki.

7.32   BOHIGAS, Oriol (1958) En el centenario del Plan Cerdà. *Cuadernos de Arquitectura*, 34.

A commentary on the Cerdà plan and its results in Barcelona.

7.33   *Ildefonso Cerdà (1815–1876)* (1976). Barcelona: Colegio de Ingenieros de Caminos, Canales y Puertos.

Catalogue of an exhibition commemorating the death of Cerdà. Relates his career and ideas to the more recent development of Barcelona. Text written mainly by Arturo Soria y Puig. Includes some discussion of extension planning in other Spanish towns.

7.34   CIRICI-PELLICER, A. (1959) Significación del Plan Cerdà. *Cuadernos de Arquitectura*, 35.

A commentary on the Cerdà plan and its results.

7.35   ESTEBAN, Julio (1978) *Los ensanches menores en la region de Barcelona (II)*. Barcelona: Escuela Tecnica Superior de Arquitectura.

Studies a number of nineteenth-century extension plans for small towns in the vicinity of Barcelona.

7.36   HEINRICH, Ernst (1962) Der 'Hobrechtplan'. *Jahrbuch für Brandenburger Landesgeschichte*, 13, pp. 41–57.

A study of the main Berlin extension plan (1858–62) of the nineteenth century.

7.37   Los planes de Barcelona (1): el Plan Cerdà y la realidad del Ensanche (1972). *Construcción de la Ciudad*, 1.

A detailed study of the Cerdà plan and its consequences.

7.38 RADICKE, Dieter (1974) Der Berliner Bebauungsplan von 1862 und die Entwicklung des Weddings: zum Verhältnis von Obrigkeitsplanung zu privatem Grundeigentum, in Poeschken, G., Radicke, D. and Heinisch, T. J. (eds.), *Festschrift für Ernst Heinrich*. Berlin: Universitäts-Bibliothek der Technishen Universität Berlin, pp. 56–74.

Demonstrates the humanity of Hobrecht's detailed planning and argues that the excesses generated by the blind and selfish application of his plan by the Berlin authorities and the exploitation of its limitations by greedy landowners cannot be blamed on Hobrecht.

7.39 RÅBERG, Marianne (1979) The development of Stockholm since the seventeenth century, in Hammarström, Ingrid and Hall, Thomas (eds.), *Growth and Transformation of the Modern City*. Stockholm: Swedish Council for Building Research, pp. 13–26.

A brief but highly informative study of the growth of Stockholm between the seventeenth and late nineteenth centuries, with main emphasis on the impact of a series of extension plans.

7.40 RÖNNEBECK, Thomas (1971) *Stadterweiterung und Verkehr im neunzehnten Jahrhundert*. Stuttgart/Berne: Karl Krämer.

Discusses the relationship between the planned extensions of German cities and traffic engineering during the nineteenth century.

7.41 SOLÀ-MORALES, Manuel de (1978) *Los ensanches, (1): el ensanche de Barcelona*. Barcelona: Escuela Tecnica Superior de Arquitectura.

A collection of articles (by the editor, M. D. Clota, and J. L. G. Ordoñez) on the Cerdà extension plan, its origins and results, in the context of the general history of extension planning in nineteenth-century southern Europe. Extensively illustrated.

7.42 WAGNER-RIEGER, Renate (ed.) (1969–) *Die Wiener Ringstrasse, Bild einer Epoche: die Erweiterung der inneren Stadt Wien unter Kaiser Franz Joseph*. Vienna: H. Böhlaus Nachfolger.

A multi-volume study of a number of themes in the history of Vienna relevant to the construction of the Ringstrasse. Still (1980) in progress.

Park planning

The planning of parks may appear no more obvious an antecedent of urban planning than the laying-out of residential estates. However, public rather than private land was usually involved, and relationships between this public open space and the rest of the town raised general planning issues as early as the mid-nineteenth century. In the United States, moreover, park design gave many landscape architects their first urban experience, and some were led on from there by the development of that unique American phenomenon, the park system, into full city planning.

See also 4.267, 5.98, 5.112, 9.43, 9.87, 9.131, Olmsted, Paxton.

7.43 CHADWICK, George F. (1966) *The Park and the Town: Public Landscape in the Nineteenth and Twentieth Centuries.* London: Architectural Press.

A history of parks throughout the advanced world, with much consideration of nineteenth-century park planning.

7.44 FRYE, Mary Virginia (1964) The historical development of municipal parks in the United States: concepts and their application. Unpublished Ph.D. thesis, University of Illinois.

A general summary of the history of public parks in the United States since colonial times, but with main emphasis on the years 1850–1914.

7.45 HENNEBO, Dieter (1974) Der Stadtpark, in Grote, Ludwig (ed.), *Die deutsche Stadt im 19. Jahrhundert: Stadtplanung und Baugestaltung im industriellen Zeitalter.* Munich: Prestel Verlag.

Mainly a study of developments in the design of urban parks in nineteenth-century Germany.

7.46 HYDE, Francis E. (1943–47) Utilitarian town planning, 1825–45. *Town Planning Review*, **19**, pp. 153–9.

Mainly a study of J. A. Roebuck's ideas for improving the British urban environment by parks in the 1830s and 1840s.

7.47 MCCARTHY, M. P. (1972) Politics and the parks: Chicago

businessmen and the recreation movement. *Journal of the Illinois State Historical Society*, **65**, pp. 158–72.
Of some relevance to the advocacy and planning of a park system in Chicago in the early 1900s.

7.48 PAETEL, Werner (1976) Zur Entwicklung des bepflanzten Stadtplatzes in Deutschland vom Beginn des 19. Jahrhunderts bis zum ersten Weltkrieg. Unpublished technical dissertation, Hannover University.
A study of developments in the design of planted urban squares in Germany in the nineteenth century.

7.49 STEWART, Ian Robert (1973) Central Park 1851–1871: urbanization and environmental planning in New York City. Unpublished Ph.D. thesis, Cornell University.
A detailed, narrative history of Central Park between 1851 and 1871.

The utopian tradition

The first half of the nineteenth century generated a spate of visions of ideal towns, many of which were associated with proposals for sweeping social reforms to be pioneered in new communities. After mid-century the increasingly solid implantation of industrial society and its concomitant large cities invalidated this approach, but the idea of the perfect, planned urban environment lived on to re-emerge triumphantly in Ebenezer Howard's Garden City proposals.

Many planning historians have been fascinated by this ideal planning. Some, most notably Benevolo, have made much of a supposed dichotomy between radical, utopian planning and mere tinkering with existing towns. Ideal visions are easy to study, and superficially exciting. Certainly, idealism, the vision of a perfect urban future, has played a key role in the evolution of urban planning. However, it continues to attract more attention than it deserves.

See also 3.11, 3.20, 3.28, 3.62, 6.27, 6.58–9, 6.78, 9.71.

7.50 ANDRIELLO, Domenico (1966) *Il pensiero utopistico e la città dell'uomo.*
Naples: Libreria Internazionale Minerva Editrice.
A general discussion of the utopian approach to urban design.

7.51 ARMYTAGE, Walter H. G. (1961) *Heavens Below: Utopian Experiments
in England, 1560–1960.* London: Routledge and Kegan Paul.
A history of English experimental communities by the main
British authority, including a number of nineteenth-century
examples with urban-design ambitions. Not primarily a piece of
planning history, however.

7.52 ARMYTAGE, Walter H. G. (1968) *Yesterday's Tomorrows: A Historical
Survey of Future Societies.* London: Routledge and Kegan Paul.
A compendium of dreams and visions, including a number of
nineteenth-century examples of relevance to urban planning.

7.53 BOLLEREY, Franziska (1974) Architekturkonzeptionen der
Utopischen Sozialisten. Unpublished doctoral thesis, Freie
Universität Berlin.
A wide-ranging study of the architectural and urban-design
ideas of the nineteenth-century utopian socialists.

7.54 CONRADS, Ulrich and SPERLICH, Hans G. (1963) *Fantastic Architecture:
Utopian Building and Planning in Modern Times.* London:
Architectural Press.
Originally published in German as *Phantastische Architektur*
(Stuttgart: G. Hatje, 1960). The English version was edited and
expanded by G. R. and C. C. Collins. Mainly a study of
expressionist architecture, but of some relevance to the utopian
tradition in urban design.

7.55 HARDY, Dennis (1979) *Alternative Communities in Nineteenth Century
England.* London: Longman.
A detailed study of a number of small alternative
communities in nineteenth- and early twentieth-century
England, grouped in four categories: utopian socialism,
agrarian socialism, communities of sectarianism, and
communities of anarchism. Comparable to the work of
Armytage in its determination to seek out the efforts of tiny
groups. The main emphasis is on the nature of utopianism

rather than on planning, which, given the small scale of many of the enterprises studied, is hardly surprising. However, the physical layout of the settlements is fully discussed.

7.56 HAWORTH, A. (1976) Planning and philosophy: the case of Owenism and the Owenite communities. *Urban Studies*, **13** (2), pp. 147–53.

A discussion of Robert Owen's ideas in theory and practice, with special emphasis on their implications for the planning of communities.

7.57 HAYDEN, Dolores (1976) *Seven American Utopias: The Architecture of Communitarian Socialism, 1790–1975*. Cambridge, Mass.: MIT Press.

A detailed study of the architecture, planning and organization of a large number of little-known American experimental communities. The approach is similar to Hardy's study of British equivalents. Concentrates on seven communities active at various times between 1790 and 1917: Hancock, Nauvoo, Phalanx, Oneida, Amana, Greeley, and Llano.

7.58 LANG, S. (1952) The ideal city: from Plato to Howard. *Architectural Review*, **112** (668), pp. 91–101.

A standard treatment of this theme, concentrating on physical design, and emphasizing the dialogue between circular and rectangular arrangements.

7.59 LORENZEN, Vilhelm Birkedal (1947) *Drømmen om den ideale By*. Copenhagen: Rosenkilde og Bagger.

An authoritative history of the utopian tradition in urban planning.

7.60 McCORMICK, E. H. (1955) The Happy Colony. *Landfall*, **9**, pp. 300–34.

This discursive paper on the nineteenth-century settlement of New Zealand includes brief discussion of Robert Pemberton's ideas for a planned town.

7.61 MEYERSON, Martin (1961) Utopian traditions and the planning of cities. *Daedalus*, **90**, pp. 180–93.

A general discussion, from More, through Owen, to Le Corbusier.

7.62 MORTON, Arthur Leslie (1952) *The English Utopia*. London: Lawrence and Wishart.

A general history of the utopian tradition in England, only marginally relevant to planning.

7.63 MUCCHIELLI, Roger (1961) *Le mythe de la cité idéale*. Paris: Presses Universitaires de France.

A general history of the utopian tradition in social reform and planning.

7.64 MUMFORD, Lewis (1923) *The Story of Utopias: Ideal Commonwealths and Social Myths*. London: Harrap.

A general history of the utopian tradition, emphasizing its relevance to urban planning.

7.65 REINER, Thomas A. (1963) *The Place of the Ideal Community in Urban Planning*. Philadelphia: University of Pennsylvania Press.

This is in fact theoretical and critical rather than historical, but a range of historical 'ideal communities' and concepts are evaluated, so that some light is thrown on the past.

7.66 RIESMAN, David (1947–48) Some observations on community plans and utopias. *Yale Law Journal*, **57**, pp. 173–200.

A critique of the post-1945 revival of utopian planning led by the Goodmans, but incorporating material on earlier examples of utopian planning.

7.67 ROCKEY, John Randolph (1977) The ideal city and model town in English Utopian thought, 1849–1902. Unpublished D.Phil. thesis, Oxford University.

A comparative study of the four major visions of the ideal town generated in Victorian England: James Silk Buckingham's 'Victoria', Robert Pemberton's 'Happy Colony', Benjamin Ward Richardson's 'Hygeia', and Ebenezer Howard's 'Garden City'.

7.68 ROSENAU, Helen (1959) *The Ideal City in Its Architectural Evolution*.

London: Routledge and Kegan Paul.
A full history of the architectural and urban design imagery associated with utopian social visions since Ancient times.

7.69 SCHUMPP, Mechthild (1972) *Stadtbau-Utopien und Gesellschaft: der Bedeutungswandel utopischer Stadtmodelle unter sozialem Aspekt*. Berlin: Bertelsmann Fachverlag.
Some historical perspective.

7.70 SERVIER, Jean (1967) *Histoire de l'utopie*. Paris: Gallimard.
A general history of utopian thought.

7.71 STRAUSSE, Gerharda (1962) Siedlungs- und Architektur-konzeptionen der Utopisten: zur Problematik und zu einigen Einzelprojekten. *Wissenschaftliche Zeitschrift der Humboldt-Universität zu Berlin. Gesellschafts- und Sprachwissenschaftliche Reihe XI*, 4, pp. 543–99.
A full discussion of the utopian socialists' approach to architecture and urban design.

7.72 WILSON, R. Jackson (1977) Experience and utopia: the making of Edward Bellamy's *Looking Backward. Journal of American Studies*, 11 (1), pp. 45–60.
Argues that much of Bellamy's vision of a future Boston was based, not on technological forecasting, but on nostalgic memories of his own home town in the days before industry transformed it.

Model communities and company housing

Industrialization produced the phenomenon of employer-built housing, usually designed to accommodate workers at some isolated production site. Many of these communities were of a low standard, but some employers grasped the opportunity to incorporate environmental qualities in their settlements. Their motives were varied; some sought to control or influence their employees in order to secure more effort or docility. At the other extreme, some wanted to educate their workers in communal awareness to the point where they could take over production on a cooperative basis. Most, perhaps, merely wanted the progress in which they placed their trust to rub off, even in minor ways, on the workforce for whom they were responsible. The better-planned of these communities were an important example to the early town-planning movement, in which some of their creators went on to play a leading part.

This section does not purport to cover all employer-built housing and factory colonies. It concentrates instead on the building of complete communities, and on examples of enlightened planning. It also includes a number of cooperative or private community-building schemes in which a high and influential standard of residential planning was achieved. Twentieth-century company towns are included in this section, but there is some overlap with the selection of titles on new towns (pp. 214–219), particularly in respect of North America.

See also 3.11, 3.22, 4.195, 4.209, 4.213, 4.251, 4.314, 6.20, 6.132, 9.2, 9.15, 9.49, 9.82, 9.93, 9.110.

7.73 ACKERS, W. (1975) Siedlung Beisenkamp in Datteln. *Stadtbauwelt*, **46**, pp. 101–4.

A study of a nineteenth-century German mining colony.

7.74 AHRENS, Hansjörg (1975) Bergarbeitersiedlungen in Nordost-england. *Stadtbauwelt*, **46**, pp. 109–12.

A study of planned nineteenth-century mining communities in north-east England.

7.75 ALLEN, James Brown (1966) *The Company Town in the American West*. Norman, Oklahoma: University of Oklahoma Press.

A full survey of the development of the company town in the West from the first half of the nineteenth century to the present. The general picture is one of rapid nineteenth-century growth, followed by slow decline in a society which, on reaching a high stage of development, no longer sees company-owned housing and facilities as necessary or desirable. Based on a University of Southern California Ph.D. thesis, The company town as a feature of western American development, 1963.

7.76 ALSOP, B. (1878) *The Late Sir Titus Salt, Bart., Founder of Saltaire*. Saltaire.

An early memoir on the life and achievement of Titus Salt, founder of the best-known industrial settlement of mid-nineteenth-century Britain.

7.77 ASHWORTH, William (1951) British industrial villages in the nineteenth century. *Economic History Review*, 2nd series, 3 (3), pp. 378–95.
A survey of the development of employer-built settlements in nineteenth-century Britain, later largely incorporated in the author's general history of British planning.

7.78 BALGARNIE, R. (1877) *Sir Titus Salt, Baronet: His Life and Lessons.* London: Hodder and Stoughton.
A hagiographical memoir on the founder of Saltaire.

7.79 BALZER, W. (1975) Einige Ansichten der Viktoria-Kolonie in Lünen. *Stadtbauwelt*, **46**, pp. 106–8.
A study of a planned mining village in nineteenth-century Germany.

7.80 BEAUREGARD, Robert A. and HOLCOMB, Briavel (1979) Dominant enterprises and acquiescent communities: the private sector and urban revitalization. *Urbanism Past and Present*, **8**, pp. 18–31.
A discussion of the implications for the quality of planning of the dominance of a town by one large, private enterprise. Includes some consideration of the history of company towns in the United States since the nineteenth century.

7.81 BLUMENFELD, Hans (1967) The Cité Ouvrière of Mulhouse, France, in Blumenfeld, Hans, *The Modern Metropolis: Its Origins, Growth, Characteristics, and Planning.* Cambridge, Mass.: MIT Press, pp. 200–12.
A brief discussion of the history and importance of the most important initiative in employer-built housing in nineteenth-century France.

7.82 BOLLEREY, Franziska and HARTMANN, Kristiana (1975) Wohnen im Revier: Siedlungen vom Beginn der Industrialisierung bis 1933: Analyse-Bewertung-Chancen. *Stadtbauwelt*, **46**, pp. 85–100.
An ambitious review and analysis of the building of

employers' housing colonies in the Ruhr between the 1840s and the 1920s. Distinguishes a phase of enlightened planning after about 1900.

7.83 BOLSTERLI, Margaret Jones (1977) *The Early Community at Bedford Park: The Pursuit of 'Corporate Happiness' in the First Garden Suburb.* London: Routledge and Kegan Paul.

A conventional account of the planning and building of Bedford Park, with strong emphasis on the cultural life of the community.

7.84 BOURNVILLE VILLAGE TRUST (1955) *The Bournville Village Trust, 1900–1955.* Bournville: Bournville Village Trust.

The standard account of the history of Bournville.

7.85 BRIGGS, Asa (1961) *Social Thought and Social Action: A Study of the Work of Seebohm Rowntree, 1871–1954.* London: Longmans.

Concentrates on Rowntree's work as a social investigator and reformer, but throws some light on the Rowntree involvement in New Earswick and in the general movement of environmental reform c.1900.

7.86 BUDER, Stanley (1967) The model town of Pullman: town planning and social control in the Gilded Age. *Journal of the American Institute of Planners,* **33,** pp. 2–10.

A resumé of his book. See next item.

7.87 BUDER, Stanley (1967) *Pullman: An Experiment in Industrial Order and Community Planning, 1880–1930.* New York: Oxford University Press.

The classic account of the rise and fall of America's most notorious company town. Much discussion of planning and architecture. Based on a University of Chicago thesis of the same title, 1966.

7.88 CUDWORTH, William (1895) *Saltaire: A Sketch History.* Saltaire.

A brief, early narrative of Saltaire's history.

7.89 DEWHIRST, Robert K. (1960–61) Saltaire. *Town Planning Review,* **31,** pp. 135–44.

A brief history of the foundation and building of Saltaire and an analysis of its plan.

7.90 GARDINER, Alfred George (1923) *Life of George Cadbury*. London: Cassell.
An early biography of the founder of Bournville.

7.91 GARNER, John S. (1971) Leclaire, Illinois: a model company town (1890–1934). *Journal of the Society of Architectural Historians*, **30** (3), pp. 219–27.
A study of the development of a company town near St. Louis, founded in 1890. The high standard of housing, environment and social facilities helps to counter the generally bad press which U.S. company towns in this period have received in recent years. The cooperative objectives of its founder, N. O. Nelson, were however untypical and Garner compares the town with Guise rather than Pullman.

7.92 GASKELL, Stuart Martin (1974) Housing estate development, 1840–1918, with particular reference to the Pennine towns (2 vols.). Unpublished Ph.D. thesis, Sheffield University.
A wide-ranging study of housing reform in northern England, including discussion of a number of employer-built communities.

7.93 GREEN, Brigid Grafton (1977) *Hampstead Garden Suburb, 1907–1977*. London: Hampstead Garden Suburb Residents' Association.
A full history of the development of the suburb by the official archivist of the Trust.

7.94 GREEVES, T. A. (1975) *Bedford Park: The First Garden Suburb: A Pictorial Survey*. London: Anne Bingley.
A popular history and architectural survey of the London planned suburb, published on the centenary of its foundation.

7.95 *The Hampstead Garden Suburb: Its Achievements and Significance* (1937). Hampstead: Hampstead Garden Suburb Trust Ltd.
An official review of the first thirty years of the suburb. Includes 'Hampstead garden suburb: thirty years of a great

experiment', an article first printed in *Country Life*, 17 October 1936.

7.96 Hampstead: the unique suburb (1957). *Town and Country Planning*, 25 (7).
An issue devoted entirely to Hampstead, with some material on its historical origins and development.

7.97 HARRISON, Michael (1976) Burnage garden village: an ideal for life in Manchester. *Town Planning Review*, 47, pp. 256–68.
A study of the most influential Manchester co-partnership housing scheme of the early 1900s, in the context of the local planning and housing debate of the period.

7.98 HELG, F. and RECKNAGEL, R. (1966) Progettazione di una città industriale: Wolfsburg. *Casabella*, 310, pp. 8–23.
An outline of the planning history of the Volkswagen factory and community since its creation in 1938.

7.99 HOLROYD, Abraham (1871) *Saltaire, and Its Founder, Sir Titus Salt, Bart.* Saltaire: author.
An early memoir on Salt and Saltaire.

7.100 HONIKMAN, Basil (1968) Port Sunlight and the Garden City movement. *System Building and Design*, October, pp. 45–52.
On Port Sunlight and its relationship to Ebenezer Howard's Garden City theory, and a comparison with Letchworth.

7.101 JACOBS, Evelyn (1978) Die *Cités ouvrières* in Mülhausen im Elsass im 19. Jahrhundert: die Entwicklung sozialpolitischer Aktivität der Unternehmerschaft und ein Beispiel ihrer Auswirkung. Unpublished Master's dissertation, University of Freiburg.
A study of employer-built housing colonies in Mulhouse and other Alsatian towns in the second half of the nineteenth century.

7.102 JONAS, Stephan (1978) Cité de Mulhouse, 1853, in Martinelli, Roberta and Nuti, Lucia (eds.), *Le città di fondazione*. Venice: Marsilio Editori, pp. 211–31.
A lively precis of Jonas's book. See next item.

7.103 JONAS, Stephan, HECKNER, Philippe and KNORR, J. M. (1975) *La cité de Mulhouse: étude critique d'un modèle d'habitat ouvrier historique.* Strasbourg: Université des Sciences Humaines de Strasbourg.

A full study of the genesis, construction, administration and subsequent evolution of the *cité ouvrière* of Mulhouse, the most famous creation of French nineteenth-century industrial philanthropy.

7.104 KLAPHECK, Richard (1930) *Siedlungswerk Krupp.* Berlin: Ernst Wasmuth.

A full history of the creation of workers' colonies by the Krupp enterprise in Essen between the 1860s and the 1920s.

7.105 KNIGHT, Rolf (1975) *Work Camps and Company Towns in Canada and the U.S.: An Annotated Bibliography.* Vancouver: New Star Books.

Covers the nineteenth and twentieth centuries.

7.106 LIEDGREN, Rut (1961) *Så bodde vi: Arbetarbostaden som typ-och tidsföreteelse.* Stockholm: Nordiska Museet.

A study of workers' housing in Sweden in the nineteenth and early twentieth centuries, including some privately and publicly planned developments.

7.107 LILLIBRIDGE, R. M. (1953) Pullman: town development in the era of eclecticism. *Journal of the Society of Architectural Historians,* 12, pp. 17–22.

Discusses the design and architecture of the model community.

7.108 MANCUSO, Franco (1977) Schio, Nuovo Schio e Alessandro Rossi. *Storia Urbana,* 1 (2), pp. 45–98.

A study of the impact on Schio, a small town in the Veneto, of the growth of the large Rossi textile company during the nineteenth century. The firm set up satellite factories with associated housing outside the town, and developed a new area of Schio itself.

7.109 METZENDORF, Rainer (1974) 65 Jahre Margarethenhöhe/Essen. *Stadtbauwelt,* 43, pp. 217–19.

Mainly an appreciation of the design qualities of the last big

Krupp community in Essen, started shortly before the First World War. The architect was Georg Metzendorf.

7.110 MORGAN, W. T. (1954) The Pullman experiment in review. *Journal of the American Institute of Planners*, **20**, pp. 27–9.
A brief comment on the rise and fall of Pullman, Illinois.

7.111 NEUMEYER, Fritz (1978) Zum Werkwohnungsbau in Deutschland um 1900, in Siepmann, Eckhard (ed.), *Kunst und Alltag um 1900*. Lahn-Giessen: Anabas Verlag, pp. 239–64.
A discussion of various strands in the development of employer-built housing in Germany in the late nineteenth and early twentieth centuries. Stresses the economic and political causation of the great boom in employer-built housing after about 1900. Main detailed emphasis is on Berlin, with the author stressing the role of employers' housing as an instrument of decentralization.

7.112 *One Man's Vision: The Story of the Joseph Rowntree Village Trust* (1954). London: Allen and Unwin.
Much of this comprises a history of New Earswick.

7.113 PENNY, Barbara R. (1976) *Pilkington Brothers' Garden Village Ventures: The End of the Garden City/Suburb Movement* (Working Paper no. 1). Liverpool: Department of Civic Design, University of Liverpool.
A brief outline of Pilkington efforts to provide housing for employees in St. Helens and in the Doncaster area in the years before and after World War I.

7.114 PETERS, Don (1974) *Darley Abbey: From Monastery to Industrial Community*. Buxton: Moorland Publishing Co.
Concentrates on the development of the settlement in the eighteenth and nineteenth centuries.

7.115 PORTEOUS, John Douglas (1969) *The Company Town of Goole: An Essay in Urban Genesis* (Occasional Papers in Geography, no. 12). Hull: University of Hull.
A study of the small Yorkshire port, an example of nineteenth-century private town planning.

116 QUILLEN, Isaac James (1942) Industrial city: a history of Gary, Indiana, to 1929. Unpublished Ph.D. thesis, Yale University. Covers the foundation and early years of one of the largest and latest of American company towns. The story of Gary, during a period of less relevance to planning history, is continued in Meister, Richard Julius (1967) A history of Gary, Indiana: 1930–1940. Unpublished Ph.D. thesis, Notre Dame University.

117 REYNOLDS, Josephine (1948) The model village of Port Sunlight. *Architects' Journal*, 107, pp. 492–6. An architectural and planning appreciation, with an outline of the history of the model community.

118 RICHARDS, J. M. (1936) Sir Titus Salt. *Architectural Review*, 80, pp. 213–18. Mainly a history and appreciation of Saltaire.

119 SAARINEN, Oiva (1975) Planning and other developmental influences on the spatial organization of urban settlement in the Sudbury area. *Laurentian University Review*, 3, pp. 38–70. Outlines the factors which have influenced the development of mining communities in and around Sudbury.

120 SCHLANDT, Joachim (1970) Die Kruppsiedlungen—Wohnungsbau im Interesse eines Industriekonzerns, in Helms, Hans G. and Janssen, Jörn (eds.), *Kapitalistischer Städtebau*, Neuwied/Berlin: Hermann Luchterhand, pp. 95–111. A critical analysis from a marxist viewpoint, stressing the social-control role of the Krupp villages, mainly during the twentieth century.

121 *Sixty Years of Planning: The Bournville Experiment* (n.d.). Bournville: Bournville Village Trust. A history of Bournville from the 1890s to the 1940s.

122 STEINHAUER, Gerhard (1956) *Gartenstadt Margarethenhöhe: 50 Jahre Margarethe-Krupp-Stiftung für Wohnungsfürsorge in Essen*. Essen: Margarethe-Krupp-Stiftung.

A commemorative history of the most ambitious Krupp workers' settlement in Essen.

7.123 STELTER, Gilbert A. (1974) Community development in Toronto's commercial empire: the industrial towns of the nickel belt, 1883–1931. *Laurentian University Review*, **6**, pp. 3–53.
A study of a series of company towns of varying degrees of planning sophistication.

7.124 STELTER, Gilbert A. and ARTIBISE, Alan F. J. (1978) Canadian resource towns in historical perspective. *Plan Canada*, **18** (1), pp. 7–16.
Outlines the development of mining and company towns in Canada since the mid-nineteenth century, with some consideration of their planning. Distinguishes three phases: (1) 1867–1920, mainly unplanned development; (2) 1920–45, beginnings of influence of City Beautiful and Garden City ideas on new foundations; (3) 1945–, more serious efforts to incorporate in new resource towns all the benefits of carefully planned new communities.

7.125 STEMMRICH, Daniel (1978) Die Siedlung als Programm: Untersuchungen zum Arbeiterwohnungsbau anhand Kruppscher Siedlungen zwischen 1861 und 1907. Unpublished dissertation, University of Bochum.
A study of the Krupp workers' colonies in Essen from their origins until the eve of the construction of Margarethenhöhe.

7.126 STRANZ, Walter (1973) *George Cadbury*. Aylesbury: Shire Publications.
A short pamphlet, with only occasional references to Bournville.

7.127 SUDDARDS, Roger W. (ed.) (1976) *Titus of Salts*. Bradford: Watmoughs Ltd.
A collection of essays on the origin, development, and present condition of Saltaire. A lively and readable account, though openly a popularization.

7.128 TARN, J. N. (1965) The model village at Bromborough Pool. *Town Planning Review*, **35** (4), pp. 329–36.

A history and design appraisal of the model town built from 1853 near Birkenhead by Price's Patent Candle Company.

7.129 THOMPSON, F. M. L. (1976) *Hampstead: Building a Borough, 1650–1964*. London: Routledge and Kegan Paul.

A history of the physical development and administration of the fashionable London suburb, including a full account of Henrietta Barnett's influential Hampstead Garden Suburb.

7.130 WHITE, P. H. (1955) Some aspects of urban development by colliery companies, 1919–1939. *Manchester School*, **23**, pp. 269–80.

Discusses the last major phase in the building of mining villages in Britain by private companies.

7.131 WILSON, Charles Henry (1954) *The History of Unilever: A Study in Economic Growth and Social Change* (2 vols.). London: Cassell.

Volume 1 includes a brief account of the foundation of Port Sunlight (pp. 144–51).

Garden cities

Since its invention by Ebenezer Howard in the 1890s, the Garden City has been the most potent single image to have been generated by the urban planning movement. It provides a direct link between the idealistic planning of the first half of the nineteenth century and the post-1945 New Town movement (for which see below, pp. 223–34). In practice, Howard's revolutionary vision of a completely new urban system was watered down to encompass suburban extensions of existing cities and even small, speculative housing promotions. Much of the literature consequently attempts to discover the true essence of Howard's thinking or to assess its practicability.

See also 3.62, 4.71, 4.154–5, 4.213, 4.266, 7.100, 9.16, 9.21, 9.92, 9.132, Howard, Letchworth, Welwyn.

132 ANDRIELLO, Domenico (1964) *Howard o della eutopia: l'idea della città giardino alla luce della Conferenza internazionale di Arnhem, giugno 1963*.

Naples: Libreria Intrernazionale Minerva Editrice.
A disquisition on the true essence of Howard's ideas and their relevance to modern needs.

7.133 BATCHELOR, Peter (1969) The origin of the garden city concept of urban form. *Journal of the Society of Architectural Historians*, **28** (3), pp. 184–200.
Sets Howard in the context of general nineteenth-century efforts to produce ideal schemes and reform existing cities. Ends with an assessment of Howard's impact on twentieth-century planning and housing. Very much an architectural approach, chasing influences and establishing precedents.

7.134 BERGMANN, Klaus (1970) *Agrarromantik und Grossstadtfeindschaft*. Meisenheim-am-Glan: Hain.
In discussing anti-urban thought in Germany c.1850–c.1940, this gives some consideration to the Garden City movement.

7.135 BERLEPSCH-VALENDÀS, Hans Eduard von (1911) *Die Garten-stadtbewegung in England: ihre Entwicklung und ihr jetziger Stand*. Munich/Berlin: R. Oldenbourg.
An effective attempt to introduce British garden city progress to a German readership. Includes some recent historical perspective.

7.136 BOLLEREY, Franziska and HARTMANN, Kristiana (1978) Der neue Alltag in der grünen Stadt: zur lebensreformerischen Ideologie und Praxis der Gartenstadtbewegung, in Siepmann, Eckhard (ed.), *Kunst und Alltag um 1900*. Lahn-Giessen: Anabas Verlag, pp. 189–238.
A discussion of the origins and development of the German Garden City movement, emphasizing its links with broader efforts by the middle classes to improve the quality of daily life.

7.137 BONHAM-CARTER, Sir Edgar (1950) Planning and development of Letchworth Garden City. *Town Planning Review*, **21** (4), pp. 362–76.
An account of the foundation and growth of the first British garden city.

7.138 CULPIN, Ewart G. (1913) *The Garden City Movement Up-to-Date*.

London: Garden Cities and Town Planning Association.
An account of the early years of the movement, with details of
Letchworth and other developments on Garden City lines.

139 DOGLIO, Carlo (1953) *L'equivoco della città giardino*. Naples: Edizioni
R. L.
A discussion of the ideological bases of the Garden City idea.
Largely polemical but with much historical relevance.

140 DOGLIO, Carlo (1953) L'equivoco della città-giardino. *Urbanistica*,
13, pp. 56–66.
A summary of his book of the same year. See previous item.

141 DOGLIO, Carlo (1974) *L'equivoco della città giardino*. Florence: C.P.
Editrice.
A new edition, with introduction and notes by Antonio
Camarda.

142 GIORDANI, Luigi (1972) *L'idea de la città giardino*. Bologna:
Calderini.
An analysis of Howard's strategy of urban development and
its twentieth-century evolution.

143 HARTMANN, Kristiana (1974) Architekturkonzeptionen der
deutschen Gartenstadtbewegung. Unpublished Diss.phil., Freie
Universität, Berlin.
Analyses the architecture and planning of Hellerau,
Falkenberg, and other early German 'garden cities'. Some of the
material was later incorporated in the author's 1977 book (see
next item).

144 HARTMANN, Kristiana (1977) *Deutsche Gartenstadtbewegung:
Kulturpolitik und Gesellschaftsreform*. Munich: Heinz Moos Verlag.
The first attempt at a full study of the German Garden City
movement, concentrating on 1900–14, but with some reference
to its antecedents from the 1880s and to its development in the
Weimar period. Detailed case-studies of Hellerau (near Dresden)
and Falkenberg (near Berlin). Strong emphasis on design and
architecture, but a number of sections attempt to set the
movement in its national economic and social context.

7.145 JOHNSON, Kenneth (1976) *The Book of Letchworth: An Illustrated Record.*
       Chesham : Barracuda Books.
       A popular history and introduction to the town.

7.146 JOLLES, Hiddo Michiel (1954) De tuinstadbeweging in Engeland.
       Tijdschrift van het Koninklijk Nederlandsch Aardrijkskundig Genootschap,
       71, pp. 137–45.
       On the historical development of the British Garden City
       movement.

7.147 JUNGHANNS, Kurt and SCHULZ, Joachim (1967) Die Gartenstadt im
       deutschen Städtebau. *Deutsche Architektur*, **16** (1), pp. 58–60.
       A brief discussion of the importance of the Garden City idea
       in German planning.

7.148 *Letchworth Garden City, 1903–1978: Catalogue of Exhibits* (1978). North
       Hertfordshire District Council.
       A well-produced and informative exhibition catalogue, with
       notes by Mervyn Miller. Conveys much of the atmosphere of life
       in early Letchworth, with sympathy and humour. Also
       informative on the international influence of the Garden City
       movement, and on the careers of Unwin and Parker.

7.149 MILLER, Mervyn (1979) Letchworth Garden City zwischen
       Romantik und Moderne. *Bauwelt*, **70** (3), pp. 96–109.
       A full study of the history of Letchworth, with main emphasis
       on architecture and urban design.

7.150 MORRIS, A. E. J. (1971) From garden cities to new towns. *Official
       Architecture and Planning*, **34** (12), pp. 922–5.
       Surveys the development of garden cities from Letchworth
       until the New Towns Act of 1946.

7.151 NITOT, Henri (1924) *Les cités-jardins: étude sur le mouvement des cités-
       jardins suivie d'une monographie de la cité-jardin de Trait (Seine-
       Inférieure).* Paris : Presses Universitaires de France.
       Includes a historical survey of the Garden City movement,
       with special emphasis on its French branch.

7.152 OSBORN, Frederic J. (1970) *Genesis of Welwyn Garden City: Some Jubilee*

Memories. London: Town and Country Planning Association.
A personal account of the town's early days.

7.153 OSBORN, Frederic J. (1946) *Green Belt Cities: The British Contribution*.
London: Faber.
Part I is a historical account of British garden cities, beginning
with Howard. A second edition, covering the post-1946 British
new towns, appeared in 1969.

7.154 OSBORN, Frederic J. (1971) The history of Howard's 'social cities'.
Town and Country Planning, **39** (12), pp. 539–45.
An outline history of the Garden City movement.

7.155 OSBORN, F. J., MUMFORD, L. and FEISS, C. (1953) L'idea della città
giardino. *Urbanistica*, **13**, pp. 37–46.
Article celebrating the fiftieth anniversary of Letchworth. It
includes an account of the historical development of the Garden
City idea.

7.156 PEPPER, Simon (1978) The garden city legacy. *Architectural Review*,
163 (976), pp. 321–4.
A brief but stimulating outline of the course, influence, and
internal tensions of the Garden City movement from its origins
to the present day. Well illustrated.

7.157 PURDOM, Charles Benjamin (1913) *The Garden City: A Study in the
Development of the Modern Town*. London: Dent.
A history of the early years of Letchworth.

7.158 PURDOM, Charles Benjamin (1925) *The Building of Satellite Towns: A
Contribution to the Study of Town Development and Regional Planning*.
London: Dent.
This includes a historical account of the Garden City
movement, with detailed studies of Letchworth and Welwyn. A
new edition, including discussion of more recent developments,
was published by Dent in 1949.

7.159 PURDOM, Charles Benjamin (1963) *The Letchworth Achievement*.
London: Dent.
An authoritative history of Letchworth and appraisal of its

importance in the general development of urban planning.

7.160 SCHIAVI, A. (1953) Industrialismo ed urbanismo. *Urbanistica*, **13**, pp. 47–55.
Of some relevance to the origins of the Garden City idea.

7.161 WATANABE, Shun-ichi (1978) Nihonteki Den-en Toshi Ron no Kenkyū II, Naimushō Chihō Kyoku Yūshi (ed.), *Den-en Toshi* (1907) o Meggute. *Nihon Toshi Keikaku Gakkai Gakujutsu Kenkyū Happyōkai Ronbunshū*, **13**, pp. 283–8.
Analyses the first introduction of the Garden City idea into Japan, in 1907, by the Ministry of the Interior.

7.162 WOLFE, Jeanne (1978) Dr. Emile Nadeau's 'Jardin de la Confédération'. *Plan Canada*, **18** (1), pp. 60–1.
Outlines a scheme for a 'garden city' in Quebec put forward by a Canadian doctor in 1913–14.

8.
Aspects of urban and regional planning

This section distinguishes the main specialisms within twentieth-century planning. Some of them are continuations of nineteenth-century proto-planning, while others have emerged from the general institutionalization of planning since the early twentieth century.

Postwar reconstruction

Most of these titles deal with the rebuilding of bombed cities after the Second World War. Mass destruction, and associated changes in public and official attitudes, greatly contributed to the wide acceptance of effective planning powers after 1945. However, in many cities the challenge appears to have been too great for the planners and their political masters, and many of these studies suggest that a great opportunity was lost.

See also 4.49, 4.61, 4.93, 4.129, 4.131, 4.171, 4.210, 5.17, 5.26–8, 5.30, 5.91–2, 8.22, 9.65, 9.75, 9.140, Coventry.

8.1 BLACKSELL, M. (1968) Recent changes in the morphology of West German townscapes, in Beckinsale, R. P. and Houston, J. M. (eds.), *Urbanisation and its Problems*. Oxford: Basil Blackwell, pp. 199–217.
 A historical account and critique of replanning and reconstruction in a number of German cities since 1945.

8.2 BRYANT, R. W. G. (1967) The reconstruction of Coventry, in Eldredge, H. Wentworth (ed.), *Taming Megalopolis, vol. II: How to Manage an Urbanized World*. New York: Praeger, pp. 765–83.
 An outline of the post-1945 reconstruction of Coventry.

8.3 CIBOROWSKI, Adolf (1964) *Warsaw, a City Destroyed and Rebuilt.*
Warsaw: Polonia Publishing House.
A full account of the rebuilding of Warsaw after 1945. Also
published in Polish as *Warszawa, o zniszczeniu i odbudowie miasta*
(Polonia, 1964).

8.4 CIBOROWSKI, Adolf and JANKOWSKI, Stanislaw (1962) *Warsaw Rebuilt.*
Warsaw: Polonia Publishing House.
An earlier version of the above item. Also published in Polish
as *Warszawa odbudowana* (Polonia, 1962).

8.5 GREENE, Ernest Thomas (1958) Politics and geography in post-war
German city planning. A field study of four German cities:
Hannover, Cologne, Kiel and Trier. Unpublished Ph.D. thesis,
Princeton University.
A comparative assessment of the achievement of each of the
four cities in postwar reconstruction, based on primary and
secondary literary sources, interviews, and visits. Concludes that
Hanover planned well and Cologne badly, while Kiel made the
best of difficult circumstances.

8.6 GREENE, Ernest Thomas (1964) Politics and planning for
reconstruction in Western Germany. *Urban Studies*, 1, pp. 71–8.
A succinct account, based on his thesis (see previous item).

8.7 GRIESER, Helmut (1978) Kontinuität und Wandel: Studien zum
Wiederaufbau Kiels nach dem Zweiten Weltkrieg. Unpublished
dissertation (*Habilitationsschrift*), University of Kiel.
Discusses aspects of the reconstruction of Kiel after the Second
World War.

8.8 INTERNATIONAL UNION OF ARCHITECTS (1958) *Construction and
Reconstruction of Towns, 1945–1957* (2 vols.). Moscow: State Building
and Architecture Publishing House. Proceedings of the Fifth
Congress of the International Union of Architects.
Covers a number of aspects of postwar reconstruction and
renewal. Also published in Russian in 1960 as *Strojitelstvo i
rekonstrukcija gorodov 1945–1957.*

8.9 JOHNSON-MARSHALL, Percy (1966) *Rebuilding Cities*. Edinburgh: Edinburgh University Press.

Most of this book studies post-1945 reconstruction and replanning, concentrating on London, Coventry and Rotterdam. These recent examples, however, are set in the context of a general history of efforts to build or rebuild cities from scratch. Much of the text is built round copious illustrations.

8.10 KURZ, Max (1953) *Frankfurt baut auf: Bauherr, Architekt, Baugewerbe berichten über Planung und Ausführung der Aufbaujahre 1948–1953*. Stuttgart: Allgemeine Werbe Agentur.

A study of the early years of the reconstruction of Frankfurt based on the impressions of leading participants.

8.11 *The Reconstruction of Berlin from 1949 to 1963* (1962). Berlin: Senator für Bau- und Wohnungswesen.

A brief, illustrated account of rebuilding in West Berlin after the Second World War.

8.12 RICHARDSON, Kenneth (1972) *Twentieth-Century Coventry*. London: Macmillan.

An official history of the city. Much attention is given to the prewar origins of the city-centre plan, the reconstruction of bomb-damaged Coventry, and general planning policies since 1945.

8.13 ROGGE, J. R. (1967–68) West Berlin and Hamburg: a comparative and selective study with special reference to the central areas in the post-war period. Unpublished Ph.D. thesis, University of London.

Includes some discussion of reconstruction after 1945.

8.14 STEPHAN, Hans (1958–59) Rebuilding Berlin. *Town Planning Review*, 29 (4), pp. 207–26.

Mainly an analysis of a contemporary problem but with some historical perspective on policies since the 1930s.

8.15 TORTORETO, Emanuele (1977) La mancata 'difesa di Milano' dal 1945 al 1950: considerazioni sulle linee politiche della

ricostruzione edilizia. *Storia Urbana*, 1 (1), pp. 97–133.
On the repair of bomb damage in Milan after World War II
and its implications for more general planning policies.

8.16 TREBBI, Giorgio (1978) *La ricostruzione di una città: Berlino 1945–1975*.
Milan: Mazzotta.
A full account of the reconstruction of Berlin after 1945.

8.17 WEAVER, John C. (1976) Reconstruction of the Richwood district
of Halifax: a Canadian episode in public housing and town
planning, 1918–1921. *Plan Canada*, **16**, pp. 36–47.
Describes the planned rebuilding of an area devastated by the
explosion of a munitions ship during the First World War.

8.18 WESTECKER, Wilhelm (1962) *Die Wiedergeburt der deutschen Städte*.
Düsseldorf: Econ-Verlag.
Discusses the postwar reconstruction of German cities.

Urban renewal, slum clearance, and redevelopment

The origins of large-scale slum clearance and urban renewal in
the context of comprehensive urban planning are to be found in
the 1930s, but little redevelopment was carried out anywhere
until the 1950s. Even then, Britain and the United States were the
main participants, and other countries make a poor showing in
this section. The British slum-clearance programme, made
necessary by a big legacy of defective housing built in the early
stages of industrialization, has been the most ambitious in the
world. Combined with mass public housing, it has brought
about a radical reshaping of the inner districts of British cities. In
the United States, urban renewal has remained a much smaller
programme, has called forth a huge participation from private
enterprise, and has become involved with the reconstruction of
commercial districts as well as residential areas. As such, it has
stimulated more criticism than the British programme. The
critical case studies generated by the American debate are
prominent below.
See also 5.79, 5.102, 5.122, 5.156, 5.198, 9.120.

8.19 ADAMS, Robert Wilson (1970) Urban renewal politics: a case study of Columbus, Ohio, 1952–1961. Unpublished Ph.D. thesis, Ohio State University.

Claims that the 1949 Housing Act was so vague that the defects of urban renewal cannot be blamed on it. Local policies were determined by the conflict between those who sought improvements in housing, and those who wanted to renew commercial districts. The case study of Columbus since 1969 reveals confusion until 1956, and then a concerted commercially-oriented programme which made housing conditions worse.

8.20 ANDERSON, Martin (1964) *The Federal Bulldozer: A Critical Analysis of Urban Renewal, 1949–62.* Cambridge, Mass.: MIT Press.

A generally critical account of Federal and local urban renewal policies in the United States.

8.21 BATEMAN, M. (1967–68) The nature and process of urban renewal in the central areas of nine towns of West Yorkshire during the postwar period. Unpublished Ph.D. thesis, University of Leeds.

Some historical perspective.

8.22 BELOV, Il'ia Ivanovich (1966) *Podnyat'ie iz ruin: istoricheskie ocherki vosstanovleniya i razvitiya stareizikh gorodov Rossii, 1943–1963 gg.* Moscow: Izd-vo lit-r'i po stroitel'stvu.

A study of urban renewal and reconstruction work in the Soviet Union between 1943 and 1963.

8.23 BRENNAN, T. (1959) *Reshaping a City.* Glasgow: Grant.

Studies the redevelopment programmes pursued in Glasgow since the 1930s.

8.24 BURNS, Wilfred (1963) *New Towns for Old: The Technique of Urban Renewal.* London: Leonard Hill.

Discusses a number of postwar reconstruction and renewal schemes.

8.25 CHRISTIE, I. (1974) Covent Garden: approaches to urban renewal. *Town Planning Review,* **45,** pp. 31–62.

Includes a historical account of the various proposals for the development of the Covent Garden district, London, after the removal of the wholesale markets.

8.26 COLLIER, Robert W. (1974) *Contemporary Cathedrals: Large-Scale Development in Canadian Cities*. Montreal: Harvest House.

Case studies of recent large-scale developments in Montreal, Vancouver, Edmonton, Winnipeg, Toronto, Ottawa, and Halifax. They represent a variety of confrontations between developers and municipal authorities.

8.27 CRESTI, Carlo and OREFICE, Gabriella (1978) Caratteri sociali, situazioni ambientali e piani di risanamento del quartiere d'Oltrarno a Firenze (1865–1940). *Storia Urbana*, 2 (6), pp. 181–207.

An account of a series of efforts to reconstruct one of the worst Florence slum districts.

8.28 DENNIS, Norman (1970) *People and Planning: The Sociology of Housing in Sunderland*. London: Faber.

A study of British slum clearance, 1930–70, with special reference to Sunderland.

8.29 DERTHICK, Martha (1972) *New Towns In-Town: Why a Federal Program Failed*. Washington, D.C.: Urban Institute.

A critique of urban renewal in the United States, with some historical perspective.

8.30 HALL, Thomas (1971) Sagerska husen: en studie i kommunal kulturmiljöpolitik. *Samfundet Sit Eriks Årsbok*, 1971, pp. 170–227.

A case study of an episode in the redevelopment of Stockholm in the 1960s and 1970s, in which efforts to incorporate a historic building in a new complex ended in failure.

8.31 HALL, Thomas (1979) The Central Business District: planning in Stockholm, 1928–1978, in Hammarström, Ingrid and Hall, Thomas (eds.), *Growth and Transformation of the Modern City*. Stockholm: Swedish Council for Building Research, pp. 181–232.

A thorough and generally critical analysis of the large-scale renewal scheme undertaken in central Stockholm in the 1960s and early 1970s, in the context of the evolution of plans for the area since the interwar years.

8.32 HARTMAN, Chester and KESSLER, Rob (1978) The illusion and reality of urban renewal: San Francisco's Yerba Buena Center, in Tabb, William K. and Sawers, Larry (eds.), *Marxism and the Metropolis: New Perspectives in Urban Political Economy.* New York: Oxford University Press, pp. 153–78.

A Marxist critique of a 1970s renewal project.

8.33 HÖGG, Hans (1967) *Istanbul: Stadtorganismus und Stadterneuerung.* Ludwigsburg: Karawane-Verlag.

A survey of redevelopment in Istanbul, with some historical perspective.

8.34 HOLLIDAY, J. (ed.) (1974) *City Centre Redevelopment: A Study of British City Centre Planning and Case Studies of Five English City Centres.* London: Charles Knight.

Includes an informative introduction by the editor (pp. 4–29) on the recent history of central-area renewal in Britain. The case studies are listed under the name of the town in Section V.

8.35 JENNINGS, Hilda (1962) *Societies in the Making: A Study of Development and Redevelopment Within a County Borough.* London: Routledge and Kegan Paul.

Studies the clearance and rebuilding of Barton Hill, a district of Bristol, and movements to suburban estates. Main period of study covers the 1950s.

8.36 KAPLAN, Harold (1961) *Urban Renewal Politics: Slum Clearance in Newark.* New York: Columbia University Press.

A historical account of urban renewal in Newark, New Jersey, between 1949 and 1960. Based on a Columbia University Ph.D. thesis, The politics of slum clearance: a study of urban renewal in Newark, New Jersey, 1961.

8.37 KOVISARS, Judith Fiorello (1970) Planned change in a changing urban environment: a social history of urban renewal in Trenton, New Jersey. Unpublished Ph.D. thesis, University of Pennsylvania.

Includes detailed studies of selected renewal projects and plans in Trenton between 1945 and 1970. Attempts to assess the impact of urban renewal on social and economic change.

Concludes that urban renewal objectives were generally inappropriate to social needs.

8.38 MALPASS, Peter (1979) Die Kehrseite der 'Mauer': das Sanierungsgebiet Byker in Newcastle. *Stadtbauwelt*, **63**, pp. 294–8.
A commentary on the Byker reconstruction scheme, with some historical perspective.

8.39 MAUSBACH, Hans (1972) *Die Planung der Stadterneuerung: ein Erfahrungsbericht mit sechs Beispielen aus Mittel- and Kleinstädten.* Stuttgart: K. Krämer.
Six case studies of urban renewal and conservation in German town centres.

8.40 MILLSPAUGH, Martin (ed.) (1964) *Baltimore's Charles Center: A Case Study of Downtown Renewal.* Washington: Urban Land Institute.
A case study of a recent renewal project.

8.41 MILLWARD, Stanley (ed.) (1977) *Urban Harvest: Urban Renewal in Retrospect and Prospect.* Berkhamsted: Geographical Publications Ltd.
A collection of papers presented at a series of seminars at Salford University. Though not primarily historical, they shed light on some aspects of the development of British slum clearance since 1945, with a digression into transport planning.

8.42 RAVETZ, Alison (1974) *Model Estate: Planned Housing at Quarry Hill, Leeds.* London: Croom Helm.
A history of the clearance, reconstruction, and rapid degeneration of the Quarry Hill district of Leeds, c.1930–c.1970.

8.43 SANDIONIGI, A. M. (1969) La politica dell'urban renewal nell'esperienza degli Stati Uniti d'America. *Città e Società*, **5**, pp. 17–39.
A review of American experience with urban renewal since 1949.

8.44 WEISMANTEL, William Louis (1969) Collision of urban renewal with zoning: the Boston experience 1950–1967. Unpublished thesis, Harvard University.
No information.

8.45 WILSON, James Q. (ed.) (1966) *Urban Renewal: The Record and the Controversy*. Cambridge, Mass: MIT Press.

A collection of articles on urban renewal in the United States between 1949 and the early 1960s. Some are historical in approach.

8.46 WOLFF, Carol Ann Ellis (1967) Urban renewal: patterns of population and housing change. Unpublished Ph.D. thesis, Michigan State University.

Measures the impact of urban renewal on housing and population in Washington and St. Louis, using Cincinnati, which did not adopt urban renewal until 1959, as a control. Main data source is the censuses of 1950 and 1960.

8.47 ZETTER, Roger (1975) Les Halles: a case study of large scale redevelopment in central Paris. *Town Planning Review*, **46** (3), pp. 267–94.

Includes an account of the building and planning history of the Halles district, and of the evolution of plans for the removal of the markets to a suburban site.

Open space

The lack of studies on this topic reflects the incorporation of open-space planning into the preparation of general development plans, and the fact that big, formal parks are rarely created nowadays.

8.48 BERNATZKY, Aloys (1960) *Von der mittelalterlichen Stadtbefestigung zu den Wallgrünflächen von heute: ein Beitrag zum Grünflächenproblem deutscher Städte*. Berlin: B. Patzer.

A history of the removal of fortifications around German towns, and the conversion of some of them into open space.

8.49 HECKSCHER, August (1977) *Open Spaces: The Life of American Cities*. New York: Harper and Row.

Reviews the development of open-space planning in the United States, with examples from numerous cities.

8.50 RICHTER, Gerhard (1969) Entstehung und Entwicklung des öffentlichen Grüns in Hannover. Unpublished dissertation, Technische Universität, Hannover.
A history of open space in Hanover.

8.51 ZAITZEVSKY, C. (1973) The Olmsted firm and the structures of the Boston park system. *Journal of the Society of Architectural Historians*, **32**, pp. 167–74.
On the early stages of the development of the Boston park system in the later nineteenth century.

Conservation (urban)

Although it has its antecedents in the *art urbain* movement of the later nineteenth century, conservation has become an important element of urban planning only in the last two decades, as opinion has swung against wholesale reconstruction. Italian and French prominence among these titles is fully merited.
See also 3.62, 9.17, 9.33, 9.73–4, 9.94, 9.119.

8.52 ARMSTRONG, Frederick H. and PHELPS, Edward C. H. (1977) In almost perpetual circles: urban preservation and the municipal advisory committee in London, Ontario. *Urban History Review*, No. 2, pp. 10–19.
A review of conservation campaigns and policies in London, Ontario, in the 1970s.

8.53 BABELON, Jean-Pierre (1975) Dix ans d'aménagement à Paris, 1965–1975. *Revue de l'Art*, **29**, pp. 9–56.
Outlines progress on a number of conservation schemes in Paris.

8.54 BRIX, Michael (ed.) (1977) *Lübeck, die Altstadt als Denkmal: Zerstörung, Wiederaufbau, Gefahren, Sanierung.* Munich: Heinz Moos Verlag.
A study of conservation in Lübeck since the post-1945 reconstruction.

8.55 DI BARI, Domenico (1968) *Bari: vicende urbanistiche del centro storico (1867–1967).* Bari: Dedalo libri.
A planning history of the historic centre of Bari since the mid-nineteenth century.

8.56 HRŮZA, Jiří and NOVY, O. (1960) Conservazione e rigenerazione dei centri storici in Cecoslovacchia. *Urbanistica,* **31,** pp. 18–52.
A full survey of Czech policies and methods in the conservation of historic town centres, including an account of the historical evolution thereof.

8.57 KAIN, Roger (1978–79) Conservation planning in France: policy and practice in the Marais, Paris. *Urbanism Past and Present,* **7,** pp. 22–34.
Sets an account of the Marais conservation project in the context of the development of French planning legislation and the national conservation strategy. Awareness of social and economic tensions generated by the 1967 conservation plan makes this a particularly valuable analysis.

8.58 MONTANARI, Armando (1978) Restaurierungspolitik in einigen Altstädten Italiens, in [Breitling, Peter, ed.] *Leben in der Altstadt* (Grazer Beiträge zu Städtebau und Stadtforschung, Band 1). Graz: Institut für Städtebau und Landesplanung der Technischen Universität Graz, pp. 31–8.
Outlines progress in renovation of central districts in Italian cities since the early 1960s, with special reference to Rome.

8.59 STUNGO, A. (1972) Conservation planning in France: an appraisal of the Malraux Act, 1962–72. Unpublished thesis (Diploma in Town Planning), University College, London.
See following item.

8.60 STUNGO, A. (1972) The Malraux Act, 1962–72. *Journal of the Royal Town Planning Institute,* **58,** pp. 357–62.

Reviews the implementation and effect of a much-praised law on urban conservation during its first ten years.

Conservation (rural)

The British coinage of 'town and country planning', a product of the interwar years, reflects a preoccupation with the conservation of the rural environment in one of the world's most crowded countries. However, North America, with its century-old tradition of national parks, is also prominent, and there is a strong link here with the development of regional planning (see pp. 234–9).
See also 8.240, 9.52, 9.86, 9.98, 9.112, 9.116.

8.61   CHERRY, Gordon E. (1975) *Environmental Planning 1939–1969. Vol. II, National Parks and Recreation in the Countryside*. London: HMSO.
One of the earliest in a planned series of official histories of British postwar planning policy, this examines the origins and implementation of the national parks, and other aspects of countryside planning, in the 1940s.

8.62   SHEAIL, John (1976) Coasts and planning in Great Britain before 1950. *Geographical Journal*, 142 (2), pp. 257–73.
Discusses the rise, from the later nineteenth century, of concern about the desecration of Britain's coastline, and early steps, both local and national, to combat it.

8.63   SHEAIL, John (1976) *Nature in Trust: The History of Nature Conservation in Britain*. Glasgow/London: Blackie.
A full history of nature conservation in Britain. Includes the development of the national parks and other planning instruments designed to protect national resources.

8.64   SHEAIL, John (1977) The impact of recreation on the coast: the Lindsey County Council (Sandhills) Act, 1932. *Landscape Planning*, 4, pp. 53–72.

A detailed study of the origins and passing of the Act, and its beneficial effects on the development of a strip of coastline which had been degenerating into a seaside slum of shacks and bungalows.

8.65 STECK, Warren F. and SARJEANT, William A. S. (1977) The history and achievements of the Saskatoon Environmental Society. *Urban History Review*, No. 2, pp. 33–54.

Outlines the activities and successes of an unusually successful environmental protection organization, founded in 1970.

Transport planning

Planning historians have been more interested in the motor vehicle than any other mode of urban transport, mainly because of the tensions it has produced within cities not designed for it. However, a number of titles on public-transport planning fill out the general picture.

See also 4.212, 5.102, 8.41, 9.59.

8.66 BUCHANAN, Colin Malcolm (1970) *London Road Plans, 1900–1970* (Research Report, no. 11). London: Greater London Council Research and Intelligence Unit.

A study of a series of road proposals for London, from the Royal Commission on London Traffic to the motorway box.

8.67 CHERRY, Gordon E. (1970) Town planning and the motor car in twentieth century Britain. *High Speed Ground Transportation Journal*, 4 (1), pp. 69–80.

A brief discussion of the impact of the motor car on British urban planning policies.

8.68 COLLINS, Michael F. and PHAROAH, Timothy M. (1974) *Transport Organisation in a Great City: The Case of London*. London: Allen and Unwin.

A detailed analysis of transport planning in London since the 1960s, with some earlier historical perspective.

8.69 COPPINI, Maria Chiara (1979) Una fase di transizione nel trasporto pubblico nell'area urbana bolognese: gli anni dal 1945 al 1964. *Storia Urbana*, 3 (7), pp. 163–89.

Analyses the impact of a concerted programme of public-transport expansion, decided in 1955, on a Bologna area which previously had enjoyed no serious transport planning.

8.70 DEELSTRA, Tjeerd, VAN TOOM, Jan and BREMER, Jaap (eds.) (1972) *De straat: vorm van samenleven*. Eindhoven: Stedelijk Van Abbemuseum.

A collection of short articles published in connection with an exhibition at the Van Abbemuseum, Eindhoven, June–August 1972. The contributions cover numerous aspects of the history and current condition of the urban street, and there is some discussion of the attitudes of planners and architects to the street since the nineteenth century.

8.71 DEHMEL, Wilhelm (1976) Platzwandel und Verkehr: zur Platzgestaltung im 19. und 20. Jahrhundert in Berlin unter dem Einfluss wachsenden und sich verändernden Verkehrs. Unpublished dissertation, Technische Universität Berlin.

On the design of squares in Berlin in the nineteenth and twentieth centuries under the impact of changing traffic requirements.

8.72 FOSTER, Mark (1979) City planners and urban transportation: the American response, 1900–1940. *Journal of Urban History*, 5 (3), pp. 365–96.

Charts the slow demise of the electric streetcar, and puts some of the blame on the planners who, at first, failed to recognize the need for a positive transport strategy, and later welcomed the automobile too naively. As a result, the streetcar was already doomed by 1940, but no alternative strategy, capable of accommodating the automobile, had emerged.

8.73 HART, D. A. (1976) *Strategic Planning in London: The Rise and Fall of the Primary Road Network*. London: Pergamon Press.

Most of the book consists of a history of the rise and fall of the G.L.C.'s plans for a 'motorway box' in London.

8.74 HUNTER, H. (1957) *Soviet Transportation Policy*. Cambridge, Mass.: Harvard University Press.

Discusses the history of Soviet transport planning, including a chapter on urban transport.

8.75 HUNTER, H. (1968) *Soviet Transport Experience: Its Lessons for Other Countries*. Washington: Brookings Institution.

Includes a chapter on the history of Soviet urban transport planning.

8.76 McSHANE, Clay (1975) American cities and the coming of the automobile. Unpublished Ph.D. thesis, University of Wisconsin.

This makes some reference to transport planning, or the lack of it, in the early twentieth century.

8.77 PLOWDEN, Stephen (1972) *Towns Against Traffic*. London: André Deutsch.

A study of the ways in which public opinion in British towns organized itself against disruptive road schemes in the 1960s, with detailed accounts of developments in Oxford and London.

8.78 RITTER, Paul (1963) *Planning for Man and Motor*. Oxford: Pergamon Press.

Mainly a discussion of the nature of transport planning in the contemporary city, but drawing on historical experience to support its arguments.

8.79 ROSE, Mark H. (1979) *Interstate: Express Highway Politics, 1941–1956*. Lawrence: Regents' Press of the University of Kansas.

Suggests that U.S. urban planners were generally unable to influence highway schemes in the interests of the better planning of their towns.

8.80 SLOAN, A. K. (1974) *Citizen Participation in Transportation Planning: The Boston Experience*. Cambridge, Mass.: Ballinger.

A study of developments in transport planning in Boston in the late 1960s and early 1970s.

8.81 STARKIE, D. N. M. (1976) *Transportation Planning, Policy and Analysis*. Oxford: Pergamon Press.

Reviews the development of transport planning in Britain since about 1960.

8.82 STEINER, Henry Malcolm (1978) *Conflict in Urban Transportation: The People Against the Planners*. Lexington, Mass.: Lexington Books.

Includes a number of case studies of episodes in American transport planning, stressing conflicts between the authorities and the residents affected by big transport projects.

8.83 TETLOW, John and Goss, Anthony (1965) *Homes, Towns and Traffic*. London: Faber.

Largely a critique of urban road planning in Britain in the 1960s, but includes a historical account of urban traffic planning in various countries since medieval times. The authors constantly link transport planning to the habitat which it permits.

8.84 TREVISINI, Giusi (1979) Il problema del traffico e dei trasporti nell'area urbana milanese, 1900–1948. *Storia Urbana*, 3 (7), pp. 81–114.

A narrative of transport developments in Milan during a period in which population growth did not radically alter the structure of the city. Municipal transport planning is discussed, though it achieved very little in those years.

Zoning and land-use planning

Zoning was developed in Germany from about 1890 as a means of adapting building regulations to the special needs of different functional districts within towns. The idea was imported into the United States after 1900 and combined with the native form of socially-discriminatory zoning which was already being used to keep undesirable uses, and the individuals who went with them, out of high-class districts. It is this American use of zoning which has attracted the most interest from historians ever since.

Elsewhere, it is a perfectly practical and non-controversial element of the general planning process.

See also 4.210, 4.259, 4.270, 5.76, 5.142, 5.210, 6.3, 6.84, 8.44, 9.63, 9.66, 9.115–6.

8.85 BABCOCK, Richard F. (1966) *The Zoning Game: Municipal Practices and Policies*. Madison: University of Wisconsin Press.

Basically a review of the contemporary practice of zoning in the United States, this has a slight degree of historical perspective on the development of zoning.

8.86 BASSETT, Edward Murray (1926) *Zoning Progress in the United States*. Washington: Division of Building and Housing.

Surveys the reaction of American courts to zoning. An amended version was republished in 1927.

8.87 BASSETT, Edward Murray (1929) *Zoning and the Courts*. Washington: Division of Building and Housing.

A review of the reaction of American courts to zoning measures since the early 1900s. An earlier version was published as Part I of *Zoning Progress in the United States* (1927).

8.88 BASSETT, Edward Murray (1936) *Zoning: The Laws, Administration and Court Decisions During the First Twenty Years*. New York: Russell Sage Foundation.

Reviews the legal successes and setbacks of New York zoning since 1916. Includes a bibliography by Katherine McNamara and an index of court cases. A new edition was published in 1940.

8.89 DANIELSON, Michael N. (1976) *The Politics of Exclusion*. New York: Columbia University Press.

Includes consideration of the development of residential zoning in the United States.

8.90 DELAFONS, John (1962) *Land-Use Controls in the United States*. Cambridge, Mass.: Joint Center for Urban Studies, MIT and Harvard University.

The historical development of U.S. zoning is outlined on pp. 16–29. Stresses the continuing influence of the New York ordinance of 1916 on zoning elsewhere. Argues that flexibility in the use of zoning is now limited by its close links with the defence of private property.

8.91   ELKIN, Stephen L. (1974) *Politics and Land Use Planning: The London Experience*. London: Cambridge University Press.

This does not set out to be a historical study, but includes a section on the history of town-planning controls in London. The case studies of Chelsea and central London have some recent historical perspective.

8.92   HASON, N. (1975) The emergence and development of zoning controls in North American municipalities. Unpublished Master's thesis, University of Toronto.

See next item.

8.93   HASON, N. (1977) *The Emergence and Development of Zoning Controls in North American Municipalities: A Critical Analysis* (Papers on Planning and Design, no. 13). Toronto: Department of Urban and Regional Planning, University of Toronto.

Based on the author's Master's thesis, this discusses the general development of zoning in twentieth-century Canada and the United States.

8.94   KOCH, Friedrich (1979) *Flächennutzungsplanung und Stadtentwicklung 1918–1978*. Augsburg: Amt für Stadtentwicklung und Statistik, Stadt Augsburg.

A brief outline of fifty years of land-use planning in Augsburg, in its relationship with the physical development of the city.

8.95   LINOWES, R. Robert (1973) *The Politics of Land Use: Planning, Zoning and the Private Developer*. New York: Praeger.

A collection of case studies of conflicts between citizen groups and private developers in the United States.

8.96   LINOWES, R. Robert and ALLENSWORTH, Don T. (1976) *The Politics of Land-Use Law: Developers vs. Citizens Groups in the Courts*. New York: Praeger.

A sequel to *The Politics of Land Use*, this traces a number of zoning disputes through into the courts of the United States. Chapter 2 provides a historical overview of land-use issues since early colonization, and the detailed studies provide much recent historical perspective, particularly since the 1960s.

8.97 LOGAN, Thomas Harvey (1972) The invention of zoning in the emerging planning profession of late-nineteenth century Germany. Unpublished Ph.D. thesis, University of North Carolina.

A standard account of the development of zoning in Germany in the 1890s and early 1900s, in the context of a general appraisal of German planning.

8.98 LOGAN, Thomas Harvey (1976) The Americanization of German zoning. *Journal of the American Institute of Planners*, 42 (4), pp. 377–85.

An informed discussion of the origins of zoning in Germany in the later nineteenth century and its adoption in the United States in the early twentieth. Argues that the weaknesses of zoning have been the product of planners' tendency to use it as an all-purpose tool, rather than as just one element in a comprehensive planning policy.

8.99 MACKESEY, Thomas William (1940) *History of Zoning in the United States*. Ithaca: author.

A mimeographed extract from the author's Master's thesis on zoning.

100 MAKIELSKI, Stanislaw J. (1966) *The Politics of Zoning: The New York Experience*. New York: Columbia University Press.

Includes full consideration of the history of zoning in New York. Based on a Columbia University Ph.D. thesis, The politics of zoning in New York City, 1910–1960 (1965).

101 MANCUSO, Franco (1978) *Le vicende dello zoning*. Milan: il Saggiatore.

A lengthy study of the development of zoning in Germany between c.1890 and the 1920s, its importation into the United States in the early 1900s and its subsequent transformation there into a means of maintaining social segregation and high suburban property values.

8.102 TOLL, Seymour I. (1969) *Zoned American*. New York: Grossman.
A racy but thorough history of zoning in the United States
since the New York ordinance of 1916.

8.103 VAN NUS, Walter (1979) Towards the City Efficient: the theory
and practice of zoning, 1919–1939, in Artibise, A. F. J. and
Stelter, G. A. (eds.), *The Usable Urban Past: Planning and Politics in the
Modern Canadian City*. Toronto: Macmillan Company of Canada,
pp. 226–46.
Argues that Canadian planners, incapable of devising fixed,
comprehensive city plans, settled instead for a flexible zoning
system which achieved little more than the protection of
property values.

Residential areas

Between 1914 and 1939 the high hopes of effective city-wide
planning were largely dispelled, except perhaps in Germany.
This meant that in many cities public-housing projects alone
offered the chance to show what planning could achieve. A new
design wave, the Modern Movement in architecture, took a
strong interest in mass housing, and historians have had plenty
to get their teeth into here. In North America, the virtual
absence of public housing precluded such an outlet, but the
spread of the low-density suburb helped generate the organizing
concept of the neighbourhood unit in the 1920s. The spread of
public housing since 1945 has generated a number of
monitoring studies of recent residential planning.
     See also 4.159, 4.252, 4.269, 5.84–5, 5.112, 6.143, 7.29, 8.42,
9.19, 9.99, 9.104, 9.129, 9.132, Unwin.

8.104 BANDEL, Hans and MACHULE, Dietmar (1974) *Der Gropiusstadt: der
städtebauliche Planungs- und Entscheidungsvorgang*. Berlin: Verlag
Kiepert.
     A study of the planning process which produced Gropiusstadt,
a high-density residential suburb, in Berlin, 1959–74.

8.105 BOUDON, Philippe (1969) *Pessac de Le Corbusier*. Paris: P. Dunod.
A full study of Le Corbusier's first mass housing scheme.

8.106 BULLOCK, Nicholas (1978) Housing in Frankfurt and the new *Wohnkultur*, 1925 to 1931. *Architectural Review*, **163** (976), pp. 335–42.
Outlines housing and planning developments in Frankfurt in the 1920s under May, stressing continuity from prewar German practice.

8.107 CASTEX, Jean, DEPAULE, Jean-Charles and PANERAI, Philippe (1975) *De l'îlot à la barre: contribution à une définition de l'architecture urbaine* (2 vols.). Versailles: ADROS (Association pour le développement de la recherche sur l'organisation spatiale) (privately circulated under auspices of the Comité de la recherche et du développement en architecture [CORDA], Ministère des Affaires Culturelles, Paris).
A detailed analysis of five approaches to the planning of building blocks: (1) Haussmann's Paris; (2) London garden suburbs 1905–25 (Hampstead and Welwyn); (3) the extensions of Amsterdam, 1913–34; (4) housing planning in Frankfurt, 1925–30; and (5) the Radiant City. Includes some consideration of the ideas and work of Unwin, Howard, Berlage, May and Le Corbusier.

8.108 DAHIR, James (1947) *The Neighbourhood Unit Plan: Its Spread and Acceptance: A Selected Bibliography With Interpretative Comments*. New York: Russell Sage Foundation.
A critical bibliography of material relating to the spread of the neighbourhood unit since the 1920s.

8.109 DROVER, Glenn (1975) London and New York: residential density planning policies and development. *Town Planning Review*, **46** (2), pp. 165–84.
Compares residential planning in London and New York since 1945.

8.110 EINSIEDEL, Sandro (1979) Idee, Anspruch und Wirklichkeit: die Nordweststadt in Frankfurt/Main. *Stadtbauwelt*, **63**, pp. 285–93.
Analyses the planning and building of a residential suburb in

Frankfurt from the origins of the idea in 1949 to realization in
the 1960s. Concentrates on the divergence of the result from the
original architectural concept.

8.111 FAGENCE, M. (1973) The Radburn idea, I. *Built Environment*, 2 (8),
pp. 467–70.
   A brief survey of the genesis of the Radburn principle, its
application in the United States between the wars, and in Britain
from the 1950s.

8.112 FEHL, Gerhard (1979) Die Legende vom Stadtbaukünstler:
Stadtgestalt und Planungsprozess der Gropiusstadt in Berlin.
Stadtbauwelt, 63, pp. 275–84.
   One of a trio of articles investigating the strengths and
weaknesses of large-scale housing schemes designed by
individual architects. Analyses the planning and building of
Gropiusstadt, in Berlin, between 1959 and 1975. Argues that in
current circumstances no architect/planner, however 'great',
can carry a project through to execution without seeing it
weakened and devalued by forces beyond his control.

8.113 GASKELL, S. Martin (1976) Sheffield City Council and the
development of suburban areas prior to World War I, in Pollard,
Sidney and Holmes, Colin (eds.), *Essays in the Economic and Social
History of South Yorkshire*. Barnsley: South Yorkshire County
Council, pp. 187–202.
   On Sheffield suburban municipal housing schemes,
c.1900–1914, and their contribution to the development of town-
planning practice.

8.114 GOLDFIELD, David R. (1979) Suburban development in Stockholm
and the United States: a comparison of form and function, in
Hammarström, Ingrid and Hall, Thomas (eds.), *Growth and
Transformation of the Modern City*. Stockholm: Swedish Council for
Building Research, pp. 139–56.
   Discusses the history of suburbs in the United States since the
nineteenth century, and in Sweden in the twentieth century (with
special reference to Stockholm). Includes consideration of the
impact of planning on trends in suburban growth.

115 HARRISON, Michael (1974) The garden suburbs of Manchester: social aspects of housing and town planning, 1895–1915. Unpublished M.A. thesis, University of Manchester.
A study of private and municipal planned housing schemes on garden suburb lines.

116 KLEIHUES, Josef Paul (1979) Berliner Baublöcke: Grundriss einer Typologie. *Werk: Archithese*, **31/32**, pp. 18–27.
Traces the development of the typical form of the Berlin building block from the nineteenth century through to the forms adopted in recent renewal schemes.

117 LINN, Björn (1974) *Storgårdskvarteret: ett bebyggelsemönsters bakgrund och karaktär*. Stockholm: Statens institut för byggnadsforskning.
A historical analysis of the evolution of the large courtyard block since Ancient times, with special emphasis on its use in public housing since the First World War in the Netherlands, Germany, Austria and Scandinavia. German summary.

118 LINN, Björn (1979) Hofraum und Stadtstruktur: gestern und heute. *Werk: Archithese*, **31/32**, pp. 8–17.
A succinct statement of the main arguments of his book (see previous item).

119 MUMFORD, Lewis (1954) The neighbourhood and the neighbourhood unit. *Town Planning Review*, **24** (4), pp. 256–70.
Surveys the whole history of neighbourhood planning since the early 1900s.

120 PASS, David (1973) *Vällingby and Farsta—from Idea to Reality: The New Community Development Process in Stockholm*. Cambridge, Mass.: MIT Press.
Case studies of the development of two planned communities in suburban Stockholm between 1945 and 1960. Presents a generally favourable view of the partnership between public and private enterprise which distinguishes Swedish planning.

121 PEPPER, Simon and SWENARTON, Mark (1978) Home front: garden suburbs for munition workers. *Architectural Review*, **163** (976), pp. 366–75.

A detailed discussion of the design of the Woolwich, Gretna and other estates built for war workers in 1914–18 under the general supervision of Raymond Unwin.

8.122 READ, James (1978) The garden city and the growth of Paris. *Architectural Review*, **163** (976), pp. 345–52.

A study of public and private housing developments in the Paris suburbs between the wars, set in the context of the development of the French planning movement since the late nineteenth century.

8.123 SAMONÀ, A. (1964) L'esperienza dei grandi 'ensembles' e il rinnovamento della struttura urbana. *Zodiac*, **13**, pp. 116–49.

Discusses the French housing strategy of large satellite estates since its interwar origins, and examines several examples in detail, with major emphasis on the Paris area. Concludes with consideration of their impact on the structure of urban areas.

8.124 SARKISSIAN, Wendy (1976) The idea of social mix in town planning: an historical review. *Urban Studies*, **13** (3), pp. 231–46.

Traces the development of the idea of social mixing in housing areas in Britain and America since the nineteenth century.

8.125 TAYLOR, Brian Brace (1972) *Le Corbusier et Pessac*. Paris: Fondation Le Corbusier.

A detailed account of Le Corbusier's first mass housing project.

8.126 TAYLOR, Brian Brace (1977) Le Corbusier at Pessac: professional and client responsibilities, in Walden, Russell (ed.), *The Open Hand: Essays on Le Corbusier*. Cambridge, Mass./London: MIT Press, pp. 162–85.

An account of some of the problems faced by Le Corbusier in his first mass housing scheme in the early 1920s.

8.127 TETLOW, J. D. (1959) Sources of the neighbourhood idea. *Journal of the Town Planning Institute*, **45** (5), pp. 113–15.

A very brief survey of the neighbourhood unit principle from dim origins in the later nineteenth century to contemporary practice.

8.128 VEAL, Anthony J. (1973) *New Communities in the U.K.: A Classified Bibliography* (C.U.R.S. Research Memorandum, no. 21). Birmingham: Centre for Urban and Regional Studies, Birmingham University.

Broader than its title suggests, this includes much reference to the planning of residential areas, not only in new towns, and there is a historical introduction.

8.129 WARNER, George A. (1954) *Greenbelt: The Cooperative Community: An Experience in Democratic Living.* New York: Exposition Press.

Includes personal reminiscences of the early years of Greenbelt, Maryland, in the 1930s.

8.130 WATANABE, Shun-ichi (1977) *Amerika Toshi Keikaku to Komyniti Rinen.* Tokyo: Gihōdō.

Traces the history of American efforts to plan local communities and neighbourhoods.

8.131 WIEDENHOEFT, Ronald Victor (1971) Workers' housing in Berlin in the 1920s: a contribution to the history of modern architecture. Unpublished Ph.D. thesis, Columbia University.

Studies twenty-two housing projects, detecting a movement in the 1920s from row-houses to apartment blocks set amid greenery in superblocks. At the end of the period a minority of influential architects were beginning to design high-rise buildings.

8.132 YOUNG, Trevor (1934) *Becontree and Dagenham: The Story of the Growth of a Housing Estate.* London: Samuel Sidders.

A sociological survey of the London County Council's largest suburban housing estate, built mainly in the 1920s. Includes a historical account of the planning and building of the area.

Urban containment and decentralization

At the end of the nineteenth century the growth of giant cities began to generate the idea that there was a limit beyond which cities ought not to be allowed to go, in terms of area, population, or both. Inevitably, this meant that the dynamic of urban growth had to be channelled elsewhere in the form of decentralization. This recognition has been one of the most potent stimuli to regional and national territorial planning in the twentieth century. Policies of urban containment were applied in their most severe form to Britain after 1945, and the titles below reflect worldwide interest in this experiment.

See also 4.40, 4.126, 4.226, 4.273, 5.36–7, 5.113, 5.163.

8.133 BOURNE, Larry S. (1975) *Urban Systems: Strategies for Regulation: A Comparison of Policies in Britain, Sweden, Australia and Canada*. Oxford: Clarendon Press.

This is a review of contemporary urban strategies in the four countries but there is some recent historical perspective.

8.134 CLAWSON, Marion and HALL, Peter (1973) *Planning and Urban Growth: An Anglo-American Comparison*. Baltimore: Johns Hopkins University Press.

Includes some historical perspective on urban growth and containment policies since 1945.

8.135 FALUDI, Andreas (1968–69) Vienna's green belt. *Transactions of the Bartlett Society*, **7**, pp. 101–25.

Includes some material on the historical development of the green-belt idea.

8.136 FARMER, Elspeth and SMITH, Roger (1972) *Glasgow Overspill, 1943–71* (Urban and Regional Studies Discussion Paper, no. 6). Glasgow: University of Glasgow.

Surveys and analyses the mixed fortunes of efforts to decant population from Glasgow since the Second World War.

8.137 FARMER, Elspeth and SMITH, Roger (1975) Overspill housing: a metropolitan case study. *Urban Studies*, **12** (2), pp. 151–68.

A later, more succinct version of the above.

8.138 FOLEY, Donald L. (1963) *Controlling London's Growth: Planning the*

Great Wen 1940–1960. Berkeley/Los Angeles: University of California Press.

A detailed study of the preparation and application of the Greater London Plan of 1944, concentrating on the problems raised by the containment strategy.

8.139 Goss, Anthony (1962) *British Industry and Town Planning*. London: Fountain Press.

Much of this book is strongly historical in emphasis, examining the development and impact of British industrial location policies.

8.140 GREGORY, David (1971) *Green Belts and Development Control: A Case Study in the West Midlands*. Birmingham: Centre for Urban and Regional Studies, Birmingham University.

An analysis of planning applications submitted in part of the proposed West Midlands Green Belt between 1957 and 1966.

8.141 HALL, John M. (1976) *London: Metropolis and Region*. Oxford: Oxford University Press.

Includes discussion of planning policies relevant to London and its region since the early 1940s.

8.142 HALL, Peter *et al.* (1973) *The Containment of Urban England* (2 vols.). London: Allen and Unwin.

A very ambitious study of the relationship between planning and the urbanization process in modern England and Wales. Its basic objective is to assess the impact of the post-1947 planning system on the location and type of new development, which involves detailed study of the progress of new towns, town development schemes, and peripheral growth. The planning system itself is also analysed and changes since the 1940s are indicated. There is also some discussion of the development of the planning and new town ideas since the nineteenth century.

8.143 HALL, Peter (1974) The containment of urban England. *Geographical Journal*, **140** (3), pp. 386–417.

A summary of his book (see previous item).

8.144 HAMSON, Paul (1969) *Green-Belt Story: A Saga of the Protection of Green*

Belt Land, With Particular Reference to Hertfordshire. Radlett: author. A brief pamphlet.

8.145 HENDERSON, R. A. (1974) Industrial overspill from Glasgow, 1958–68. *Urban Studies*, 11, pp. 61–79.
Assesses the success of efforts to relocate Glasgow industry during a period of energetic redevelopment.

8.146 MANDELKER, Daniel Robert (1962) *Green Belts and Urban Growth: English Town and Country Planning in Action*. Madison: University of Wisconsin Press.
Analyses a series of green-belt decisions and points to inconsistencies.

8.147 MINISTRY OF HOUSING AND LOCAL GOVERNMENT (1962) *The Green Belts*. London: HMSO.
An official publicity pamphlet on this distinctive British planning policy. Includes a historical survey.

8.148 MOSELEY, M. J. (1973) Some problems of small expanding towns. *Town Planning Review*, 44, pp. 263–78.
Throws some light on the experiences of towns designated for expansion under British overspill arrangements.

8.149 OSBORN, Frederic J. (1945) The country-belt principle: its historical origins. *Town and Country Planning*, 13 (49), pp. 10–19.
Traces the growth of the green-belt idea from its origins in the Old Testament (!) to Ebenezer Howard, via Adelaide.

8.150 REPS, John W. (1960) The green belt concept. *Town and Country Planning*, 28 (7), pp. 246–50.
A brief discussion of aspects of the development of the idea in eighteenth and nineteenth-century colonial planning.

8.151 RODWIN, Lloyd (1970) *Nations and Cities: A Comparison of Strategies for Urban Growth*. Boston: Houghton Mifflin.
A collection of studies on the implementation of urban growth and containment strategies since the Second World War. Includes articles on national urban growth strategies in Venezuela and Turkey, development and decentralization

policies in Britain and France, efforts to save the central cities in the United States, and the general experience of urban growth strategies.

152 SELF, Peter (1957) *Cities in Flood*. London: Faber.
An account of planning policies pursued in Britain since 1945, with special emphasis on land and densities.

153 STRANZ, Walter (1972) *Overspill—Anticipation and Reality: A Case Study of Redditch*. Birmingham: Centre for Urban and Regional Studies, Birmingham University.
Analyses the impact of overspill population from Birmingham on a small Midland town under the Town Development Act of 1952.

154 THOMAS, David (1964) The green belt, in Coppock, J. T. and Prince, H. C. (eds.), *Greater London*. London: Faber, pp. 265–91.
Outlines the origins of the green-belt principle, the establishment of the London green belt, and its effects on building development in the London region.

155 THOMAS, David (1970) *London's Green Belt*. London: Faber.
A study of the application of the green-belt principle to the London region, with strong historical perspective.

156 WURZER, Rudolf (1966) 60 Jahre Wald- und Wiesengürtel der Stadt Wien. *Berichte zur Raumforschung und Raumplanung*, 9 (4), pp. 266–86.
A history of the Vienna green belt.

157 WYNN, Michael G. and SMITH, Roger J. (1978) Spain: urban decentralization. *Built Environment*, 4 (1), pp. 49–55.
A brief but full review of the impact of the idea of planned decentralization in Spain between the turn of the century and the limited new-town programme of the 1970s.

New towns

Even in Britain, the new towns house only a tiny fraction of the population. However, the planning of new urban communities from scratch can scarcely fail to attract droves of historians. Most of the titles below relate to the British new-town policy, the most ambitious (and the most faithful to Howard's ideals) in the world. Elsewhere, the concept has been watered down much as the garden city had been earlier. In France, for instance, many so-called new towns are merely planned suburbs. However, in Israel, the Soviet Union and other developing areas, new towns have been built as growth poles in a strategy of regional development, and a number of new capital cities have been built, from Canberra to Brasilia.

See also 3.62, 3.88, 4.74, 4.209, 5.116, 6.129–30, 7.153, 8.128–9, 9.5, 9.10, 9.31, 9.39, 9.64, 9.85, 9.111, 9.117, 9.121, Brasilia, Canberra, Chandigarh, Islamabad.

8.158 ADAMS, Eric (1963) *The Development of the New Town of Harlow.* Harlow: Harlow Development Corporation.
The official history of the new town.

8.159 ALTMAN, E. A. and ROSENBAUM, B. R. (1973) Principles of planning and Zionist ideology: the Israeli development town. *Journal of the American Institute of Planners*, **39**, pp. 316–25.
A survey of the Israeli new-town programme.

8.160 ARNOLD, Joseph Larkin (1971) *The New Deal in the Suburbs: A History of the Greenbelt Town Program, 1935–1954.* Columbus: Ohio State University Press.
A full history of the conception, planning, construction, management and eventual sale of the greenbelt towns. Tries to explain why they made so little impact on community planning between 1935 and 1950. Based on an Ohio State University Ph.D. thesis, The New Deal in the suburbs: the Greenbelt town program, 1935–1952 (1968).

8.161 BAILEY, James (1973) *New Towns in America: The Design and Development Process.* New York: John Wiley.
Some historical relevance.

8.162 BATEMAN, L. H. (ed.) (1969) *History of Harlow.* Harlow: Harlow Development Corporation.
The history of the new town is summarized on pp. 127–46.

8.163 BERKMAN, H. G. (1972) The new town and the changing urban form. *Land Economics*, **48**, pp. 93–103.
Includes a historical survey of U.S. experience with new towns.

8.164 BERLER, Alexander (1970) *New Towns in Israel*. Jerusalem: Israel Universities Press.
A translation of the Hebrew version of the same year, *Arim hadashot be-Yisrael*.

8.165 BEST, Robin H. (1964) New towns in the London region, in Coppock, J. T. and Prince, H. C. (eds.), *Greater London*. London: Faber, pp. 313–32.
Includes some historical material on the development of the new-town strategy for London.

8.166 BROOKS, Richard O. (1974) *New Towns and Communal Values: A Case Study of Columbia, Maryland*. New York: Praeger.
A study of a recent American new town.

8.167 CHALINE, Claude (1971) La nouvelle génération des 'new towns' britanniques. *Annales de Géographie*, **442**, pp. 666–86.
Discusses the Mark II new towns of the 1960s in the context of the history of the British new-town programme.

8.168 CLAPP, James A. (1971) *New Towns and Urban Policy: Planning Metropolitan Growth*. New York: Dunellen.
Includes a summary of the history of British and U.S. new towns.

8.169 COMAY, Y. and KIRSCHENBAUM, A. (1973) The Israeli new town: an experiment at population redistribution. *Economic Development and Cultural Change*, **22**, pp. 124–34.
Provides some historical perspective on the Israeli new-town programme.

8.170 CORDEN, Carol (1978) *Planned Cities: New Towns in Britain and America*. Beverley Hills: Sage.
A comparative analysis of the British new towns and what pass for new towns in the United States, with much historical

perspective. Includes a discussion of the historical roots of the new-town idea.

8.171 DE MICHELIS, Marco (1978) La politica delle città nuove in URSS, in Martinelli, Roberta and Nuti, Lucia (eds.), *Le città di fondazione.* Venice: Marsilio Editori, pp. 256–70.
   A summary of the debates on new-town planning which took place in the Soviet Union in the late 1920s and early 1930s, and a description of some of the physical results.

8.172 DIAMOND, Derek (1972) New towns in their regional context, in Evans, Hazel (ed.), *New Towns: The British Experience.* London: Charles Knight for Town and Country Planning Association, pp. 54–65.
   Outlines the new role of new towns as an element in British regional planning since the 1960s, and contrasts it with the apparent lack of concern for regional development in the first-generation new towns.

8.173 EVANS, Hazel (ed.) (1972) *New Towns: The British Experience.* London: Charles Knight for Town and Country Planning Association.
   A collection of articles by advocates of new towns, and individuals involved in their promotion or administration. Main aim is to show (i) that the British new towns programme has been a success, and (ii) that it has proved adaptable to changing needs.

8.174 *L'expérience française des villes nouvelles* (1970). Paris: Armand Colin.
   Reviews progress on 'new town' developments in France in the 1960s.

8.175 FERGUSON, K. (1974) *Glenrothes: The First Twenty-Five Years.* Glenrothes: author.
   A history of the Scottish Mark I new town.

8.176 GALANTAY, Ervin Y. (1975) *New Towns: Antiquity to the Present.* New York: George Braziller.
   Briefly covers the entire history of created towns since Ancient times, with main concentration on the industrial period. Emphasis on design, somewhat hurried treatment. Fully illustrated.

8.177 GOLANY, G. (1973) *New Towns Planning and Development: A World-Wide Bibliography* (Urban Land Institute, Research Report no. 20). Washington: Urban Land Institute.

An impressively comprehensive collection, providing world-wide coverage, and including many historical items.

8.178 HARDOY, Jorge E. (1969) The planning of new capital cities, in United Nations, Department of Economic and Social Affairs, *Planning of Metropolitan Areas and New Towns.* New York: United Nations, pp. 232–49.

Outlines some of the main features of the planning and development of Canberra, Brasilia, and Islamabad.

8.179 HERTZEN, Heikki von and SPREIREGEN, Paul D. (1971) *Building a New Town: Finland's New Garden City, Tapiola.* Cambridge, Mass.: MIT Press.

A detailed study of the planning and development of Finland's most famous new town, which the authors discuss in the context of new-town strategies world-wide. A revised edition appeared in 1974.

8.180 HOLE, W. V., ADDERSON, I. M. and POUNTNEY, M. T. (1979) *Washington New Town: The Early Years.* London: HMSO.

A description and analysis, by members of the staff of the Building Research Establishment, of the first ten years of Washington new town, designated in 1964. Emphasizes the special problems raised by new-town development in an area of economic decline. Very thorough treatment, with strong statistical support.

8.181 KNITTEL, R. E. (1973) New town knowledge, experience and theory: an overview. *Human Organization,* **32**, pp. 37–48.

A brief survey of the historical experience of new towns.

8.182 KOROSCIL, P. M. (1978) Planning and development in Whitehorse, Yukon Territory. *Plan Canada,* **18** (1), pp. 30–45.

A study of new-town development in a resource-rich Canadian territory.

8.183 McCANN, L. D. (1978) The changing internal structure of

Canadian resource towns. *Plan Canada*, **18** (1), pp. 46–59.
A critical analysis of developments in the physical and social
planning of Canadian resource towns since the 1920s.

8.184 McFARLAND, John R. (1966) The administration of the New Deal
greenbelt towns. *Journal of the American Institute of Planners*, **32**,
pp. 217–25.
A succinct review of the greenbelt town programme from its
origins in the early 1930s to the present, with emphasis on
finance and administrative organization.

8.185 MANGIAMELE, Joseph Francis (1962) The development of new
towns: an analysis of growth control policies. Unpublished Ph.D.
thesis, University of London.
Evaluates the methods used to control the growth of British
new towns. Not primarily a historical piece, but throws some
light on the experience of the Mark I new towns.

8.186 MARIANI, Riccardo (1976) *Fascismo e 'città nuove'*. Milan: Feltrinelli.
Discusses the 'new town' projects promoted in Italy under
Mussolini.

8.187 MARSONI, L. (1968) Vent'anni di New Towns: rilettura di un
intervento parametrico. *Zodiac*, **18**, pp. 188–200.
A rapid discussion of the 1940s background to the British new-
town programme and changing objectives and methods
thereafter.

8.188 MARTINELLI, Roberta and NUTI, Lucia (1978) Città nuove in
Sardegna durante il periodo fascista. *Storia Urbana*, **2** (6),
pp. 291–323.
A study of the three new towns founded by Mussolini's
government in Sardinia.

8.189 MÉOLI, María Enriqueta, CERUSO, Nilda María and WEILAND,
Edgardo G. (1969) *Londres y las nuevas ciudades inglesas: una teoría de
planeamiento que pasó a ser realidad.* La Plata: Facultad de
Arquitectura y Urbanismo, Universidad Nacional de La Plata.
A critique of the British new-towns programme.

8.190 MERLIN, Pierre (1971) *New Towns: Regional Planning and Development.* London: Methuen.

First published in French as *Les villes nouvelles* (Paris: Presses Universitaires de France, 1969). Discusses the new-town strategies of a number of countries. The most historical in flavour is the one devoted to Britain, which outlines the history of the new-town programme since the 1940s. This remains the authoritative, standard work on the new-town phenomenon, worldwide.

8.191 MITCHELL, Elizabeth B. (1967) *The Plan That Pleased.* London: Town and Country Planning Association.

Personal memoirs of a planner closely involved in the early history of the Scottish new towns, and particularly in East Kilbride.

8.192 MUNZER, Martha E. and VOGEL, John (1974) *New Towns: Building Cities from Scratch.* New York: Knopf (distributed by Random House).

A children's book. Outlines the growth of the new-town idea since Howard, and sets out the British and American achievement.

8.193 NATIONAL CAPITAL DEVELOPMENT COMMISSION (1972) Development of the New Towns of Canberra. *Studies in Comparative Local Government,* **6,** pp. 5–25.

Discusses the satellite communities built in recent years in the vicinity of the Australian capital.

8.194 *New Communities: A Bibliography* (1970). Washington D.C.: Department of Housing and Urban Development.

An official compilation relating mainly to new towns and suburban developments in North America.

8.195 New towns come of age (1968). *Town and Country Planning,* **36** (1, 2).

A special issue of the journal, including a number of contributions bearing on the history of British new towns since 1946.

8.196 NUTI, Lucia and MARTINELLI, Roberta (1978) Le città nuove del ventennio: da Mussolinia a Carbonia, in Martinelli, Roberta and Nuti, Lucia (eds.), *Le città di fondazione*. Venice: Marsilio Editori, pp. 271–93.

A full discussion of the new-town policy pursued in Fascist Italy, with analysis of the planning and architecture of some of the more outstanding examples.

8.197   ORLANS, Harold (1952) *Stevenage: A Sociological Study of a New Town*. London: Routledge and Kegan Paul.

This includes an account of the early years of the growth of Stevenage. It was published in the United States as *Utopia Ltd. : The Story of the English New Town of Stevenage* (New Haven: Yale University Press, 1953).

8.198   OSBORN, Frederic J. and WHITTICK, Arnold (1963) *The New Towns: The Answer to Megalopolis*. London: Leonard Hill.

The context is partly historical, beginning with Howard and the garden cities. Covers Britain only. A second edition was published in 1969, and a third in 1978.

8.199   PAGNINI ALBERTI, Maria P. (1969) *Columbia, una città nuova nel corridoio Baltimora-Washington: ricerca di geografia urbana*. Udine: Del Bianco.

A brief study of the development and function of a recent American new town.

8.200   PETERSEN, W. (1968) The ideological origins of Britain's New Towns. *Journal of the American Institute of Planners*, **34** (3), pp. 160–9.

A study of the intellectual currents in which garden cities and later the new towns were born.

8.201   POCOCK, D. C. D. (1960) The growth of British new towns. *Tijdschrift voor Economische en Sociale Geografie*, **51**, pp. 2–9.

Outlines the growth of population, employment, and facilities since 1946.

8.202   POWELL, David R. and BURG, Nan C. (1972) *New Towns Bibliography* (Council of Planning Librarians Exchange Bibliography no. 249). Monticello, Ill.: Council of Planning Librarians.

Some historical material.

8.203 PRAKASH, Ved (1969) *New Towns in India.* Distributed by the Cellar Bookshop, Detroit.
Some recent historical perspective.

8.204 PRESSMAN, Norman E. P. (1973) *A Comprehensive Bibliography of New Towns in Canada* (Council of Planning Librarians Exchange Bibliography no. 483). Monticello, Ill.: Council of Planning Librarians.
Includes some historical material.

8.205 PRESSMAN, Norman E. P. (1975) *Planning New Communities in Canada.* Ottawa: Ministry of State for Urban Affairs.
A concise discussion of Canadian new-town planning, with some historical perspective.

8.206 ROBINSON, Albert J. (1975) *Economics and New Towns: A Comparative Study of the United States, the United Kingdom, and Australia.* New York: Praeger.
Pays much attention to the historical development of new town policies, and is particularly eager to point to their economic weaknesses, notably in the British case.

8.207 RODWIN, Lloyd (1956) *The British New Towns Policy: Problems and Implications.* Cambridge, Mass.: Harvard University Press.
The first part of the book discusses the development of the new-town idea since Howard.

8.208 ROSNER, Rolf (1962) *Neue Städte in England.* Munich: Verlag Callwey.
Historical accounts of the first fifteen new towns.

8.209 RUSHMAN, Gordon (1976) Towards new cities in Australia. *Town Planning Review,* **47** (1), pp. 4–25.
Covers developments in the planning of new towns in Australia in recent years.

8.210 SAARINEN, Oiva (1979) The influence of Thomas Adams and the British New Towns movement in the planning of Canadian resource communities, in Artibise, A. F. J. and Stelter, G. A.

(eds.), *The Usable Urban Past: Planning and Politics in the Modern Canadian City.* Toronto: Macmillan Company of Canada.

Discusses the ways in which the British Garden City movement influenced Canadian planning, via Thomas Adams. Includes detailed case studies of two towns built to further the exploitation of forest products—Iroquois Falls and Témiscaming.

8.211 SCHAFFER, Frank (1972) 'The new town movement', in Evans, Hazel (ed.), *New Towns: The British Experience.* London: Charles Knight for Town and Country Planning Association, pp. 11–21.

Outlines the progress of the British movement since Howard.

8.212 SCHAFFER, Frank (1970) *The New Town Story.* London: MacGibbon and Kee.

Part of the book is a historical survey of the British new-town movement, since Howard.

8.213 SHKVARIKOV, V. A. (1964) *Stroitel'stvo nov'ik gorodov v SSSR.* Moscow: Strojisdat.

A study of the construction of new towns in the Soviet Union.

8.214 SMITH, P. J. (1966) Changing objectives in Scottish new towns policy. *Annals of the Association of American Geographers,* **56,** pp. 492–507.

A chronological survey of the development of Scottish new towns, beginning with Howard's theories, and ending in the early 1960s.

8.215 SMITH, Roger (1974) The origins of Scottish New Towns policy and the founding of East Kilbride. *Public Administration,* **52,** pp. 143–60.

A detailed account of the genesis of a new-town strategy for Glasgow in the 1940s.

8.216 SPIEGEL, Erika (1966) *New Towns in Israel.* Stuttgart/Berne: Karl Krämer Verlag.

Studies a number of new town projects, with recent historical perspective.

8.217 STEIN, Clarence (1951) *Towards New Towns for America*. Liverpool: Liverpool University Press.

Studies a number of American planned suburbs, settlements, and new towns since the early twentieth century.

8.218 SUTCLIFFE, Anthony (1978) New towns and the urbanisation process in Britain since industrialisation, in Martinelli, Roberta and Nuti, Lucia (eds.), *Le città di fondazione*. Venice: Marsilio Editori, pp. 239–55.

Discusses the origins and development of postwar British new-town policy, arguing that it was too abrupt a departure from the established pattern of urbanization to secure success without major modifications which eventually undermined much of the attraction of the original idea.

8.219 THOMAS, Ray and CRESSWELL, Peter (1973) *The New Town Idea*. Milton Keynes: Open University Press.

A unit of an Open University course. Includes material on the history of new towns in Britain since Howard.

8.220 TOLLEY, R. S. (1972) Telford New Town: conceptions and reality in West Midlands industrial overspill. *Town Planning Review*, 43, pp. 343–60.

Discusses some of the successes and failures in persuading industry to locate in the new town of Telford.

8.221 TROW-SMITH, Robert (1958) *The History of Stevenage*. Stevenage: Stevenage Society.

A history of the settlement from its origins, with a section devoted to the period since its designation as a new town.

8.222 TUPPEN, J. (1979) New towns in the Paris region: an appraisal. *Town Planning Review*, 50, pp. 55–70.

Outlines the Parisian 'new towns' policy from its origins in 1965 until 1978.

8.223 VASIL'EV, Boris Leonidovich (1958) *Goroda-sputniki: Harlow, Wythenshawe, Vällingby: iz op'ita gradostroitel'stva za rubezhom*. Leningrad: Gos.izd-vo lit-r'i po stroitel'stvu, arkhitekture i stroit. materialam.

A comparison of British and Swedish new-town planning and design, with some historical material.

8.224 WARNER, G. A. (1954) *Greenbelt: The Co-operative Community*. New York: Exposition Press.

A history of Greenbelt, Maryland, the best known of the new communities founded under the New Deal.

8.225 WEINER, Howard R. (1976) New towns in twentieth century Italy. *Urbanism Past and Present*, **2**, pp. 13–23.

A wide-ranging article, tracing new-town theory and practice in Italy from the Futurists through the Fascist programme of rural new towns to the company towns of the 1950s and 1960s.

8.226 WEINER, Howard R. (1978) New towns for Italians in Libya (1933–1941). *South Atlantic Urban Studies*, **2**, pp. 236–54.

On an aspect of the extension of Mussolini's new-town programme to North Africa.

8.227 WEINER, Howard R. (1978–79) New communities in Franco Spain: the rural towns of the *Instituto Nacional de Colonizacion*. *Urbanism Past and Present*, **7**, pp. 13–20.

A study of the Franco Government programme for rural new towns, which produced almost three hundred new settlements between 1942 and 1973. Strong echoes of Mussolini's new-town strategy, but Weiner stresses the continuity from earlier Spanish traditions of planned colonization.

8.228 WEISS, Shirley F. (1973) *New Town Development in the United States: Experiment in Private Entrepreneurship*. Chapel Hill: Centre for Urban and Regional Studies, University of North Carolina.

Includes a number of case studies of privately-developed new towns in the United States.

Regional planning

In the twentieth century a constant tendency is visible towards regional planning as the process of urban deconcentration has accelerated. The United States took an early lead in this area between the wars, and the Tennessee Valley Authority remains a model of ambitious regional development. However, in Germany and some other parts of Europe the origins of regional planning can be detected in the later nineteenth century, and this tradition has been reinforced since 1945.

See also 4.47, 4.48, 4.64, 4.96, 4.107, 4.112, 4.117, 4.260, 4.267, 4.270, 5.38–9, 5.116, 5.141, 5.143–4, 5.154, 5.156–7, 5.198–9, 6.3, 6.12, 8.141, 8.172, 9.38, 9.106, 9.113, 9.118.

8.229 ADAMS, Thomas (1927) *Planning the New York Region: An Outline of the Organization, Scope and Progress of the Regional Plan.* New York: Committee on Regional Plan of New York and Its Environs.

Includes a full account (pp. 31–70) of the origins and development of regional planning in the New York area between 1903 and 1926.

8.230 CHRISTIE, Jean (1970) The Mississippi Valley Committee: conservation and planning in the early New Deal. *The Historian,* 32 (3), pp. 449–69.

A narrative of the initial high hopes and eventual failure of a rural and regional planning body which might have emulated the TVA.

8.231 DAHIR, James (1955) *Region Building: Community Development Lessons from the Tennessee Valley.* New York: Harper and Bros.

A study of some of the successes and failures of the TVA.

8.232 FRIEDMANN, John (1964) The concept of a planning region: the evolution of an idea in the United States, in Friedmann, John and Alonso, William (eds.), *Regional Development and Planning: A Reader.* Cambridge, Mass.: MIT Press, pp. 497–518.

A joint reprinting of two earlier articles.

8.233 FRIEDMANN, John and WEAVER, Clyde (1979) *Territory and Function: The Evolution of Regional Planning.* London: Edward Arnold.

A worldwide history of regional planning from its American

beginnings in the 1920s, ending with proposals for an 'agropolitan' planning suitable for the Third World.

8.234 HAMILTON, F. E. Ian (1976) *The Moscow City Region*. London: Oxford University Press.

This includes a great deal of historical material on the evolution and planning of the Moscow area since the Revolution, with full discussion of the Moscow plan of 1935 and its successors.

8.235 HAYS, Forbes B. (1965) *Community Leadership: The Regional Plan Association of New York*. New York/London: Columbia University Press.

A history of the activities of the Association from its foundation in 1929 until the early 1960s, concentrating on its internal organization and motivation. Stresses the great difficulties which it has faced in mobilizing opinion and in coordinating the study of the planning of the New York region. Includes (pp. 5–21) an outline of the development of the regional planning idea in New York between the early 1900s and 1929.

8.236 HEBEBRAND, W., KEIL, G. and SPECKTER, H. (1962) La città regione di Amburgo. *Casabella*, **270**, pp. 26–59.

On planning developments in Hamburg and its region since the nineteenth century.

8.237 JACHNIAK-GANGULY, Danuta (1978) Spatial planning in Poland and local government reorganization, 1961–75, in Hayward, Jack and Narkiewicz, Olga A. (eds.), *Planning in Europe*. London: Croom Helm, pp. 147–68.

Includes brief discussion of recent changes in the organization of regional planning in Poland, with main emphasis on developments since the later 1960s.

8.238 JOHNSON, David Alan (1974) The emergence of metropolitan regionalism: an analysis of the 1929 Regional Plan of New York and its Environs. Unpublished Ph.D. thesis, Cornell University.

A full study of one of the world's earliest regional plans, published in 1930, product of developments under way in New York reforming circles since before the First World War.

8.239 KANTOR, Harvey A. (1973) Charles Dyer Norton and the origins of the Regional Plan of New York. *Journal of the American Institute of Planners*, **39** (1), pp. 35–42.

A narrative of Norton's involvement in urban reform and planning in New York from the early 1900s until his death in 1923, followed by a brief assessment of the value of the Regional Plan.

8.240 KOCHER, Sandra (1979) *Appalachian Trail*. Portland, Or.: Graphic Arts Center Publishing Company.

Discusses the conception and realization of the Trail as an episode in the development of regional planning in the United States between the wars. Throws some light on Benton MacKaye, creator of the Trail.

8.241 LAPPO, G. M. (1973) Trends in the evolution of settlement patterns in the Moscow region. *Soviet Geography: Review and Translation*, **14** (1), pp. 13–24.

Contrasts the intentions of the Moscow regional plan with the actual course of development.

8.242 LOJKINE, Jean (1972) *La politique urbaine dans la région parisienne, 1945–72*. Paris: Mouton.

An analysis of the progress of planning policies in the Paris area since 1945, with main emphasis on transport planning.

8.243 LOJKINE, Jean (1974) *La politique urbaine dans la région lyonnaise, 1945–1972*. Paris: Mouton.

An analysis and critique of urban and regional planning in the Lyons region since the end of the Second World War.

8.244 McCRAW, Thomas K. (1971) *TVA and the Power Fight, 1933–1939*. Philadelphia: J. B. Lippincott.

A political history of the early years of the TVA.

8.245 MARTIN, Roscoe C. (ed.) (1956) *TVA: The First Twenty Years: A Staff Report*. Knoxville: University of Tennessee Press.

A progress report on the work of the Tennessee Valley Authority.

8.246 MORGAN, Arthur E. (1974) *The Making of the TVA*. Buffalo: Prometheus Books.
An autobiographical account of the history of the TVA in the 1930s by the one-time chairman of its board of directors.

8.247 MUGGLI, Hugo W. (1968) *Greater London und seine New Towns: Studien zur kulturräumlichen Entwicklung und Planung einer großstädtischen Region*. Basle: Helbing and Lichtenhahn for Geographisch-Ethnologische Gesellschaft.
A study of the postwar planning and development of the London region.

8.248 PRITCHETT, C. Herman (1943) *The Tennessee Valley Authority: A Study of Public Administration*. Chapel Hill: University of North Carolina Press.
A full analysis of the workings of the TVA between its establishment in 1933 and the early 1940s.

8.249 REBENTISCH, Dieter (1975) Anfänge der Regionalplanung und Raumordnung im Rhein-Main-Gebiet. *Hessisches Jahrbuch für Landesgeschichte*, **25**, pp. 307–39.
Discusses the development of regional organization and planning in the Frankfurt area before and after the First World War.

8.250 REBENTISCH, Dieter (1978) Politik und Raumplanung im Rhein-Main-Gebiet: Kontinuität und Wandel seit hundert Jahren. *Archiv für Frankfurts Geschichte und Kunst*, **56**, pp. 191–210.
A discussion of the development of regional government and planning in the Frankfurt region since the later nineteenth century.

8.251 RODWIN, Lloyd (1969) *Planning Urban Growth and Regional Development: The Experience of the Guayana Program of Venezuela*. Cambridge, Mass.: MIT Press.
A thorough, historical study of the planning of the Ciudad Guayana region since the early 1960s.

8.252 STANDING CONFERENCE ON LONDON AND SOUTH-EAST REGIONAL PLANNING (1974) *A History of the Conference and Its Work, 1962–1974*. London: S.C.L.S.E.R.P.

A brief and anodyne 'official' account of the work of this South-East regional planning body between its inauguration in 1962 and its re-establishment on the occasion of local government reorganization in 1974.

8.253 STANDING CONFERENCE ON LONDON AND SOUTH-EAST REGIONAL PLANNING (1974) *London and South-East England: Regional Planning, 1943–1974*. London: S.C.L.S.E.R.P.

A brief 'official' account of major developments in the planning of the region.

8.254 STRUTHERS, W. A. K. and WILLIAMSON, C. B. (1979) Local economic development: integrated policy planning and implementation in Merseyside. *Town Planning Review*, 50, pp. 164–84.

Outlines progress in local economic planning between 1947 and 1979.

8.255 SUSSMAN, Carl (ed.) (1976) *Planning the Fourth Migration: The Neglected Vision of the Regional Planning Association of America*. Cambridge, Mass.: MIT Press.

A collection of texts generated by the Association during its key period of activity in the 1920s and 1930s, preceded by a lengthy introduction by the editor on the pioneering significance of the Association's work.

8.256 TAYLOR, Brian Brace (1978) The 'villes nouvelles' in France, in Martinelli, Roberta and Nuti, Lucia (eds.), *Le città di fondazione*. Venice: Marsilio Editori, pp. 232–8.

A brief sketch of developments in the planning of the Paris region from the 1920s to the 1970s.

8.257 *West Midland Group Handlist: Guide to the Papers of the West Midland Group on Post-War Reconstruction and Planning* (1969). Birmingham: Centre for Urban and Regional Studies, Birmingham University.

A guide to the archives (deposited in Birmingham University Library) of the West Midland Group, a semi-official regional planning committee which published a series of influential reports in the 1940s.

Additional entries

9.1 AKAGI, Suruki (1968) Toshi keikaku no keikaku-sei, in *Toshi Kōzō to Toshi Keikaku*. Tokyo: Tokyo Toritsu Daigaku Toshi Kenkyū-kai, pp. 499–566.

Discusses the enactment of the Japanese City Planning Act of 1919 and explains why its powers subsequently lost their comprehensive character.

9.2 ALANEN, Arnold R. (1979) The planning of company communities: the Lake Superior mining region. *Journal of the American Planning Association*, 45 (3), pp. 256–78.

A study of the building and planning of company towns in Wisconsin and Minnesota.

9.3 ALBERS, Gerd (1980) Das Stadtplanungsrecht im 20. Jahrhundert als Niederschlag der Wandlungen im Planungsverständnis. *Stadtbauwelt*, 65, pp. 485–90.

Discusses the development of planning law in Germany since the early twentieth century, arguing that it has generally reflected progress in planning practice.

9.4 ALBERS, Gerd (1980) Town planning in Germany: change and continuity under conditions of political turbulence, in Cherry, Gordon E. (ed.), *Shaping an Urban World: Planning in the Twentieth Century*. London: Mansell, pp. 145–60.

The English translation of 4.57.

9.5 ALDRIDGE, Meryl (1979) *The British New Towns: A Programme Without a Policy*. London: Routledge and Kegan Paul.

A full, critical history of the British new-towns programme, from its origins in Howard's ideas to its partial eclipse in the later

1970s. It questions whether there has ever been a single, coherent new-town strategy, rather than an amalgam of more or less related policies.

9.6   ALDUY, Jean-Paul (1979) L'aménagement de la région de Paris entre 1930 et 1975: de la planification à la politique urbaine. *Sociologie du Travail*, no. 2, pp. 167–200.
Outlines the course of the planning of the Paris region since the 1930s.

9.7   ALTEZOR, Carlos and BARACCHINI, Hugo (1971) *Historia urbanística y edilicia de la ciudad de Montevideo*. Montevideo: Junta Departamental de Montevideo.
A full planning and building history of Montevideo.

9.8   APPLEYARD, Donald (1978) The major published works of Kevin Lynch: an appraisal. *Town Planning Review*, **49** (4), pp. 551–7.
Assesses the impact of Lynch's thinking on worldwide planning orthodoxy since *The Image of the City* was published in 1960.

9.9   ARTIBISE, Alan F. J. and STELTER, Gilbert A. (1980) Conservation planning and urban planning: the Canadian Commission of Conservation in historical perspective, in Kain, Roger (ed.), *Planning for Conservation: An International Perspective*. London: Mansell, pp. 17–36.
Discusses the activities of Canada's first national planning body during its brief existence, 1909–21. Stresses the close link in Canada between conservation and urban planning. All this is incorporated into a broader consideration of Canadian urbanization and urban policy since the later nineteenth century. Some reference is made to the contribution of Thomas Adams.

9.10 ASH, Joan (1974) The progress of new towns in Israel. *Town Planning Review*, **45** (4), pp. 387–400.
A full review of the Israeli new-town programme since 1948.

9.11 BARNETT, Henrietta (1918) *Canon Barnett: His Life, Work and Friends* (2 vols.). London: John Murray.

Reissued in one volume in 1921. Includes a chapter on Hampstead Garden Suburb, and throws intermittent light elsewhere on the involvement of Samuel and Henrietta Barnett in urban reform.

9.12 BATER, James (1980) *The Soviet City*. London: Edward Arnold.

An introduction to the Soviet experience of urbanization, aimed mainly at undergraduates. Includes much discussion of planning, with historical perspective.

9.13 BEBBINGTON, D. W. (1979) The city, the countryside and the social gospel in late Victorian nonconformity, in Baker, Derek (ed.), *The Church in Town and Countryside*. Oxford: Basil Blackwell, pp. 415–26.

In an unusual interpretation, this stresses the contribution of Nonconformity to the genesis of the town-planning idea in Britain, c. 1880–1900.

9.14 BLIJSTRA, Reinder (1969) *2000 jaar Utrecht: stedebouwkundige ontwikkeling van castrum tot centrum*. Utrecht: Bruna.

A lengthy building and planning history of Utrecht.

9.15 BOLLEREY, Franziska and HARTMANN, Kristiana (1980) *Kappes – Kohle – Kolonie: Wohnen und Wohnumwelt im Ruhrgebiet*. Munich: H. Moos Verlag.

Information incomplete at time of going to press, but presumably includes more of these authors' work on employers' housing in the Ruhr, c. 1840–1940. Illustrated.

9.16 BOLLEREY, Franziska and HARTMANN, Kristiana (1980) A patriarchal utopia: the garden city and housing reform in Germany at the turn of the century, in Sutcliffe, Anthony (ed.), *The Rise of Modern Urban Planning, 1800–1914*. London: Mansell, pp. 135–65.

A survey of the rise of the housing-reform movement in nineteenth-century Germany, and its apotheosis in the German version of the garden-city movement. Includes case studies of Hellerau and Falkenberg. Also informative on employers' housing in the Ruhr.

9.17 BREITLING, Peter (1980) The origins and development of a conservation philosophy in Austria, in Kain, Roger (ed.), *Planning for Conservation: An International Perspective*. London: Mansell, pp. 49–61.

Includes a brief survey of the development of the urban conservation movement in Austria since the nineteenth century.

9.18 BREITLING, Peter (1980) The role of the competition in the genesis of urban planning: Germany and Austria in the nineteenth century, in Sutcliffe, Anthony (ed.), *The Rise of Modern Urban Planning, 1800–1914*. London: Mansell, pp. 31–54.

Argues that open competitions contributed substantially to the evolution of planning theory and technique in the German-speaking world in the nineteenth century. Makes special reference to competitions at Vienna and Munich.

9.19 BRENNE, Winfried and PITZ, Helga (1980) *Siedlung Onkel Tom— Berlin Zehlendorf: Einfamilien-Reihenhäuser 1929; Architekt Bruno Taut*. Berlin: Mann.

A lengthy, illustrated study of a housing estate by Bruno Taut.

9.20 BROWNELL, Blaine A. (1980) Urban planning, the planning profession, and the motor vehicle in early twentieth-century America, in Cherry, Gordon E. (ed.), *Shaping an Urban World: Planning in the Twentieth Century*. London: Mansell, pp. 59–78.

A discussion of major tendencies in U.S. urban planning between c. 1910 and c. 1930, with special reference to the impact of the motor vehicle. Argues that planners used the motor vehicle as an excuse to move away from broader concerns of urban reform, and to establish their professional credibility by providing technical solutions to specific physical problems.

9.21 BUSBY, Richard J. (1976) *The Book of Welwyn: The Story of the Five Villages and the Garden City*. Chesham: Barracuda Books.

Includes an account of the planning and development of Welwyn Garden City, both before and after its designation as a New Town.

9.22 CALABI, Donatella (1980) The genesis and special characteristics of town-planning instruments in Italy, 1880–1914, in Sutcliffe,

Anthony (ed.), *The Rise of Modern Urban Planning, 1800–1914*. London: Mansell, pp. 55–70.

Argues, with special reference to a number of medium-sized towns in the Veneto, that mature urban planning did not emerge in Italy before 1914.

9.23 CARTER, F. W. (1979) Prague and Sofia: an analysis of their changing internal city structure, in French, R. A. and Hamilton, F. E. Ian (eds.), *The Socialist City: Spatial Structure and Urban Policy*. Chichester: John Wiley and Sons, pp. 425–59.

Assesses the impact of socialist planning on Prague and Sofia since 1945.

9.24 CHERRY, Gordon E. (1980) Introduction: aspects of twentieth-century planning, in Cherry, Gordon E. (ed.), *Shaping an Urban World: Planning in the Twentieth Century*. London: Mansell, pp. 1–22.

Identifies a number of key issues in the discussion by historians of the development of urban and regional planning in the twentieth century.

9.25 CHERRY, Gordon E. (1980) The place of Neville Chamberlain in British town planning, in Cherry, Gordon E. (ed.), *Shaping an Urban World: Planning in the Twentieth Century*. London: Mansell, pp. 161–80.

Investigates a neglected phase in the career of Neville Chamberlain, as Minister of Health in the 1920s. Argues that Chamberlain's national achievement in housing and slum improvement was an extension of his earlier involvement in Birmingham's pioneering planning and environmental policies.

9.26 *City Planning of Tokyo* (TMG Municipal Library, no. 13) (1978). Tokyo: Tokyo Metropolitan Government.

Includes a brief outline of the history of planning legislation in Japan, and provides some slight historical perspective on Tokyo planning since the 1850s.

9.27 CIUCCI, Giorgio, DAL CO, Francesco, MANIERI-ELIA, Mario and TAFURI, Manfredo (1980) *The American City: From the Civil War to the New Deal*. London: Granada.

The English translation of 4.267.

9.28 COHEN, Yehoshua (1972) *Diffusion of an Innovation in an Urban System: The Spread of Planned Regional Shopping Centers in the United States, 1949–1968* (Department of Geography Research Paper no. 140). Chicago: Department of Geography, University of Chicago.

A study of the diffusion of large suburban shopping centres in the context of urban planning policies, and their impact on surrounding urban areas.

9.29 COLLINS, George R. and COLLINS, Christiane C. (1980) Camillo Sitte reappraised, in Kain, Roger (ed.), *Planning for Conservation: An International Perspective*. London: Mansell, pp. 63–73.

Updates the conclusions published in 6.120, in the light of more recent literature and debate. Reiterates the central importance of Sitte's contribution to the emergence of modern planning.

9.30 COLLINS, John (1980) Lusaka: urban planning in a British colony, 1931–64, in Cherry, Gordon E. (ed.), *Shaping an Urban World: Planning in the Twentieth Century*. London: Mansell, pp. 227–42.

A history of the planning and building of a new administrative capital for Northern Rhodesia (Zambia), and its evolution up to independence.

9.31 CULLINGWORTH, J. B. (1979) *Environmental Planning 1939–1969. Vol. III: New Towns Policy*. London: H.M.S.O.

A detailed study of the formulation and application of the British new-towns policy, from the early 1940s until 1969, based almost entirely on central government documents. Also covers the town development programme, from 1952 onwards. Sober, 'official history' approach.

9.32 CUNNINGHAM, Susan M. (1980) Brazilian cities old and new: growth and planning experiences, in Cherry, Gordon E. (ed.), *Shaping an Urban World: Planning in the Twentieth Century*. London: Mansell, pp. 181–202.

An analysis of the progress of urban planning in Brazil since the 1920s, stressing its defects, with special reference to Rio de Janeiro, São Paulo, Belo Horizonte and Brasilia.

9.33 DE MARTINO, U. (1966) Cento anni di dibattito nel risanamento dei centri storici: note bibliografiche. *Rassegna dell'Istituto di Architettura e Urbanistica*, **4**, pp. 75–116.

Outlines the debate on the conservation of isolated monuments and historic areas in Italian towns between its mid-nineteenth-century beginnings and the present day.

9.34 DE PAOLIS, Saverio and RAVAGLIOLI, Armando (eds.) (1971) *La Terza Roma: lo sviluppo urbanistico, edilizio e tecnico di Roma capitale*. Rome: Fratelli Palombi.

A collection of articles providing comprehensive coverage of the planning of Rome since the later nineteenth century.

9.35 DIX, Gerald (1978) Little plans and noble diagrams. *Town Planning Review*, **49** (3), pp. 329–52.

A survey of the career, and some of the planning schemes, of Patrick Abercrombie until about 1940.

9.36 DONNISON, David with SOTO, Paul (1980) *The Good City: A Study of Urban Development and Policy in Britain*. London: Heinemann.

Includes (pp. 3–37) a brief but perceptive survey of the development of planning since 1947. Argues that while urban planners have become increasingly aware of their dependence on economic factors, social reformers have recognized that their own work has a spatial dimension.

9.37 DÜLFFER, Jost, THIES, Jochen and HENKE, Josef (1978) *Hitlers Städte: Baupolitik im Dritten Reich*. Vienna: Böhlau Verlag.

A collection of documents relating to plans for Berlin, Munich, Hamburg, Nuremburg and Linz, with an introduction on Hitler's general planning objectives.

9.38 ESTALL, Robert (1977) Regional planning in the United States: an evaluation of experience under the 1965 Economic Development Act. *Town Planning Review*, **48** (4), pp. 341–64.

Assesses progress in regional planning in the United States, 1965–75.

9.39 *L'expérience française des villes nouvelles* (1970). Paris: Fondation Nationale des Sciences Politiques.

An appraisal of the French new-towns policy up to 1970.

9.40 EVENSON, Norma (1980) The city as an artifact: building control in modern Paris, in Kain, Roger (ed.), *Planning for Conservation: An International Perspective*. London: Mansell, pp. 000–00.
Analyses the impact of changing building regulations on the Parisian townscape since the nineteenth century.

9.41 FANELLI, Giovanni (1978) *Architettura, edilizia, urbanistica: Olanda 1917–1940*. Monteoriolo: F. Papafeva.
A lengthy, illustrated study of architecture and town planning in the Netherlands between the wars.

9.42 FEHL, Gerhard (1980) Stadtbaukunst contra Stadtplanung: zur Auseinandersetzung Camillo Sittes mit Reinhard Baumeister. *Stadtbauwelt*, 65, pp. 451–61.
Analyses and sets in context Sitte's attack on Baumeister's approach to urban planning.

9.43 FISCHER, Friedrich (1971) *Die Grünflächenpolitik Wiens bis zum Ende des Ersten Weltkrieges*. Vienna/New York: Springer in Komm.
Based on the author's university thesis of 1959, this outlines the development of park design and open-space policy in Vienna in the nineteenth century.

9.44 FISHMAN, Robert (1980) The anti-planners: the contemporary revolt against planning and its significance for planning history, in Cherry, Gordon E. (ed.), *Shaping an Urban World: Planning in the Twentieth Century*. London: Mansell, pp. 243–52.
Discusses the contribution to planning's current malaise of a number of critics of rational, scientific, inhuman planning.

9.45 FRENCH, R. A. (1979) The individuality of the Soviet city, in French, R. A. and Hamilton, F. E. Ian (eds.), *The Socialist City: Spatial Structure and Urban Policy*. Chichester: John Wiley and Sons, pp. 73–104.
Though primarily an analysis of the outstanding geographical features of the contemporary Russian city, this makes much reference to the development of Soviet planning theory and practice since 1917, and their effect on urban form and living conditions.

9.46 FRENCH, R. A. and HAMILTON, F. E. Ian (1979) Is there a socialist city?, in French, R. A. and Hamilton, F. E. Ian (eds.), *The Socialist City: Spatial Structure and Urban Policy*. Chichester: John Wiley and Sons, pp. 1–22.

Includes a brief but incisive discussion of the main trends and elements in the socialist approach to urban planning since 1917. Stresses the difficulty of translating ideal forms into practice, and suggests important similarities between socialist and capitalist cities.

9.47 FUKUOKA, Shunji (1971–72) Taishō-kiino toshi seisaku: jūtaku toshi keikaku kōso no tenkai. *Tokyo Toritsu Daigaku Hōgakkai Zasshi*, 11 (2), 12 (1), 13 (1), pp. 1–81.

A study of the origins, development and collapse of the 'housing-planning vision' developed in the 1920s by Goto Shimpei, Ikeda Hiroshi, and their group (Toshi Kenkyu-kai).

9.48 GALANTAY, Ervin Y. (1978) The planning of Owerri: a new capital for Imo state, Nigeria. *Town Planning Review*, 49 (3), pp. 371–86.

A study of the planning and building of a new town in Nigeria since the early 1960s.

9.49 GASKELL, Martin (1979) Model industrial villages in S. Yorkshire/ N. Derbyshire and the early town planning movement. *Town Planning Review*, 50 (4), pp. 437–58.

Discusses the economic and social context of the model mining communities of Bolsover, Cresswell, Woodlands and Edlington, and assesses their contribution to early British town-planning theory and practice. Also discusses early regional planning in the Doncaster area.

9.50 GEHRMANN, Werner (1980) Die Baugeschichte Berlins von 1648 bis 1918. *Stadtbauwelt*, 65, pp. 491–7.

A brief survey of the building and planning history of Berlin, 1648–1918.

9.51 GEROSA, Pier Giorgio (1979) Le Corbusier: éléments architecturaux pour la synthèse urbaine. *Cahiers de l'Institut d'Urbanisme et d'Aménagement régional* (Université des Sciences Humaines de Strasbourg), 1, pp. 26–44.

Discusses the various elements which combined to create Le Corbusier's concept of the ideal urban structure.

9.52 GILG, Andrew W. (1980) Planning for nature conservation: a struggle for survival and political respectability, in Kain, Roger (ed.), *Planning for Conservation: An International Perspective*. London: Mansell, pp. 97–116.

Discusses the fundamental philosophy of nature conservation, with much reference to developments since the nineteenth century.

9.53 GILLIE, Blaise (1980) Landmarks in the history of British town and country planning (1909–1939). *Planning History Bulletin*, 2 (1), pp. 5–11.

Seeks to establish what can be universally agreed about the contribution of the major pieces of planning legislation, 1909–1939, in order to clear the ground for debate on their more contentious aspects.

9.54 GOLDFIELD, David R. (1980) Planning for urban growth in the Old South, in Sutcliffe, Anthony (ed.), *The Rise of Modern Urban Planning, 1800–1914*. London: Mansell, pp. 11–30.

Surveys the environmental policies pursued in a number of Southern cities before the Civil War, arguing that they amounted to a coherent planning policy.

9.55 GOTTMANN, Jean (1980) Planning and metamorphosis in Japan: a note. *Town Planning Review*, 51 (2), pp. 171–6.

Briefly surveys the development of urban and regional planning in Japan since the 1960s.

9.56 GRANATSTEIN, J. L. (1971) *Marlborough Marathon: One Street Against a Developer*. Toronto: A. M. Hakkert.

Case study of an episode in Toronto urban renewal in the 1960s.

9.57 GUTHEIM, Frederick (1977) *Worthy of the Nation: The History of Planning for the National Capital*. Washington, D.C.: Smithsonian Institution Press.

An exhaustive, richly-illustrated history of the planning of

Washington 1790–1976, including some discussion of recent regional planning. Author indexes in some libraries may classify this book under National Capital Planning Commission rather than Gutheim.

9.58 HAJDU, J. G. (1979) Phases in the post-war German urban experience. *Town Planning Review*, **50** (3), pp. 267–86.

Reviews the major features of, and tendencies in, West German planning since 1945.

9.59 HALL, Peter (1980) *Great Planning Disasters*. London: Weidenfeld and Nicolson.

A collection of case studies of engineering and planning projects since the 1950s, which were completed at costs out of all proportion to those originally envisaged, which failed to bring about the results expected of them, or were abandoned before completion owing to an accumulation of problems. The main emphasis is on transport projects, and the most relevant to the interests of this bibliography are the studies of Bay Area Rapid Transit (San Francisco–Oakland), the London motorway box, and the third London airport. The book is written with all this author's customary panache, and is held together by a stimulating theory of planning inertia and obsolescence in long-term projects.

9.60 HAMILTON, F. E. Ian (1979) Spatial structure in East European cities, in French, R. A. and Hamilton, F. E. Ian (eds.), *The Socialist City: Spatial Structure and Urban Policy*. Chichester: John Wiley and Sons, pp. 195–261.

A very thorough analysis of the impact of socialist urban planning policies in the countries of Eastern Europe incorporated into the Communist world since 1945. The main emphasis is on Poland. Despite the weight of the pre-1945 legacy, Hamilton argues that a distinctive socialist urban structure is emerging.

9.61 HARRISON, M. L. (1974) British town planning ideology and the Welfare State. *Journal of Social Policy*, **4** (3), pp. 259–74.

Discusses the links between urban planning and social policy in Britain.

9.62 HEINEBERG, Heinz (1979) Service centres in East and West Berlin, in French, R. A. and Hamilton, F. E. Ian (eds.), *The Socialist City: Spatial Structure and Urban Policy*. Chichester: John Wiley and Sons, pp. 305–34.
A thorough study of the planning of the business and administrative districts of East and West Berlin since 1945.

9.63 HORIUCHI, Ryōichi (1978) *Toshi keikaku to yōto chiikisei: Tokyo-to ni okeru sono enkaku to tenbō*. Tokyo: Nishida Shoten.
A study of zoning in Tokyo, with some historical perspective.

9.64 HOUGHTON-EVANS, W. (1980) Schemata in British new town planning, in Cherry, Gordon E. (ed.), *Shaping an Urban World: Planning in the Twentieth Century*. London: Mansell, pp. 101–28.
Isolates and appraises some of the distinctive design features of the British new towns.

9.65 ISHIDA, Yorifusa (1968) Daitoshi-ken no hattatsu to keikaku: sengo no Tokyo daitoshi keikaku no hensen, in *Toshi Kōzō to Toshi Keikaku*. Tokyo: Tokyo Toritsu Daigaku Toshi Kenkyū-kai, pp. 621–64.
On reconstruction planning in postwar Tokyo.

9.66 ISHIDA, Yorifusa (1978) Nihon ni okeru shigaika yokusei no tame no chiikisei no hatten: 1945 nen made, in *Toshi Keikaku to Kyojū Kankyō: Kawana kichiemon sensei taikan kinen ronbun-shū*. Tokyo: Tokyo Toritsu Daigaku Toshi Keikaku Kenkyū-shitsu, pp. 181–202.
Analyses the historical development of zoning techniques in Japan.

9.67 ISHIDA, Yorifusa and IKEDA, Takayuki (1979) Kenchiku-sen seido ni kansuru kenkyū (1). *Sōgō Toshi Kenkyū*, 6, pp. 33–72.
On the history of building-line control in Japan.

9.68 ISHIZUKA, Hiromichi (1971) 19 seiki ni okeru Tokyo kaizō-ron to chikkō mondai. *Toshi Kenkyu Hōkoku*, 22, pp. 33–59.
An analysis of the planning process of the Tokyo City Improvement Programme of 1888.

9.69 IWAMI, Ryōtaro (1978) *Tochi Kukaku Seiri no Kenkyū: Kukakū Seiri no Mondaiten to Sono Kōzō*. Tokyo: Jichitai Kenkyūsha.
Outlines the historical development of land consolidation, a key instrument of Japanese urban planning.

9.70 JOHNSON, Donald Leslie (1979) *Canberra and Walter Burley Griffin* (Architecture Series: Bibliography A-97). Monticello, Ill.: Vance Bibliographies.
A brief collection of printed items relating to Griffin's work at Canberra.

9.71 JONAS, Stephan (1979) De la famille au quartier: la conception d'unités de vie sociale dans la pensée et les projets utopiques-socialistes chez Thomas More, Owen et Fourier. *Cahiers de l'Institut d'Urbanisme et d'Aménagement régional* (Université des Sciences Humaines de Strasbourg), 1, pp. 91–115.
An analysis of the architectural implications of the ideas of More, Owen and Fourier on the articulation of the various social units envisaged in their ideal schemes.

9.72 KAHN, Judd (1979) *Imperial San Francisco: Politics and Planning in an American City, 1897–1906*. Lincoln: University of Nebraska Press.
A full analysis of the rise of the city-planning movement in San Francisco from about 1900, and an explanation of why it failed to produce an enlightened reconstruction of the city after the fire of 1906. Includes full discussion of the Burnham plan of 1905, but, in contrast to earlier work on this episode, seeks to elucidate the economic and political context which restricted the men of vision.

9.73 KAIN, Roger (1980) Conservation planning in France: policy and practice in the Marais, Paris, in Kain, Roger (ed.), *Planning for Conservation: An International Perspective*. London: Mansell, pp. 199–233.
A detailed study of the Marais conservation scheme since the 1950s, in the context of general developments in French urban conservation policy and legislation.

9.74 KAIN, Roger (1980) Introduction: definitions, attitudes and debates, in Kain, Roger (ed.), *Planning for Conservation: An International Perspective*. London: Mansell, pp. 1–15.

Includes some reference to the historic development of the urban and rural conservation movements since the nineteenth century.

9.75 KAWAKAMI, Hidemitsu and ISHIDA, Yorifusa (1960) Henbō suru toshi: tenki o mukaeta sengo Nihon no toshi keikaku, in *Kenchiku Nenkan, 1960*. Tokyo: Bijutsu Shuppansha.
A study of postwar urban reconstruction in Japan until 1960.

9.76 KAWANA, Kichiemon (1968) Shōwa shoki no toshi keikaku, in *Toshi Kōzō to Toshi Keikaku*. Tokyo: Tokyo Toritsu Daigaku Toshi Kenkyū-kai, pp. 567–76.
A brief history of Japanese planning during the Second World War.

9.77 KING, A. D. (1980) Exporting planning: the colonial and neo-colonial experience, in Cherry, Gordon E. (ed.), *Shaping an Urban World: Planning in the Twentieth Century*. London: Mansell, pp. 203–26.
A revised version of 3.58.

9.78 KNEILE, Heinz (1979) *Stadterweiterungen und Stadtplanung im 19. Jahrhundert: Auswirkungen des ökonomischen und sozialen Strukturwandels auf die Stadtphysiognomie im Grossherzogtum Baden*. Freiburg: Wagner.
Discusses the impact of town-extension and other town-planning schemes on towns in Baden in the nineteenth century. Illustrated.

9.79 KONVITZ, Josef W. (1980) L'urbanisme des ports et du littoral (1780–1980). *Urbi*, 4.
A wide-ranging survey of urban design and planning in seaports and other coast and lakeside cities (including Nice, Antwerp and Chicago).

9.80 KOSHIZAWA, Akira (1978) *Shokuminchi Manshū no Toshi Keikaku*. Tokyo: Asia Kenkyu-jo.
A study of Japanese planning in Manchuria during the occupation period.

9.81 KRABBE, Wolfgang R. (1978) Das Verhältnis von Staat,

Gesellschaft und Gemeinde und die unterschiedliche Einschätzung der industriellen Zukunft: der Fall des Dortmunder Bebauungsplans von 1858. *Beiträge zur Geschichte Dortmunds und der Grafschaft Mark*, **71**, pp. 163–98.

A study of the Dortmund extension plan of 1858, in its administrative and economic context.

9.82 LANE, James B. (1978) *'City of the Century': A History of Gary, Indiana.* Bloomington: Indiana University Press.

A history of one of the largest U.S. company towns.

9.83 Leslie Patrick Abercrombie: a centenary note (1979). *Town Planning Review*, **50** (3), pp. 257–64.

An outline of Abercrombie's career and assessment of his contribution to British planning.

9.84 LEVERHULME (William Hulme Lever, 2nd Viscount) (1927) *Viscount Leverhulme, By His Son.* Boston: Houghton Mifflin.

A full biography of W. H. Lever, including his work at Port Sunlight, in the British town-planning movement, and in the regeneration of the Western Isles.

9.85 LEVIN, P. H. (1976) *Government and the Planning Process: An Analysis and Appraisal of Government Decision-making Processes with Special Reference to the Launching of New Towns and Town Development Schemes.* London: Allen and Unwin.

A study in public administration, thoroughly investigating the decision-making processes employed in launching new-town and town-development schemes. Includes case studies of Central Lancashire New Town and Swindon.

9.86 MABEY, Richard (1980) *The Common Ground: A Place for Nature in Britain's Future?* London: Hutchinson.

Includes a review of the history of nature conservancy in Britain.

9.87 McKEE, William C. (1979) The Vancouver park system, 1886–1929: a product of local businessmen. *Urban History Review*, no. 3, pp. 33–49.

A history of the early decades of park planning in Vancouver.

9.88 MAKIELSKI, Stanislaw J. (1969) *Local Planning in Virginia: Development, Politics and Prospects*. Charlottesville: Institute of Government, University of Virginia.
Some historical perspective.

9.89 MARCUSE, Peter (1980) Housing in early city planning. *Journal of Urban History*, 6 (2), pp. 153–76.
A more succinct version of the following item.

9.90 MARCUSE, Peter (1980) Housing policy and city planning: the puzzling split in the United States, 1893–1931, in Cherry, Gordon E. (ed.), *Shaping an Urban World: Planning in the Twentieth Century*. London: Mansell, pp. 23–58.
Points out the early split (c. 1909) between the housing-reform and city-planning movements in the United States, and argues that both movements have been irreparably weakened and distorted by it.

9.91 MELLER, Helen (1980) Cities and evolution: Patrick Geddes as an international prophet of town planning before 1914, in Sutcliffe, Anthony (ed.), *The Rise of Modern Urban Planning, 1800–1914*. London: Mansell, pp. 199–224.
A succinct survey and analysis of the development of Geddes's ideas in their relationship to planning. Stresses the complexity of his thinking, and his (not entirely unrelated) difficulties in getting his message across.

9.92 MILLER, Mervyn (1979) Garden City influence on the evolution of housing policy. *Local Government Studies*, 5 (6), pp. 5–22.
Not seen at time of going to press.

9.93 MUNN, Robert F. (1979) Development of model towns in the bituminous coal fields. *West Virginia History*, 40 (3), pp. 243–54.
One of a swelling wave of publications on U.S. company towns.

9.94 MUTHESIUS, Stefan (1980) The origins of the German conservation movement, in Kain, Roger (ed.), *Planning for Conservation: An International Perspective*. London: Mansell, pp. 37–48.
A brief discussion of the urban conservation movement in

Germany c. 1900, relating it to trends in art, philosophy, social reform and politics.

9.95 NISHIYAMA, Uzō and YOSHINO, Shōji (1973) Toshi keikaku gakusetsu-shi gaisetsu, in Kawano, Yoshikatsu (ed.), *Toshi Jichi Gakusetsu-shi Gaisetsu: Tokyo Shisei Shōsa-kai 50 Shūnen Kinen Ronbunshū*. Tokyo: Tokyo Shisei Chosa-kai, pp. 100–29.
An interpretation of the development of Japanese planning theories between 1868 and the end of the Second World War.

9.96 NOVY, Klaus and UHLIG, Günther (1980) Stadt – Land – Wirtschaft: Begründungsdilemma eines wirtschaftlichen Städtebaus am Beispiel des Werkes Martin Wagners. *Stadtbauwelt*, 65, pp. 468–72.
A discussion of German urban planning under the Weimar Republic with special reference to the work of Martin Wagner (1885–1957).

9.97 NOWLAN, David and Nadine (1970) *The Bad Trip: The Untold Story of the Spadina Expressway*. Toronto: New Press/House of Anansi.
Blow-by-blow account of a Toronto planning episode of the 1960s.

9.98 ORAVEC, C. (1979) Studies in the rhetoric of the conservation movement in America, 1865–1913. Unpublished Ph.D. thesis, University of Wisconsin-Madison.
No information at time of going to press.

9.99 PELTZ-DRECKMANN, Ute (1978) *Nationalsozialistischer Siedlungsbau: Versuch einer Analyse der die Siedlungspolitik bestimmenden Faktoren am Beispiel des Nationalsozialismus*. Munich: Minerva.
A lengthy study of the design of residential areas in Germany during the Third Reich.

.100 PENDERGRASS, Lee F. (1977) Urban reform and voluntary association: the Municipal League of Seattle, 1910–1916, in Ebner, Michael H. and Tobin, Eugene M. (eds.), *The Age of Urban Reform: New Perspectives on the Progressive Era*. Port Washington: Kennikat Press, pp. 55–67.
Includes a brief discussion of a civic improvement plan for

Seattle by Virgil Bogue, finally rejected in 1912 as too visionary.

9.101 PEPPER, Simon and SWENARTON, Mark (1980) Les banlieues-jardins des travailleurs de l'armement en Grande-Bretagne (1915–1918). *Urbi*, **3**, pp. 68–80.
A French translation of 8.121.

9.102 PERKS, William T. and ROBINSON, Ira M. (1979) *Urban and Regional Planning in a Federal State: The Canadian Experience*. Stroudsburg, Penn.: Dowden, Hutchinson and Ross.
Information on contents not available at time of going to press.

9.103 PETERSON, Jon Alvah (1979) The impact of sanitary reform upon American urban planning, 1840–1890. *Journal of Urban History*, **13** (1), pp. 83–104.
Makes some reference to drainage and park planning, and to Frederick Law Olmsted.

9.104 POPENOE, David (1977) *The Suburban Environment: Sweden and the United States*. Chicago: University of Chicago Press.
Contrasts the planning of suburban residential areas in Sweden and the United States since 1945. Includes detailed studies of Levittown, near Philadelphia, and Vällingby. Concludes that the Swedish decision to plan high-density neighbourhoods produced the more satisfactory environment.

9.105 PRESTON, Howard Lawrence (1979) *Automobile Age Atlanta: The Making of a Southern Metropolis, 1900–1935*. Athens: University of Georgia Press.
Includes much discussion of the impact of the automobile on planning policies for Atlanta.

9.106 REBENTISCH, Dieter (1980) Regional planning and its institutional framework: an illustration from the Rhine-Main area, 1890–1945, in Cherry, Gordon E. (ed.), *Shaping an Urban World: Planning in the Twentieth Century*. London: Mansell, pp. 79–100.
A narrative and analysis of the development of regional planning in Rhine-Main (Frankfurt region) between the Liberal 1890s and the National Socialist period. Suggests a great degree of continuity.

9.107 REINER, Thomas A. and WILSON, Robert H. (1979) Planning and decision-making in the Soviet city: rent, land and urban form, in French, R. A. and Hamilton, F. E. Ian (eds.), *The Socialist City: Spatial Structure and Urban Policy*. Chichester: John Wiley and Sons, pp. 49–72.

Includes an outline of the history of urban planning in the Soviet Union.

9.108 RODRIGUEZ-LORES, Juan (1980) Die Grundfrage der Grundrente: Stadtplanung von Ildefonso Cerdà für Barcelona und James Hobrecht für Berlin. *Stadtbauwelt*, 65, pp. 443–50.

Compares and contrasts the Cerdà plan for Barcelona and Hobrecht's contemporary effort for Berlin, arguing that the maximizing of ground rents provides the key to both.

9.109 ROSSI, Angelo (1979) *Sviluppo urbano e politica urbana in Svizzera*. Porza-Lugano: Edizioni Trelingue.

A general study of Swiss urban development in its relationship to planning policies, 1945–75. Includes detailed studies of the experiences of the larger Swiss cities.

9.110 ROTH, Leland M. (1979) Three industrial towns by McKim, Mead and White. *Journal of the Society of Architectural Historians*, 38 (4), pp. 317–47.

Appraises the industrial and public buildings, and housing, built in three company towns (Niagara Falls, Roanoke Rapids, and Naugatuck) by the noted architectural partnership. Throws some light on the general development of company towns in the United States.

9.111 RUBENSTEIN, James M. (1978) *The French New Towns*. Baltimore: Johns Hopkins University Press.

Discusses the formulation and execution of the French 'new towns' strategy since the 1950s, with main emphasis on the Paris region.

9.112 SANDBACH, Francis (1980) The early campaign for a national park in the Lake District, in Kain, Roger (ed.), *Planning for Conservation: An International Perspective*. London: Mansell, pp. 117–40.

A detailed narrative of certain antecedents of the creation of the Lake District National Park in the activities of pressure-groups in the 1920s and 1930s.

9.113 SATŌ, Atsushi (1965) *Nihon no Chiiki Kaihatsu.* Tokyo: Miraisha.
A study of regional development in Japan, including a historical survey of regional planning since the Meiji era.

9.114 SHAW, Denis J. B. (1979) Recreation and the Soviet city, in French, R. A. and Hamilton, F. E. Ian (eds.), *The Socialist City: Spatial Structure and Urban Policy.* Chichester: John Wiley and Sons, pp. 119–43.
Primarily a description of current recreational and cultural provision in Soviet cities, but with much perspective on the history of policy in these areas since 1917.

9.115 SHEAIL, John (1979) The Restriction of Ribbon Development Act: the character and perception of land use control in inter-war Britain. *Regional Studies,* **13** (6), pp. 501–12.
Discusses the origins and effect of the 1935 Act restricting ribbon development, which foreshadowed the universal planning controls set up in 1947.

9.116 SHEAIL, John (1980) Changing perceptions of land-use controls in interwar Britain, in Kain, Roger (ed.), *Planning for Conservation: An International Perspective.* London: Mansell, pp. 141–57.
Investigates three planning episodes in the 1920s and 1930s: the protection of the Downs (Eastbourne), the Woodbridge bypass, and seacoast protection in Lindsey.

9.117 SHKVARIKOV, V. A., HAUCKE, M. and SMIRNOVA, O. (1964) The building of new towns in the U.S.S.R. *Ekistics,* **18,** pp. 307–19.
This study includes some historical perspective and complements Shkvarikov's Russian-language book of the same year (8.213).

9.118 SMALLWOOD, J. B. (1980) An American way to conservation: comment on Federal river basin development, in Kain, Roger (ed.), *Planning for Conservation: An International Perspective.* London: Mansell, pp. 159–76.
A general survey of the development of river-valley planning

in the United States, including the Tennessee Valley Authority.

.119 SMITH, Paul Bryan (1979) Conserving Charleston's architectural heritage. *Town Planning Review*, **50** (4), pp. 459–76.

Throws light on the history of conservation in Charleston since the early twentieth century.

.120 SMITH, P. J. (1980) Planning as environmental improvement: slum clearance in Victorian Edinburgh, in Sutcliffe, Anthony (ed.), *The Rise of Modern Urban Planning, 1800–1914*. London: Mansell, pp. 99–134.

A detailed investigation of slum clearance and redevelopment in Edinburgh and Leith between the 1860s and the turn of the century.

.121 SMITH, Roger (1979) *East Kilbride: The Biography of a Scottish New Town, 1947–1973*. London: H.M.S.O.

One of a series of new town studies supported by the Building Research Establishment. A full planning history and social survey of the town, set in the context of the economic and social history of the Clyde Valley.

.122 SPEARRITT, Peter (1973) *Selected Writings of Sydney Planning Advocates, 1900–1947: A Preliminary Bibliography*. Canberra: Metropolitan Research Trust.

A brief listing of books, articles and pamphlets relevant to the planning history of Sydney.

.123 SPEER, Albert (1978) *Architektur: Arbeiten 1933–1942*. Frankfurt-am-Main: Propyläen Verlag.

An illustrated study of Speer's architectural and urban design work from the beginning of the Third Reich until his transfer to more important duties.

.124 *Stadtplanung Wien 1963–1969* (1971). Vienna: Jugend und Volk Verlagsgesellschaft.

Edited by Georg Conditt, this is an illustrated survey of planning developments in Vienna in the 1960s.

.125 SUTCLIFFE, Anthony (1980) Introduction: the debate on

nineteenth-century planning, in Sutcliffe, Anthony (ed.), *The Rise of Modern Urban Planning, 1800–1914*. London: Mansell, pp. 1–10.

Identifies a number of salient characteristics of the historiography of the rise of planning in the nineteenth century, stressing the contrast between British, American and Continental approaches, and isolating three major interpretations: liberal-progressist, Marxist and functionalist.

9.126 SUTCLIFFE, Anthony (1980) Vorstadtplanung im Vergleich mit anderen Ländern: die geplante Wanderung an die Peripherie als Reformmoment um die Jahrhundertwende. *Stadtbauwelt*, **65**, pp. 462–7.

Discusses the impact of tendencies of spontaneous urban decentralization on urban planning before 1914, with principal reference to Britain and Germany.

9.127 TARN, John Nelson (1980) Housing reform and the emergence of town planning in Britain before 1914, in Sutcliffe, Anthony (ed.), *The Rise of Modern Urban Planning, 1800–1914*. London: Mansell, pp. 71–98.

A wide-ranging discussion of English nineteenth-century urban growth, residential development, and model housing, in their relation to the emergence of town planning before 1914.

9.128 *Town Planning in Maharashtra, 1914–1964: With Special Reference to New Trends and Future Development* (1965). Poona: Town Planning and Valuation Department.

No information other than title.

9.129 ÜHLIG, Gunther (1979) Town planning in the Weimar Republic. *Architectural Association Quarterly*, **11** (1), pp. 24–38.

Not seen at time of going to press.

9.130 WALZ, Manfred (1980) Gegenbilder zur Grossstadt: von den nationalsozialistischen Versuchen zur Auflösung der Stadt bis zu den Wiederaufbauphasen nach 1945. *Stadtbauwelt*, **65**, pp. 473–82.

Analyses the development of anti-urban thinking in Germany between about 1930 and 1950, and discusses its impact on the urban planning policies pursued during this period.

9.131 WANETSCHEK, Margret (1971) *Die Grünanlagen in der Stadtplanung Münchens von 1790–1860*. Munich: R. Wölfle.

A study of the planning of open spaces in Munich in the first half of the nineteenth century, based on the author's university thesis.

9.132 WATANABE, Shun-ichi J. (1960) Garden City Japanese style: the case of Den-en Toshi Company Ltd., 1918–28, in Cherry, Gordon E. (ed.), *Shaping an Urban World: Planning in the Twentieth Century*. London: Mansell, pp. 129–44.

A study of Japan's first 'garden city', a speculatively-built low-density suburb of Tokyo. Originally published in Japanese as: Nihon-teki den-en toshi-ron no kenkyū (1): den-en toshi Kabushiki Kaisha (1918–28) no baai. *Nihon Toshi Keikaku Gakkai Gakujutsu Kenkyū Happyō-Kai Ronbun-shū*, **12**, 1977, pp. 151–6.

9.133 WATANABE, Shun-ichi J. (1980) Planning history in Japan. *Urban History Yearbook*, pp. 63–75.

A review of historical investigations of planning in Japan, including a brief historical outline of the growth of planning there since 1868.

9.134 WATANABE, Shun-ichi J. (1979) Toshi keikaku-shi kenkyu e no izanai. *Tochi Jūtaku Mondai*, **53**, pp. 35–43.

Urges Japanese planners and historians to devote more attention to the history of planning in Japan. Argues that the character of planning in each country is determined by the socio-historical context in which it first emerges.

9.135 WATANABE, Shun-ichi J. and SADAYUKI, Yasuhiro (1979) Ikeda Hiroshi den shiron. *Tochi Jūtaku Mondai*, **56**.

A study of the work and influence of Ikeda Hiroshi (1881–1939), who drafted Japan's Planning Act of 1919 and who was the main administrator and theorist of Japanese planning in the interwar years.

9.136 WHITE, Paul M. (1980) *Soviet Urban and Regional Planning: A Bibliography With Abstracts*. London: Mansell.

An extended version of 4.186.

9.137 WHITE, Paul M. (1980) Urban planning in Britain and the Soviet Union: a comparative analysis of two planning systems. *Town Planning Review*, 51 (2), pp. 211–26.
A summary of 4.187.

9.138 WILLIAMS, Allan (1980) Conservation planning in Oporto: an integrated approach in the Ribeira-Barredo. *Town Planning Review*, 51 (2), pp. 177–94.
Studies a renovation project in a working-class district of Oporto, throwing light on the planning history of Oporto, and of Portugal, since the 1940s.

9.139 WILSON, William H. (1980) The ideology, aesthetics and politics of the City Beautiful movement, in Sutcliffe, Anthony (ed.), *The Rise of Modern Urban Planning, 1800–1914*. London: Mansell, pp. 166–98.
The most recent general evocation of the City Beautiful movement, maintaining its centrality in the development of planning in the United States.

9.140 ZAREBSKA, Teresa (1980) The reconstruction of Kalisz, Poland, following its destruction in 1914, in Kain, Roger (ed.), *Planning for Conservation: An International Perspective*. London: Mansell, pp. 75–96.
A study of the reconstruction of a war-damaged Polish town, foreshadowing the rebuilding of Warsaw after 1945.

9.141 (ZUKOWSKY, John [ed.]) (1979) *The Plan of Chicago: 1909–1979*. Chicago: Art Institute of Chicago.
Catalogue of an exhibition held at the Burnham Library of Architecture. Includes contributions by John Zubowsky, Sally Chappell and Robert Bruegmann on the origins, elaboration and impact of the Burnham plan. Extensively illustrated.

Index of names

Abercrombie, P. 9.35, 9.83
Adams, T. 4.9, 6.1, 8.210, 9.9
Addams, J. 4.309
Addis Abeba 4.103
Adelaide 4.2, 5.1, 8.149
Adickes, F. 4.59, 4.301
Alberta 4.22
Amana 7.57
American Institute of Planners 4.264,
    4.290, 4.318
Amsterdam 8.107
Antwerp 9.79
Appalachian Trail 8.240
Argyll, Dukes of 5.97
Athens Charter 3.2, 3.96, see also
    CIAM
Atlanta 5.2–4, 9.105
Augsburg 8.94
Australia 4.1–3, 8.133, 8.206, 8.209
Austria 4.4–5, 4.94, 9.17–18
Autun 5.5

Baden 5.6, 9.78
Baltimore 8.40
Barcelona 4.136, 5.7–13, 7.32–4, 7.37,
    7.41, 9.108, see also Sert, J.
Bari 8.55
Barnett, H. see Hampstead
Barnett, S. 4.232, 9.11
Bartholomew, H. 6.2
Barton Hill 8.35
Basle 5.14
Bassett, E. 6.3
Baumeister, R. 9.42
Bay Area Rapid Transit 9.59
Bedford Park 7.83, 7.94

Beisenkamp 7.73
Belfast 5.15
Belgium 7.23
Bellamy, E. 7.72
Belo Horizonte 9.32
Berlage, H. 8.107
Berlin 3.42, 3.97, 4.83, 5.16–29, 6.47,
    7.30, 7.36, 7.38, 7.111, 8.11,
    8.13–14, 8.16, 8.71, 8.116, 8.131,
    9.19, 9.37, 9.50, 9.62, 9.108, see
    also Falkenberg, Gropiusstadt
Bettman, A. 6.4
Bielefeld 5.30
Bilbao 5.31–2
Birmingham 4.207, 4.218, 4.223,
    5.33–7, 8.140, 8.153, 8.257, 9.25,
    see also Bournville
Blumenfeld, H. 6.5
Bogue, V. 9.100
Bold, W. 5.165
Bologna 8.69
Bolsover 9.49
Boston 3.42, 5.38–9, 7.72, 8.44, 8.51,
    8.80
Boundary Street 7.29
Bournville 7.84, 7.90, 7.121, 7.126
Brasilia 5.40–4, 8.178, 9.32
Brazil 4.6–7, 9.32
Bristol 8.35
Broadacre City 4.267, see also Wright,
    F. L.
Bromborough Pool 7.128
Brussels 7.23
Buckingham, J. 6.6–7, 7.67
Budapest 3.42, 5.45
Buenos Aires 5.46

Bund deutscher Bodenreformer 4.59
Burnage 7.97
Burnham, D. 4.267, 4.322, 5.62,
   6.8–10, 9.72, 9.141
Byker 8.38

Cadbury, G. see Bournville
Calgary 5.47–8
Cambridge 5.49
Canada 2.8, 4.8–25, 7.105, 7.123–4,
   8.92–3, 8.103, 8.133, 8.183,
   8.204–5, 8.210, 9.9, 9.102
Canberra 4.305, 5.50, 6.44–5, 8.178,
   8.193, 9.70
Canton 4.31
Caracas 5.51–2
Carbonia 8.196
Catalonia 4.136, 4.138
Catania 5.53
Central Lancashire New Town 9.85
Cerdà, I. 5.7–13, 6.11–19, 7.32–4, 7.37,
   7.41, 9.108
Chamberlain, N. 9.25
Chandigarh 5.54–9, 6.77
Charles Center see Baltimore
Charleston 9.119
Chelsea 8.91
Chicago 3.42, 4.265, 4.303, 4.305,
   5.60–2, 7.47, 9.79, 9.141, see also
   Pullman
Chicago School of Sociology 4.270,
   4.277
Chile 4.26
China 4.27–31, 4.176, 9.80
CIAM 3.24, 3.92, 3.96, see also Athens
   Charter
Cincinnati 8.46
Cité industrielle see Garnier, T.
Cité(s) ouvrière(s) (Mulhouse, etc.) 7.81,
   7.101–3
Ciudad Guayana 8.251
Ciudad lineal 3.26, see also Soria y
   Mata, A.
Cleveland 5.63, 6.66
Clyde Valley 9.121
Cologne 3.42, 5.64, 8.5
Colombia 4.32
Columbia (Maryland) 8.166, 8.199

Columbus 8.19
Commission of Conservation
   (Canada) 4.9, 9.9
Congrès internationaux
   d'architecture moderne see CIAM
Copeland, R. 6.20
Copenhagen 5.65–6
Covent Garden 8.25
Coventry 5.67–8, 8.2, 8.9, 8.12
Cracow 6.65
Cresswell 9.49
Croydon 7.4
Cuba 4.33–5
Czechoslovakia 3.50–1, 4.36–8, 8.56

Dakar 5.69
Dallas 5.70
Dar Es Salaam 5.71
Darley Abbey 7.114
Datteln 7.73
Dawley see Telford
Dayton 5.3–4
Delhi 3.57, 6.81–2
Denmark 4.39–42
Derbyshire 9.49
Detroit 4.286, 5.72
Deutsche Akademie für Städtebau
   und Landesplanung 4.80
Dock, M. 5.93
Dodecanese 4.108
Doncaster 7.113, 9.49
Dortmund 5.73, 9.81
Downs, The 9.116
Dresden see Hellerau
Düsseldorf 6.47

Earswick see New Earswick
Eastbourne 9.116
East Kilbride 8.191, 8.215, 9.121
Easton 5.74
Edinburgh 9.120
Edlington 9.49
Edmonton 5.75–7, 8.26
Eggeling, F. 6.21
Essen 5.78, 7.104, 7.120, 7.125, see also
   Margarethenhöhe
Ethiopia 4.103

Falkenberg 7.143–4, 9.16
Farsta 8.120
Fassbender, E. 6.22
FIHUAT 4.113
Fischer, T. 6.23
Florence 4.107, 5.79–80, 7.2, 7.5, 7.18,
    7.28, 8.27
Forlí 5.81
Fourier, C. 9.71
France 3.9, 4.43–52, 7.151, 8.59–60,
    8.151, 8.174, 9.39, 9.73, 9.111
Frankfurt 4.301, 5.82–6, 6.88, 8.10,
    8.106–7, 8.249–50, 9.106, see also
    Nordweststadt
Futurism 3.25, 8.225, see also
    Sant'Elia, A.

Garden Cities and Town Planning
    Association 4.225
Garden City Association 4.225
Garnier, T. 3.56, 3.72, 4.52, 6.18,
    6.24–7
Gary 7.116, 9.82
GATCPAC 5.11–12
Geddes, P. 4.232, 6.29–43, 9.91
Genoa 5.87–8
German Democratic Republic 4.61,
    4.95–6
Germany 2.1, 2.14, 3.43, 3.83, 4.53–94,
    4.301, 7.45, 7.48, 7.111, 7.134,
    7.136, 7.143, 7.144, 7.147, 8.1,
    8.5–6, 8.18, 8.39, 8.48, 8.97–8,
    8.101, 9.3–4, 9.16, 9.18, 9.37, 9.58,
    9.78, 9.94, 9.96, 9.99, 9.106, 9.126,
    9.129–30
Glasgow 7.1, 8.23, 8.136–7, 8.145,
    8.215
Glenrothes 8.175
Goodman, P. 7.66
Goole 7.115
Gosplan 4.157
Greece 4.108
Greeley 7.57
Green, A. 5.146
Greenbelt (Maryland) 8.129, 8.224
Greenbrook 6.143
Gretna 6.132, 8.121
Griffin, W. 4.305, 6.44–5, 9.70

Grôlée 7.25
Gropius, W. see Gropiusstadt
Gropiusstadt 8.104, 8.112
Guayana 8.251

The Hague 5.89
Halifax 8.17, 8.26
Halles 8.47
Hallman, P. 4.145
Hamburg 4.59, 5.90–1, 6.115–16, 7.27,
    8.13, 8.236, 9.37
Hampstead Garden Suburb 6.132,
    7.93, 7.95–6, 7.129, 8.107, 9.11
Hancock 7.57
Hanover 5.92, 8.5, 8.50
Happy Colony see Pemberton, R.
Harlow 8.158, 8.162, 8.223
Harrisburg 5.93
Hartford 5.94
Haussmann, G. 3.62, 7.3, 7.8–10,
    7.12–13, 7.15, 7.17, 7.19, 7.21–2,
    7.24, 7.26
Havana 5.95
Hegemann, W. 6.46–7
Hellerau 7.143–4, 9.16
Helsinki 7.31
Hénard, E. 3.72, 6.48–51
Hertfordshire 8.144
Hesse 4.59
Hilberseimer, L. 6.18, 6.53
Hiroshi, I. 9.47, 9.135
Hitler, A. 9.37
Hobrecht, J. 9.108, see also Berlin
Horsfall, T. 6.54–5
Howard, E. 3.72, 6.56–65, 7.67, 8.107,
    9.5
Howe, F. 4.309, 6.66–7
Hungary 3.78, 4.97–8
Hygeia 6.111, see also Richardson, B.

India 4.99, 6.43, 8.203, 9.128
Indianapolis 5.96
Inverary 5.97
Iroquois Falls 8.210
Islamabad 8.178
Israel 4.100, 8.159, 8.164, 8.169, 8.216,
    9.10
Istanbul 8.33

Italy 1.4, 4.101–18, 8.58, 8.186, 8.196,
    8.225–6, 9.22, 9.33

Japan 4.119–23, 7.161, 9.1, 9.47, 9.55,
    9.66–7, 9.69, 9.75–6, 9.80, 9.95,
    9.113, 9.132–4
Jardin de la Confédération 7.162
Jaussely, L. 5.12
Jeanneret, C.-E. see Le Corbusier
Johnson, T. 5.63
Josimović, E. 6.68

Kahn, L. 6.69
Kalisz 9.140
Kansas City 5.98
Kent 4.191
Kiel 8.5, 8.7
Korn, A. 6.70
Krupp 7.104, 7.109, 7.120, 7.125

Lake District 9.112
Lake Superior Region 9.2
Lancashire 4.212
Landmann, L. 5.86
Le Corbusier 3.72, 6.58–9, 6.72–9,
    6.118, 8.107, 9.51, see also
    Chandigarh, Pessac
Le Havre 4.49
Leclaire 7.91
Leeds see Quarry Hill
Leghorn 5.99
Leicester 5.100–01
Leiden 5.102
Leith 9.120
L'Enfant, C. 5.231–4
Leningrad 4.171, 5.103–5
Léopold II 7.23
Letchworth 6.132, 7.48, 7.137–8,
    7.145, 7.157–9
Lever, W. 9.84, see also Port Sunlight
Levittown 9.104
Lex Adickes 4.59
Libya 4.116, 8.226
Lichtwark, A. 6.80
Light, Col. 5.1
Lindhagen, A. 5.195
Lindley, W. 7.27
Lindsey 8.64, 9.116

Linz 4.4, 9.37
Lisbon 5.106
Liverpool 4.221, 5.107–8, 8.254
Livorno see Leghorn
Llano 7.57
London 3.42, 3.97, 4.187, 5.109–19,
    6.70, 7.6–7, 7.11, 7.29, 8.9, 8.66,
    8.68, 8.73, 8.77, 8.91, 8.109, 8.138,
    8.141, 8.154–5, 8.165, 8.189, 8.247,
    8.252–3, 9.59, see also Becontree,
    Bedford Park, Covent Garden,
    Dagenham, Hampstead Garden
    Suburb
London (Ontario) 8.52
Lübeck 8.54
Lünen 7.79
Lusaka 9.30
Lutyens, E. 6.81–3
Lynch, K. 9.8
Lyons 4.52, 7.14, 7.25, 8.243, see also
    Garnier, T.

McAneny, G. 6.84
MacKaye, B. 8.240
McKim, Mead and White
    (partnership) 9.110
Maharashtra 9.128
Manchester 5.120–2, 8.115, see also
    Burnage, Wythenshawe
Manchuria 9.80
Manila 6.8
Marais 8.57, 9.73
Margarethenhöhe 7.109, 7.122
MARS 6.70
Marsh, B. 6.85–6
Mawson, T. 6.87
May, E. 5.84–5, 6.88, 8.106–7
Melbourne 4.2
Memphis 5.2
Merseyside 8.254
Metzendorf, G. 7.109
Mexico 4.124
Middlesbrough 4.221
Midlands 4.223, 8.140, 8.220, 8.257
Milan 5.123–31, 8.15, 8.84
Miliutin, N. 6.18, 6.89
Minnesota 9.2
Mississippi Valley Committee 8.230

Moabit 5.24
Molotov see Perm
Montevideo 9.7
Montreal 5.132, 8.26
More, T. 9.71
Moscow 4.187, 5.133–6, 8.234, 8.241
Moses, R. 5.139
Mulhouse see Cité ouvrière
Mumford, L. 1.6
Munich 3.42, 9.18, 9.37, 9.131
Mussolinia 8.196
Muthesius, H. 4.75

Nadeau, E. 7.162
Napoleon III see Haussmann, G.
Naples 5.137–8, 7.16
National Resources Planning Board
    4.274, 4.299
Naugatuck 9.110
Nauvoo 7.57
Netherlands 4.125–7, 9.41
Nettlefold, J. S. 4.207
New Delhi see Delhi
New Earswick 6.132, 7.112
New Orleans 5.2
New York 4.270, 4.295, 5.139–46, 6.3,
    6.84–5, 7.49, 8.100, 8.109, 8.229,
    8.235, 8.238–9, see also
    Olmsted, F.
Newark 8.36
Newcastle 5.147, 8.38
Niagara Falls 9.110
Nice 9.79
Nolen, J. 6.90–2
Nordweststadt 8.110
Northern Ireland 4.236
Norton, C. 8.239
Norway 4.128
Nuovo Schio see Schio
Nuremburg 5.148, 9.37

Oak Bluffs 6.20
Oakland 9.59
Odessa 5.149
Ohio Planning Conference 4.321
Olmsted, F. L. 4.322, 6.93–107, 7.49,
    8.51, 9.103
Oneida 7.57

Onkel Tom Siedlung 9.19
Oporto 9.138
Oslo 5.150
Ottawa 5.151, 8.26
Owen, R. 7.56, 9.71
Owerri 9.48
Oxford 8.77

Padua 5.152
Palermo 5.153
Paris 3.42, 3.97, 4.49, 5.119, 5.154–62,
    7.3, 7.8–10. 7.12–13, 7.15, 7.17,
    7.19–22, 7.24, 7.26, 8.53, 8.107,
    8.123, 8.222, 8.242, 8.256, 9.6, 9.40,
    9.73, 9.111, see also Halles,
    Hénard, E., Marais
Park, R. 4.309
Parker, B. 6.132, 6.134, see also
    Letchworth
Paxton, J. 6.108
Pemberton, R. 7.60, 7.67
Perm 5.163
Perth 5.165
Perugia 5.164
Pessac 8.105, 8.125–6
Phalanx 7.57
Philadelphia 5.166, 6.69
Philippines 6.8
Pilkington Brothers 7.113
Pittsburgh 5.167
Poggi, G. 7.2
Poland 4.129–32, 8.237, 9.60
Port Sunlight 7.100, 7.117, 7.131
Portmeirion 5.168
Portugal 9.138
Prague 9.23
Pray, J. S. 4.262
Pretoria 5.169
Price's Patent Candle Co. 7.128
Prost, H. 6.109–10
Prussia 4.59
Pullman 7.86–7, 7.107, 7.110

Quarry Hill 8.42

Radburn layout 8.111
Radiant City 8.107, see also Le
    Corbusier

Redditch 8.153
Regional Planning Association of
    America 4.266, 4.277, 4.296, 8.255
Regional Plan Association of New
    York 8.235
Rhein-Main Region 8.249–50, 9.106
Rheinische Verein zur Förderung des
    Wohnungswesens 4.59
Ribeira-Barredo 9.138
Richardson, B. 6.111, 7.67
Richwood see Halifax
Rio de Janeiro 5.42, 9.32
Rixdorf 5.24
Roanoke Rapids 9.110
Robinson, C. M. 4.308
Roebuck, J. 7.46
Rome 5.170–83, 9.34
Rossi, A. 7.108
Rotterdam 5.184, 8.9
Rowntree, J. see New Earswick
Rowntree, S. see New Earswick
Royal Town Planning Institute 4.205
Ruhr 7.82, 9.15–16
Rumania 3.93
Russia see U.S.S.R.

St. Helens 7.113
St. Louis 5.185, 8.46
Salt, T. 7.76, 7.78, 7.88–9, 7.99, 7.118,
    7.127
Saltaire see Salt, T.
San Francisco 9.59, 9.72, see also
    Yerba Buena Center
Sant'Elia, A. 6.112–14
São Paulo 9.32
Sardinia 8.188
Saskatoon 5.186, 8.65
Schio 7.108
Schumacher, F. 6.115–16
Scotland 4.189, 8.214–15, 9.121
Seattle 5.3–4, 9.100
Serbia 4.329, 6.68
Sert, J. 6.18, 6.117
Sheffield 4.221, 5.187–8, 8.113
Shenyang 4.31
Shimpei, G. 9.47
Sienna 5.189
Siracusa 5.190

Sitte, C. 6.118–21, 9.29, 9.42
Société française des urbanistes 4.44,
    4.50
Sofia 9.23
Soria y Mata, A. 3.26, 3.72, 6.18,
    6.122–5
South Africa 4.133–4
South Australia 5.1
South Hampshire 4.221
Spain 4.135–40, 7.33, 8.157, 8.227
Speer, A. 4.83, 5.21, 9.123
Stein, Clarence 4.276
Stevenage 8.197, 8.221
Stockholm 3.42, 4.145, 5.64,
    5.191–200, 7.39, 8.30–1, 8.114, see
    also Farsta, Vällingby
Sudbury 7.119
Sunderland 8.28
Sweden 4.141–6, 7.106, 8.133, 9.104
Swindon 5.202, 9.85
Switzerland 9.109
Sydney 4.2, 9.122

Tange, K. 6.126
Tapiola 8.179
Taut, B. 6.127, 9.19
Taylor, F. 6.128
Telford 8.220
Témiscaming 8.210
Tennessee Valley Authority 4.270,
    8.231, 8.244–6, 8.248, 9.118
Tokyo 9.26, 9.63, 9.65, 9.68, 9.132
Toronto 5.205–12, 8.26, 9.56, 9.97
Toshi Kenkyu-kai 9.47
Town and Country Planning
    Association 4.216, 4.220, 4.225–6
Trait 7.151
Trentino 4.102
Trenton 8.37
Trier 8.5
Tripolitania 4.116
Tugwell, R. 6.129–30
Turin 5.213–14
Turkey 8.151

Ujung Pandang 5.215
Unilever 7.131

U.S.S.R. 3.83, 4.147–88, 6.88, 8.22,
   8.74–5, 8.171, 8.213, 9.12–13, 9.45,
   9.107, 9.117, 9.136–7
United Kingdom 2.15–16, 3.3, 3.46,
   4.75, 4.78, 4.189–261, 7.55, 7.67,
   7.74, 7.77, 7.92, 7.130, 7.135, 7.146,
   7.150, 7.153, 8.34, 8.41, 8.61–3,
   8.67, 8.77, 8.81, 8.83, 8.111,
   8.133–4, 8.139, 8.146–8, 8.151–2,
   8.167–8, 8.170, 8.172–3, 8.185,
   8.187, 8.189, 8.195, 8.198, 8.200–1,
   8.206–8, 8.211–12, 8.218–19, 9.5,
   9.25, 9.31, 9.36, 9.61, 9.64, 9.85–6,
   9.92, 9.101, 9.112, 9.115–16,
   9.126–7, 9.137
United States 1.2, 2.8, 3.4, 3.35, 3.46,
   3.70, 4.262–328, 6.91, 7.44, 7.75,
   7.80, 7.105, 8.20, 8.29, 8.43, 8.45,
   8.49, 8.72, 8.76, 8.79, 8.82, 8.85–90,
   8.92–3, 8.95–6, 8.98–9, 8.101–2,
   8.111, 8.114, 8.134, 8.146, 8.151,
   8.160–1, 8.163, 8.168, 8.170, 8.184,
   8.194, 8.206, 8.217, 8.228, 8.232,
   9.20, 9.27–8, 9.38, 9.53–4, 9.88–90,
   9.93, 9.98, 9.103–4, 9.110, 9.118,
   9.139
Unwin, R. 3.56, 4.235, 6.131–8, 8.107,
   8.121, see also Hampstead Garden
   Suburb, Letchworth
Upper Austria 4.4
Urbino 4.107, 5.216
Utrecht 9.14

Vällingby 8.120, 8.223, 9.104
Västerås 5.217
Valencia 5.218
Vancouver 5.219, 8.26, 9.87
Vaux, C. 6.95, see also Olmsted, F. L.
Veneto 9.22
Venezuela 8.151, 8.251

Venice 4.107, 5.220–2
Verein Reichswohnungsgesetz 4.59
Verhaeren, E. 6.136–7
Verona 5.223
Victoria (Australia) 4.1
Victoria (B.C.) 5.224
Victoria (model town) see
   Buckingham, J.
Vienna 3.42, 5.225–8, 7.42, 8.135,
   8.156, 9.18, 9.43, 9.124
Viktoria-Kolonie 7.79
Ville radieuse see Radiant City
Virginia 9.88
Volkswagen see Wolfsburg

Wagner, M. 9.96
Wagner, O. 6.139–41
Warsaw 5.229, 8.3–4
Washington 5.230–4, 8.46, 8.180, 9.57
Wels 4.4
Welwyn 7.152, 7.158, 8.107, 9.21
West Midland Group 8.257
West Midlands 8.140
Whitehorse 5.235, 8.182
Winnipeg 5.236–7, 8.26
Wisconsin 9.2
Wolfsburg 7.98
Woodbridge 9.116
Woodlands 9.49
Woolwich 8.121
Wright, F. L. 4.267, 6.58–9, 6.142
Wright, H. 6.143
Wythenshawe 6.132, 8.223

Yerba Buena Center 8.32
Yorkshire 8.21, 9.49
Yugoslavia 4.329–30

Zehlendorf 9.19

Index of authors

Abercrombie, P. 3.1, 4.214, 5.225, 6.6, 6.136, 7.30
Ackers, W. 7.73
Acosta, M. 4.33–4
Adams, E. 8.158
Adams, F. 4.262
Adams, I. 4.189
Adams, J. 4.190–1
Adams, R. 8.19
Adams, T. 3.3–4, 8.229
Adamson, A. 4.8
Adderson, I. 8.180
Adshead, S. 6.118
Ahrens, H. 7.74
Akademie für Raumforschung und Landesplanung 2.1
Akademiia Arkhitektury S.S.S.R. 4.147
Akagi, S. 9.1
Alanen, A. 9.2
Albers, G. 3.5, 4.53–7, 9.3–4
Albrecht, G. 4.58
Aldridge, M. 9.5
Alduy, J. 9.6
Alessandri, G. 4.192
Allan, C. 7.1
Alex, W. 4.169, 6.93
Allen, J. 7.75
Allensworth, D. 8.96
Alonso, W. 4.263
Alsop, B. 7.76
Altezor, C. 9.7
Altman, E. 8.159
Amaral, F. 5.106
Amos, F. 5.107
Anderson, M. 8.20

Andriello, D. 7.50, 7.132
Anthony, H. 6.72
Antonini, E. 4.101
Åström, K. 4.141
Åström, S.-E. 7.31
Apollonio, U. 6.122
Appleyard, D. 9.8
Architekten- und Ingenieur-Verein, Hamburg 5.90
Armstrong, A. 4.9
Armstrong, F. 8.52
Armytage, W. 7.51–2
Arnold, J. 8.160
Artibise, A. 4.10, 4.22, 5.236–7, 7.124, 9.9
Ashworth, W. 4.193, 7.77
Association of Engineers and Architects in Israel 4.100
Ash J. 9.10
Ashworth, G. 2.2
Astengo, G. 5.91
Auzelle, R. 2.3, 3.6, 4.43
Aymonino, C. 3.7, 5.65

Babcock, R. 8.85
Babelon, J.-P. 8.53
Bacon, E. 3.8
Bailey, J. 8.161
Balgarnie, R. 7.78
Balzer, W. 7.79
Bandel, H. 8.104
Bangert, W. 5.82
Baracchini, H. 9.7
Baranov, N. 4.148, 5.103
Bardet, G. 3.9–10, 6.48
Barey, A. 5.7

Barkin, D. 4.35
Barlow, E. 6.93
Barnett, H. 9.11
Barnett, S. 4.232
Bassett, E. 6.3, 8.86–8
Bastié, J. 5.154
Bastlund, K. 6.117
Batchelor, P. 7.133
Bateman, L. 8.162
Bateman, M. 8.21
Bater, J. 4.149, 9.12
Batty, M. 4.194
Baumgarten, I. 5.12
Beaudouin, E. 4.44
Beauregard, R. 7.80
Bebbington, D. 9.13
Beckett, J. 5.15
Bell, C. 4.195
Bell, G. 5.94
Bell, Reginald 5.112
Bell, Rose 4.195
Belov, I. 8.22
Bender, T. 6.94
Benevolo, L. 3.11–13, 5.170–1
Berend, I. 4.97
Bergamin, R. 5.51
Berger-Thimme, D. 4.59
Bergmann, K. 7.134
Berkman, H. 8.163
Berlepsch-Valendàs, H. 7.135
Berler, A. 8.164
Bernatzky, A. 8.48
Berndt, H. 3.14
Best, R. 8.165
Bestor, G. 2.4
Bettison, D. 4.11
Beveridge, C. 6.95
Bhardwaj, R. 4.99
Biarez, S. 4.45
Bidagor Lasarte, P. 4.135
Bidstrup, K. 4.39
Bigwood, R. 4.119
Birrell, J. 6.44
Black, R. 4.264
Blacksell, M. 8.1
Blijstra, R. 4.125, 5.89, 5.184, 9.14
Bliznakov, M. 4.150
Blodgett, G. 6.96

Blumenfeld, H. 3.15, 4.151, 7.81
Boardman, P. 6.29–30
Boato, A. 4.102
Bobek, H. 5.226
Boesiger, W. 6.73
Bohigas, O. 4.136, 5.8, 7.32
Boileau, I. 6.122
Bollerey, F. 7.53, 7.82, 7.136, 9.15–16
Bolsterli, M. 7.83
Bonham-Carter, E. 7.137
Bor, W. 4.196, 5.109
Boralevi, A. 4.103
Borg, N. 5.33
Borsi, F. 7.2
Bortollotti, L. 5.99
Boscarino, S. 5.53
Bottomley, J. 5.219
Boudon, P. 8.105
Bourne, L. 8.133
Bournville Village Trust 7.84
Boyarsky, A. 6.119
Boyd, A. 4.27
Bozarth, D. 5.230
Branch, M. 2.7
Breitling, P. 9.17–18
Bremer, J. 8.70
Brennan, T. 8.23
Brenne, W. 9.19
Briggs, A. 5.34, 7.85
Brion-Guerry, L. 6.113
Brix, J. 4.60, 8.54
Brooks, R. 8.166
Brown, A. 5.100
Brownell, B. 5.2, 9.20
Bruegmann, R. 9.141
Bryant, R. 8.2
Buchanan, C. 4.197, 8.66
Buck, D. 4.28
Buder, S. 6.56, 7.86–7
Buekschmitt, J. 6.88
Bullock, N. 8.106
Bunin, A. 3.16–7
Burg, D. 4.265
Burg, N. 8.202
Burke, G. 4.198
Burns, W. 8.24
Busby, R. 9.21
Butler, A. 6.81

Byplankontoret, Oslo 5.150

Cabianca, V. 5.190
Cady, D. 4.266
Calabi, D. 4.199, 4.270, 6.46–7, 6.49, 9.22
Calgary City Planning Department 5.47
Camarda, A. 7.141
Caracciolo, A. 5.172
Caramel, L. 6.114
Cardarelli, U. 3.18
Caro, R. 5.139
Carozzi, C. 4.104
Carter, F. 9.23
Carver, H. 3.19, 4.12
Castex, J. 8.107
Castronovo, V. 5.213
Ceccarelli, P. 4.152
Centre de Recherche d'Urbanisme 4.46
Centre for Urban Studies 4.200
Ceruso, N. 8.189
Chadwick, G. 6.108, 7.43
Chaline, C. 5.110–11, 8.167
Chan-Magomedov, S. 4.184
Chapman, B. 7.3
Chappell, S. 9.141
Cherry, G. 1.1, 4.201–8, 8.61, 8.67, 9.24–5
Chirivi, R. 5.220
Chiumeo, R. 5.128
Choay, F. 3.20–2
Christen, A. 3.23
Christie, I. 8.25
Christie, J. 8.230
Churchill, H. 6.143
Ciborowski, A. 4.129, 8.3–4
Cid, S. 6.11–12
Circulo de Economia 5.9
Cirici-Pellicer, A. 7.34
Ciucci, G. 4.267, 9.27
Clapp, J. 8.168
Clawson, M. 8.134
Clota, M. 7.41
Clough, R. 3.25
Cohen, Y. 9.28
Collier, R. 8.26

Collins, C. 6.120, 9.29
Collins, G. 3.26, 4.169, 6.120, 6.124–5, 9.29
Collins, J. 9.30
Collins, M. 8.68
Colombo, L. 4.61
Comay, Y. 8.169
Committee on the City Plan [New York] 5.140
Committee on Town Planning of the American Institute of Architects 4.268
Condit, C. 5.60–1
Conditt, G. 9.124
Congatti, A. 6.114
Conkin, P. 4.269
Conrads, U. 3.27, 5.17, 7.54
Cooke, C. 4.153–5
Cooper, I. 4.13
Coppa, M. 5.164
Coppini, M. 8.69
Corden, C. 8.170
Cornu, M. 5.155
Cort, C. 6.13
Cosh, M. 5.97
Costa, F. 5.173
Cowan, P. 3.28
Cox, A. 4.230
Cox, M. 4.253
Cox, R. 7.4
Creese, W. 4.209, 6.131
Creixell, S. 6.14
Cresswell, P. 8.219
Cresti, C. 7.5, 8.27
Crosta, P. 4.270
Cudworth, W. 7.88
Cullingworth, J. 4.210–11, 9.31
Culpin, E. 7.138
Cunningham, S. 9.32
Curl, J. 3.29
Czerny, W. 3.30

Dahir, J. 8.108, 8.231
Dakin, A. 5.205–8
Dal Co, F. 3.99, 4.267, 9.27
Dale, E. 5.75–6
Daniels, R. 4.212
Danielson, M. 8.89

Darley, G. 4.213
Day, M. 6.132–3
De Carlo, G. 5.216
De Casseres, J. 4.214
De Finetti, G. 5.123
De Marpillero, G. 5.87
De Martino, U. 9.33
De Michelis, M. 4.156, 8.171
De Paolis, S. 9.34
De Seta, C. 4.105–7
Dean, E. 4.108
Deelstra, T. 8.70
Defries, A. 6.31
Dehmel, W. 8.71
Delafons, J. 8.90
Dennis, N. 8.28
Depaule, J.-C. 8.107
Derthick, M. 8.29
Despo, J. 3.31
Dewhirst, R. 7.89
Di Bari, D. 8.55
Diaconoff, P. 4.157
Diamond, D. 4.215, 8.172
Dickhoff, E. 5.78
Dickins, I. 4.253
Diehl, R. 5.83
Dix, G. 9.35
Doblhamer, G. 4.4
Dodi, L. 5.124
Doglio, C. 7.139–41
Dolcetta, B. 5.221
Donnelly, D. 4.216
Donnison, D. 9.36
Dorsett, L. 4.271
Drakenberg, S. 5.217
Drover, G. 8.109
Dülffer, J. 9.37
Dyos, H. 7.6
Dziewulski, S. 5.229

Edaleo, A. 5.125–7
Eden, W. 6.57
Edwards, P. 7.7
Eggleston, W. 5.151
Egli, E. 3.32
Einsiedel, S. 8.110
Eisner, S. 3.35
Elkin, S. 8.91

Epstein, D. 5.41
Eskew, G. 4.272
Estall, R. 9.38
Estapé, F. 6.15
Esteban, J. 7.35
Evans, H. 8.173
Evenson, N. 5.42–3, 5.54–5, 5.156,
    6.74, 9.40
Eversley, D. 4.217

Fabos, J. 6.97
Fagence, M. 8.111
Fagin, H. 4.273
Fallenbuchl, Z. 4.130
Faludi, A. 8.135
Fanelli, G. 9.41
Farmer, E. 8.136–7
Fawcett, A. 4.260
Fehl, G. 8.112, 9.42
Fein, A. 6.98–9
Feiss, C. 5.231, 7.155
Ferguson, K. 8.175
Ferrari, M. 5.191
Ferras, R. 5.10
Fischer, A. 6.80
Fischer, F. 9.43
Fischer, I. 6.100
Fisher, J. 3.33–4, 4.131
Fishman, R. 6.58–9, 6.75, 9.44
Fitch, R. 5.141
Flores, C. 6.125
Floyd, T. 4.133–4
Fogarty, M. 4.218
Foley, D. 4.219–20, 8.138
Folin, M. 4.270, 6.47, 6.49
Foran, M. 5.48
Ford, G. 4.268, 5.142
Foster, M. 8.72
Frampton, K. 4.158, 6.76
Franchi, D. 5.128
Franke, T. 5.12
Frecot, J. 4.62
Fregna, R. 5.81
Frei, S. 7.5
French, R. A. 9.45–6
Frick, D. 6.21
Fried, R. 5.174
Friedmann, J. 8.232–3

Fritsch, A. 4.47
Frolic, B. 4.159, 5.133
Fry, M. 6.70, 6.77
Frye, M. 7.44
Fukaoka, S. 9.47
Fullaondo, J. 5.31
Funigiello, P. 4.274

Gabrielli, B. 5.88, 5.214
Gaillard, J. 7.8
Galantay, E. 8.176, 9.48
Galley, K. 5.147
Gallion, A. 3.35
Gardiner, A. 7.90
Gardner, J. 4.6
Garner, J. 7.91
Garnier, J.-P. 5.95
Garstang, K. 6.133
Gaskell, S. 7.92, 8.113, 9.49
Gavinelli, C. 4.29–30
Geddes, A. 6.36
Geddes, P. 4.232
Gehrmann, W. 9.50
Gejvall, B. 5.192
Gelfand, M. 4.275
Geretsegger, H. 6.139
Gerecke, K. 4.14
Gerosa, P. 9.51
Gertler, L. 4.15
Gibbon, G. 5.112
Gibelli, M. 4.29
Giedion, S. 3.36, 3.92
Giles, J. 6.128
Gilg, A. 9.52
Gillette, H. 4.276
Gillie, B. 9.53
Gioja, R. 4.7
Giordani, L. 7.142
Girard, L. 7.9
Giovannoni, G. 3.37
Giura Longo, T. 3.13
Gladstone, F. 4.221
Glasscock, R. 5.15
Goist, P. 4.277–8, 6.32
Golany, G. 8.177
Goldfield, D. 1.2, 8.114, 9.54
Goodman, R. 4.279
Goss, A. 8.83, 8.139

Gottmann, J. 9.55
Grabow, S. 6.142
Graf, O. 6.140
Granatstein, J. 9.56
Green, B. 7.93
Greene, E. 8.5–6
Greeves, T. 7.94
Gregory, D. 8.140
Gregory, T. 5.67
Grieser, H. 8.7
Grote, L. 4.63
Grubb, W. 4.1
Grushka, E. 3.38 (see also Hruška, E.)
Guenoun, M. 3.39
Guidi, F. 5.182
Guidi, L. 5.137
Gunton, T. 4.16
Gut, A. 4.58
Gutheim, F. 9.57
Guttenberg, A. 4.280

Hackett, B. 3.40
Hajdu, J. 9.58
Hall, J. 8.141
Hall, P. 3.41, 4.64, 4.126, 5.113, 5.134,
    5.143, 5.157, 5.203, 8.134, 8.142–3,
    9.59
Hall, T. 8.30–1
Hamilton, F. 8.234, 9.46, 9.60
Hamson, P. 8.144
Hancock, J. 4.281, 6.90–2
Hardoy, J. 4.33–4, 8.178
Hardy, D. 7.55
Harloe, M. 5.202
Harmsworth, C. 6.60
Harrison, M. 7.97, 8.115
Harrison, M. L. 9.61
Hart, D. 8.73
Hartman, C. 8.32
Hartmann, K. 7.82, 7.136, 7.143–4,
    9.15–16
Hartog, R. 4.65
Hason, N. 8.92–3
Haucke, M. 9.117
Haussmann, G. 7.10
Hawkes, D. 6.134
Haworth, A. 7.56
Hawson, H. 5.187

Hawtree, M. 4.222
Hayden, D. 7.57
Hays, F. 8.235
Healey, P. 5.218
Hebebrand, W. 4.66, 8.236
Hecker, H. 4.67
Heckner, P. 7.103
Heckscher, A. 8.49
Hegemann, W. 3.42, 4.282–4, 5.18
Heifetz, R. 4.285
Heiligenthal, R. 3.43
Heineberg, H. 9.62
Heinrich, E. 5.19, 7.36
Helg, F. 7.98
Helms, H. 3.44, 4.68
Hemdahl, R. 5.64
Hendelson, R. 5.185
Henderson, R. 8.145
Henke, J. 9.37
Hennebo, D. 7.45
Herbert, G. 3.45
Hertzen, H. von 8.179
Hilberseimer, L. 6.53
Hillebrecht, R. 5.92
Hines, T. 5.63, 6.8–9
Hiorns, F. 3.46
Hodge, G. 4.262
Hodgkinson, G. 5.68
Hofmann, W. 4.69
Hogg, H. 8.33
Holcomb, B. 7.80
Hole, W. 8.180
Holford, W. 5.50
Holliday, J. 8.34
Holroyd, A. 7.99
Honikman, B. 7.100
Honjo, M. 4.120, 5.204
Horiuchi, R. 9.63
Houghton-Evans, W. 3.47, 9.64
House, J. 4.48
Hruška, E.   3.48, 3.83, see also
    Grushka, E.
Hrůza, J. 3.49–51, 4.36–7, 8.56
Hubbard, H. 4.287, 4.286–8
Huff, R. 6.66
Huggins, K. 4.289
Hughes, T. 3.52
Hugo-Brunt, M. 3.53

Hulchanski, J. 2.8, 4.13, 4.17–18, 6.1
Humphries, H. 4.223
Hunter, H. 8.74–5
Hussey, C. 6.82
Hyde, F. 7.46

Ikeda, T. 9.67
Ikonnikov, A. 4.224
Illeris, S. 4.40
Inman, J. 5.122
Insolera, I. 5.175–8
International Federation for Housing
    and Planning 4.46
International Union of Architects 8.8
Ishida, Y. 9.65–7, 9.75
Ishizuka, H. 9.68
Istituto Nazionale di Urbanistica 4.109
Itō, M. 4.121
Ivanitskii, A. 4.162
Iwami, R. 9.69

Jachniak-Ganguly, D. 8.237
Jackson, W. 5.114
Jacobs, E. 7.101
Jankowski, S. 8.4
Janssen, J. 4.68
Jellicoe, G. 3.54
Jellicoe, S. 3.54
Jennings, H. 8.35
Jensen, R. 3.55
Johnson, D. A. 8.238
Johnson, D. L. 6.45, 9.70
Johnson, K. 7.145
Johnson, L. 5.102
Johnson-Marshall, P. 6.71, 8.9
Johnston, N. 4.290, 6.2
Jolles, H. 7.146
Jonas, S. 3.56, 7.102–3, 9.71
Jones, G. 7.11
Jones, H. 2.4
Jones, P. 6.137
Judd, D. 5.185
Jürgens, O. 4.137
Junghanns, K. 6.127, 7.147
Justement, L. 5.233

Kabel, E. 4.70
Kahn, J. 9.72

Kain, R. 7.12, 8.57, 9.73-4
Kallmorgen, W. 6.115
Kantor, H. 5.144-5, 6.85, 8.239
Kaplan, B. 5.146
Kaplan, H. 8.36
Kaufmann, E. 4.41
Kaufmann, R. 5.14
Kawakami, H. 9.75
Kawana, K. 9.76
Keable, G. 4.225
Keeble, D. 4.226
Keeble, L. 4.227
Keil, G. 8.236
Kessler, R. 8.32
Kimball, T. 4.291, 6.102
King, A. 3.57-8, 9.77
Kirschenbaum, A. 8.169
Kitchen, P. 6.33-4
Klapheck, R. 7.104
Kleihues, J. 8.116
Knappe, C. 5.209
Kneile, H. 9.78
Knight, R. 7.105
Knittel, R. 8.181
Knorr, J. M. 7.103
Koch, F. 8.94
Kocher, S. 8.240
Konvitz, J. 9.79
Kopp, A. 4.163-4
Korn, A. 3.59
Koroscil, P. 5.235, 8.182
Koshizawa, A. 9.80
Kostof, S. 5.179-80
Kotarbiński, A. 4.132
Kovisars, J. 8.37
Krabbe, W. 4.71, 9.81
Krause, R. 5.20
Kulski, J. 4.292
Kultermann, U. 6.126
Kunze, E. 5.6
Kurz, M. 8.10

Lacava, A. 5.190
Lamborn, E. 3.52
Lameyre, G. 7.13
Lane, B. 4.72
Lane, J. 9.82
Lang, S. 7.58

Lange, G. 4.127
Lappo, G. 8.241
Larsson, L. 5.21
Latini, A. 3.60
Lavedan, P. 3.61-2, 4.49, 5.158
Lee, C. 5.224
Lees, A. 4.73
Leonard, C. 7.14
Lepawsky, A. 4.293
Lesser, W. 6.35
Leverhulme, 9.84
Levin, P. 9.85
Lewis, D. 4.228
Lichtenberger, E. 5.226
Liebknecht, K. 5.17
Liedgren, R. 7.106
Lillibridge, R. 7.107
Linden, G. 4.142
Lindsay, I. 5.97
Linn, B. 8.117-18
Linowes, R. 8.95-6
Lissitzky, E. 4.165-6
Lo, C. 4.31
Logan, T. 8.97-8
Lojkine, J. 8.242-3
Lorenzen, V. 4.42, 7.59
Lubove, R. 4.294-7, 5.167, 6.67
Lundén, T. 5.193
Lutyens, R. 6.83

Mabey, R. 9.86
McAllister, E. 4.229
McAllister, G. 4.229
McAneny, G. 6.84
McCann, L. 8.183
McCarthy, M. 5.62, 7.47
Macchi Cassia, C. 5.129
McCormick, E. 7.60
McCraw, T. 8.244
MacFadyen, D. 6.61
McFarland, J. 8.184
McGegan, E. 6.36
Machule, D. 8.104
McKay, D. 4.230
McKee, W. 9.87
Mackesey, T. 8.99
McLaughlin, C. 6.101
Macmorran, J. 5.35

MacNalty, A. 6.111
McNamara, K. 4.288, 4.298
McShane, C. 4.317, 8.76
McTaggart, W. 5.215
Mairet, P. 6.37
Makielski, S. 8.100, 9.88
Maksimović, B. 4.329, 6.68
Malcolmson, R. 3.63
Malet, H. 7.15
Malpass, P. 8.38
Mancuso, F. 4.270, 7.108, 8.101
Mandelker, D. 8.146
Mangiamele, J. 8.185
Manieri-Elia, M. 4.267, 9.27
Mann, P. 4.231
Manson-Smith, P. 5.208
Marconi, P. 5.223
Marcuse, P. 9.89–90
Mariani, R. 8.186
Marienbach, J. 4.167
Markelius, S. 5.194
Marmo, M. 5.138, 7.16
Marsan, J.-C. 5.132
Marsh, B. 6.86
Marshall Kaplan, Gans, and Kahn 5.3–4
Marsoni, L. 8.187
Martin, R. 8.245
Martinelli, R. 8.188, 8.196
Martorell Portas, V. 5.11
Matzerath, H. 5.22
Mausbach, H. 8.39
Mawson, T. 6.87
May, E. 4.168
Mears, F. 6.36
Meister, R. 7.116
Meller, H. 4.232, 6.38, 9.91
Mellor, J. 4.233
Melograni, C. 3.13, 5.181
Méoli, M. 8.189
Mercandino, A. 4.111
Merino, J. 5.38–9
Merlin, P. 8.190
Merriam, C. 4.299
Merruau, C. 7.17
Metzendorf, R. 7.109
Meyerson, M. 3.64, 7.61
Michelucci, G. 7.18

Migliorini, F. 7.18
Milde, G. 6.97
Miliutin, N. 4.169, 6.89
Miller, B. 6.17
Miller, M. 7.148–9, 9.92
Millspaugh, M. 8.40
Millward, S. 8.41
Minett, M. 4.234–5
Ministry of Housing and Local Government 8.147
Mioni, A. 4.104, 4.112
Mitchell, E. 8.191
Mitchell, R. 3.64
Moholy-Nagy, S. 3.65
Mollenkoff, J. 4.300
Montanari, A. 8.58
Moore, C. 6.10
Moore, P. 5.210
Morgan, A. 8.246
Morgan, W. 7.110
Morini, M. 3.66
Morizet, A. 5.159
Morris, A. 7.150
Morton, A. 7.62
Moseley, M. 8.148
Moss, G. 5.160
Moss-Eccardt, J. 6.62
Mucchielli, R. 7.63
Muggli, H. 8.247
Mullin, J. 4.74, 4.301, 5.84–5
Mumford, L. 3.67–9, 6.39, 7.64, 7.155, 8.119
Munn, R. 9.93
Munzer, M. 8.192
Murie, A. 4.236
Murphy, L. 4.237
Mušič, V. 4.330
Muthesius, S. 4.75, 9.94
Myrha, D. 6.129

Nader, G. 4.19–20
National Capital Development Commission 8.193
National Conference on City Planning 4.302
Neufield, M. 4.303
Neumeyer, F. 7.111
Newton, N. 3.70

Nicolini, L. 6.40
Nihon Kenchiku Gakkai 4.122
Nishiyama, U. 9.95
Nitot, H. 7.151
Nolen, J. 4.304
Novy, K. 9.96
Novy, O. 8.56
Nowlan, D. 9.97
Nowlan, N. 9.97
Nuti, L. 8.188, 8.196
Nuttgens, P. 4.238

Ochert, E. 6.116
Ödmann, E. 4.143
Olmo, C. 3.71
Olmsted, F. 6.102
Oravec, C. 9.98
Ordoñez, J. 7.41
Orefice, G. 8.27
Orlans, H. 8.197
Ortíz, A. 6.18
Ortmann, W. 4.76
Osborn, F. 6.63–4, 7.152–5, 8.149, 8.198
Ostrowski, W. 3.72–3, 6.65

Paetel, W. 7.48
Pagnini Alberti, M. 8.199
Palla, M. 5.79
Panerai, P. 8.107
Pannell, C. 4.31
Parés, S. 6.14
Parker, B. 6.135
Parker, J. 4.171
Parkins, M. 4.171–3
Pasini, E. 4.156
Pass, D. 8.120
Patricios, N. 3.74
Paulsson, T. 3.75, 4.144–5
Pawley, M. 3.76
Pawlowski, C. 6.24
Pedersen, S. 4.128
Peets, E. 4.284, 6.121, 7.19
Peintner, M. 6.139
Peisch, M. 4.305
Peltz-Dreckmann, U. 9.99
Pendergrass, L. 9.100
Penny, B. 7.113

Pepler, G. 4.240–1, 6.41
Pepper, S. 7.156, 8.121, 9.101
Perényi, I. 3.77–8, 4.174
Perks, W. 9.102
Perloff, H. 4.306
Peters, D. 7.114
Petersen, W. 8.200
Peterson, J. 4.307–8, 9.103
Petino, A. 5.53
Petsch, J. 3.79, 4.77
Pevsner, N. 4.78
Pfister, R. 6.23
Pfretzschner, P. 5.74
Pharoah, T. 8.68
Phelps, E. 8.52
Philipp-Nehring, D. 6.103
Piacentini, M. 5.182
Piccinato, G. 4.79
Piccinato, L. 1.3, 4.113–14, 5.189
Pierotti, P. 1.4, 3.80
Pinkney, D. 7.20–2
Pirchan, E. 6.141
Piroddi, E. 4.115
Pirrone, G. 5.153
Pitz, H. 9.19
Plowden, S. 8.77
Pocock, D. 8.201
Poliakov, N. 3.17
Pooley, B. 4.243
Popenoe, D. 9.104
Porteous, J. 7.115
Portoghesi, P. 2.9
Posch, W. 5.227
Potenza, S. 4.270
Pountney, M. 8.180
Powell, D. 8.202
Prager, S. 4.80
Prakash, V. 8.203
Preisich, G. 5.45
Presnall, P. 5.70
Pressman, N. 1.5, 6.5, 8.204–5
Preston, H. 9.105
Presthus, R. 4.244
Pritchett, C. 8.248
Purdom, C. 7.157–9

Quandt, J. 4.309
Queen, S. 4.310

Quilici, V. 4.175
Quillen, I. 7.116

Radicke, D. 7.38
Ragon, M. 3.81
Ranieri, L. 7.23
Råberg, M. 7.39
Rasmussen, S. 3.82, 5.66, 5.115–16
Ratcliffe, J. 4.245
Ravaglioli, A. 9.34
Ravetz, A. 4.246, 8.42
Ravis, D. 5.186
Read, J. 8.122
Réau, L. 7.24
Rebentisch, D. 5.86, 8.249–50, 9.106
Recknagel, R. 7.98
Redford, A. 5.120
Reed, H. 4.325
Reeve, F. 5.49
Reggiori, F. 5.130
Reiner, T. 7.65, 9.107
Reitani, G. 4.116
Reps, J. 4.311–15, 5.234, 8.150
Reynolds, J. 6.54–5, 7.117
Ribas y Piera, M. 4.138–9
Richards, J. 7.118
Richardson, K. 8.12
Richter, G. 8.50
Riesman, D. 7.66
Rimbert, S. 5.201
Rippel, J. 5.92
Ritter, P. 8.78
Rivet, F. 7.25
Robin, J. 4.26, 4.32
Robinson, A. 8.206
Robinson, I. 9.102
Robson, W. 5.117
Rockey, J. 7.67
Rodgers, C. 4.316
Rodríguez-Lores, J. 5.12, 9.108
Rodwin, L. 8.151, 8.207, 8.251
Rönnebeck, T. 7.40
Rogge, J. 8.13
Romando, M. 5.131
Romanelli, G. 5.222
Roper, L. 6.104
Roscioli, S. 5.190
Rose, M. 8.79

Rosenau, H. 7.68
Rosenbaum, B. 8.159
Rosenberg, F. 3.83
Rosner, R. 8.208
Rossi, A. 5.17, 9.109
Roth, L. 9.110
Rotival, M. 6.50
Roweis, S. 3.84, 3.91
Royer, J. 4.50
Rubenstein, J. 9.111
Rushman, G. 8.209
Russell, I. 5.120

Saalman, H. 7.26
Saarinen, E. 3.85
Saarinen, O. 7.119, 8.210
Sadayuki, Y. 9.135
Salazar, J. 3.86, 5.32
Salvioli, L. 5.80
Samonà, G. 3.87, 8.123
Sandbach, F. 9.112
Sandercock, L. 4.2
Sandionigi, A. 8.43
Sarin, M. 5.57–8
Sarjeant, W. 8.65
Sarkissian, W. 8.124 .
Satō, A. 9.113
Sawers, L. 4.176
Schaffer, F. 4.247, 8.211–12
Schiavi, A. 7.160
Schinz, A. 5.23
Schlandt, J. 7.120
Schneider, W. 3.88
Schultz, S. 4.317
Schultze, J. 3.89
Schulz, J. 4.81, 7.147
Schumacher, F. 4.82, 7.27
Schumpp, M. 7.69
Scimemi, G. 5.152
Scully, V. 6.69
Selling, G. 5.195
Servier, J. 7.70
Shvidkovskii, O. 4.38, 4.184
Schwan, B. 3.90
Schweitzer, R. 4.5
Scott, A. 3.91
Scott, M. 4.318
Scully, V. 4.319

Séassal, R. 6.110
Self, P. 8.152
Sernini, M. 4.117
Sert, J. 3.92
Sfintescu, C. 3.93
Shade, P. 5.96
Shaw, D. 5.105, 9.114
Shaw, J. 4.3
Sheail, J. 8.62–4, 9.115–16
Shepherd, J. 5.118
Shillaber, C. 2.10
Shkvarikov, V. 3.17, 4.177–8, 8.213, 9.117
Shurtleff, F. 4.320
Sica, P. 3.94–5
Sidenbladh, G. 5.196–8
Simon, E. 5.122
Simon, S. 5.121
Simpson, M. 4.321–2
Simutis, L. 6.105–6
Skinner, F. 5.149
Sloan, A. 8.80
Smallwood, F. 5.211
Smallwood, J. 9.118
Smigielski, W. 5.101
Smirnova, O. 9.117
Smith, P. B. 9.119
Smith, P. J. 4.21, 8.214, 9.120
Smith, R. 5.36–7, 8.136–7, 8.157, 8.215, 9.121
Solà-Morales, M. 7.41
Solesbury, W. 4.248
Sommer, J. 5.69
Sori, E. 4.118
Soria y Puig, A. 6.19, 6.125, 7.33
Sosnovy, T. 4.180
Soto, P. 9.36
Spadolini, G. 7.28
Spagnoli, L. 4.95
Spearritt, P. 9.122
Speckter, H. 5.161, 8.236
Speer, A. 4.83, 9.123
Sperlich, H. 7.54
Spiegel, E. 8.216
Spielvogel, S. 2.11
Spreiregen, P. 8.179
Spyer, G. 4.249
Stadt Bielefeld 5.30

Staeubli, W. 5.44
Stainton, J. 5.188
Stalley, M. 6.42
Standing Conference on London and South-East Regional Planning 8.252–3
Starkie, D. 8.81
Starr, S. 4.181–3
Steck, W. 8.65
Steffel, R. 7.29
Stein, C. 8.217
Steiner, H. 8.82
Steinhauer, G. 7.122
Steinmann, M. 3.96
Stelter, G. 4.10, 4.22, 7.123–4, 9.9
Stemmrich, D. 7.125
Stepanov, M. 5.163
Stephan, H. 8.14
Sternsher, B. 6.130
Stewart, C. 4.250
Stewart, I. 7.49
Stranz, W. 7.126, 8.153
Strausse, G. 7.71
Struthers, W. 8.254
Stübben, J. 4.84
Stungo, A. 8.59–60
Suddards, R. 7.127
Sundström, T. 5.200
Sussman, C. 8.255
Sutcliffe, A. 2.12, 3.97, 5.37, 5.119, 5.162, 6.78, 8.218, 9.125–6
Sutton, S. 6.107
Švidkovskij, O. 4.38, 4.184
Swenarton, M. 8.121, 9.101

Tafuri, M. 3.98–9, 4.85, 4.185, 4.267, 5.136, 5.228, 9.27
Tajima, M. 4.123
Tarn, J. 4.251, 7.128, 9.127
Taylor, B. 8.125–6, 8.256
Taylor, N. 4.252
Taylor, R. 4.86, 4.253
Teodori, M. 4.254
Terzo, F. 4.26, 4.32
Tesdorpf, J. 2.13
Tetlow, J. 8.127
Teut, A. 4.87
Thiele, K. 5.17

Thienel, I. 5.22, 5.24
Thies, J. 4.88–91, 9.37
Thomas, D. 8.154–5
Thomas, L. 4.310
Thomas, R. 8.219
Thompson, F. 7.129
Toll, S. 8.102
Tolley, R. 8.220
Tombola, G. 3.100
Torres Balbás, L. 4.140
Tortoreto, E. 8.15
Travis, A. 4.52
Trebbi, G. 8.16
Trevisini, G. 8.84
Triggs, H. 3.101
Troedsson, C. 3.102
Trow-Smith, R. 8.221
Tunnard, C. 1.6–7, 4.323–5
Tuppen, J. 8.222
Turner, R. 6.7
Tyrwhitt, J. 6.43

Uhlig, G. 4.92, 9.96, 9.129
Uribe Uribe, L. 3.103

Van Nus, W. 4.23–5, 8.103
Van Toom, J. 8.70
Vasil'ev, B. 8.223
Veal, A. 4.255, 8.128
Vercelloni, V. 4.30
Veronesi, G. 6.25
Violich, F. 5.52
Virágh, P. 4.98
Vitz, M. 6.4
Vogel, J. 8.192
Von Moos, S. 5.59, 6.79
Vorlaufer, K. 5.71
Vuillemot, G. 5.5

Wagner-Rieger, R. 7.42
Walz, M. 9.130
Wandersleb, H. 2.14
Wanetschek, M. 9.131
Ward, C. 4.256
Ward, S. 4.257–8
Warner, G. 8.129, 8.224
Warner, S. 5.166

Watanabe, S. 7.161, 8.130, 9.132–5
Weaver, C. 8.233
Weaver, J. 5.77, 5.212, 8.17
Webb, M. 5.165
Wedepohl, E. 4.93
Weiland, E. 8.189
Weimer, D. 4.326
Weiner, H. 8.225–7
Weinmayr, V. 6.97
Weismantel, W. 8.44
Weiss, E. 6.20
Weiss, S. 8.228
Welch, R. 4.31
Wermuth, A. 5.25
Werner, F. 5.26–8
Westecker, W. 8.18
Westergaard, J. 4.259
Westerman, A. 4.146
Weyl, J. 5.92
White, B. 2.15–16, 5.108
White, P. H. 7.130
White, P. M. 4.186–7, 9.136–7
Whittick, A. 2.17, 3.104, 8.198
Wiebenson, D. 6.26–8
Wiedenhoeft, R. 8.131
Williams, A. 9.138
Williams, M. 5.1
Williams-Ellis, C. 5.168
Williamson, C. 8.254
Willis, F. 3.105
Wilson, C. 7.131
Wilson, J. 8.45
Wilson, R. H. 9.107
Wilson, R. J. 7.72
Wilson, W. 4.327, 5.93, 5.98, 9.139
Wittwer, G. 6.21
Wolf, P. 6.51–2
Wolfe, J. 7.162
Wolff, C. 8.46
Wolters, R. 5.29
Woodford, G. 4.260
Worster, D. 4.328
Wright, H. 4.261
Wróbel, T. 3.106
Wurmb, D. von 5.148
Wurms, C. 4.96
Wurzer, R. 4.94, 6.22, 8.156
Wynn, M. 5.13, 8.157

Yoshino, S. 9.95
Young, T. 8.132

Zaitzevsky, C. 8.51
Zarebska, T. 9.140

Zetter, R. 8.47
Zevi, B. 3.107
Zile, Z. 4.188
Zukowsky, J. 9.141
Zweig, S. 6.138